AF379317

This Glorious Mess

Creating a New Paradigm for Relationships

Roman Ramsey

SunflowerSun   Boulder, Colorado

Printed in the United States of America

Second Printing, 2018

ISBN 978-0996904308

SunflowerSun

3754 Telluride ln.

Boulder, CO 80305

www.romanramsey.com

To those women whose paths have crossed mine, starting with my Ma, including my daughter Zascha and those in between and beyond, who, in ways both subtle and grand, have led me to reassess and redefine the possibilities and limitations, the very definition, of what is it to be a man.

"We waste time looking for the perfect lover,

instead of creating the perfect love."

Tom Robbins

TABLE OF CONTENTS

Preface

This is not a typical self-help book. I prefer to think of it as a how-to/how-not-to/confessional. There are personal stories included in this book, recounted through a veil of historical embellishment, so it's possible that there may be some distortion, which may have occurred even in the moment. Such is the case with perception. There is also a tone in some places of flippancy and humor that can be interpreted as sarcasm, bitterness, cynicism and even resignation. Sarcasm maybe, but resignation, bitterness? Nah, I ain't got time for that, not anymore anyway. In some places, "colorful" language has been implemented to punctuate a point, or perchance, to entertain, but not to hurt or offend.

Truth is, I have loved every woman I have ever been with, either in the rapture of the infatuation experience or the much deeper and profound experience of endeavoring to create a lasting union. Any "darkness" in the telling of the stories reflects the way we all sometimes feel about relationship when we are not getting the outcomes we would like. I have always been and continue to be a hopeful romantic and an optimist. I believe we can do better, all of us, and this book is my attempt to move us collectively in that direction.

Also, the telling of the stories is in no way meant to be disrespectful. Their narration is meant as a tool to illustrate how wondrous, growth-inducing, educational, difficult, challenging, painful, heart-breaking, stimulating and poignant the path of love can be. Where appropriate I have also included the stories of friends and clients to show the universality of our experiences.

In the original conversations I had with friends, partners and acquaintances, some bristled at the idea of a "contract" in a romantic relationship. It does have a very cut-and-dried, clinical, legalistic feel to it. As the idea for this new paradigm has evolved, I have at times substituted the words "proposal" (which, despite the matrimonial reference, has a feeling of "let's-try-this-and-see-how-it-goes" feeling to it), "vows" (another matrimonial reference, but with a bit more feeling of commitment) and "agreement" for "contract." I will use the terms interchangeably throughout the book. As you apply this new perspective in your relationship, use whichever term feels best for you and your partner.

The ideas contained in this book will not be for everyone. I have borrowed from my own experiences and those of others to try and create a new perspective around relationship. I don't claim to have the answers for everyone. Hell, I may not have the answers for anyone, but what I am trying to engender is the possibility of proactive, deeper, more conscious, fulfilling, meaningful, joyful engagement between partners.

Every relationship I have ever entered into I have done so with the intent of it lasting, and finding a life partner. I believed The Faerietale, I drank the Kool-Aid. In marrying, when I promised to spend the rest of my life with someone, at the time, I meant it.

"At the time." That is the operative phrase here isn't it? Sounds like a backpedal, an excuse, not a statement made by someone who knows the meaning of commitment.

That is true; I thought I did, but I didn't.

I had a lot to learn. And hopefully, in the reading of this book, others can learn from my experiences and the road to creating an extraordinary union will have fewer potholes in it than it has for me.

For the purpose of this book, we are discussing male-female relationship, but some of the ideas for this new paradigm have been inspired by agreements and dynamics of same sex relationships, necessitated by antiquated, traditional marriage laws. So, not only do many of the ideas apply to same sex relationship, in some ways have been inspired by them.

Love is love.

Introduction

If you are reading this book, it stands to reason that you are disenchanted with either your current relationship or series of relationships or maybe you are "in-between" relationships and you are looking to take it to the next level should you meet someone promising. If you are happily married: I mean deeply, truly, blissfully, *I-just-cannot-believe-how-lucky-I-am-to-have-met-you* married, and have been for a while, you know you are in the minority and you probably won't be reading this anyway. If your relationship or marriage is new, and you are still in the honeymoon phase, you won't be reading this book either. More likely, you WERE at that blissful stage once, or even numerous times (lucky you, you infatuation junkie) and now you are not.

I know, bummer, right? That feeling, according to every song, every Hollywood movie, every love story, every Fairyfuckingtale says it's supposed to last forever because we have found THE ONE.

No? Not resonating with that particular myth?

Well, join the ranks of the disenchanted, but not in a "Woe is me; I'll never find my soulmate" kind of way, but in a "Clearly we have been laboring under some false assumptions, there has to be a better way and let's find it!" kind of way.

As in all things in life, we are faced with choice points, and there are those decisions we make that take us backward or simply not ahead, and there are those that move us forward. We will look at those actions and inactions that keep us from extraordinary relationship, and those that have helped us evolve.

Whether you are in need of some relationship repair or relationship construction (for an upcoming "project") we will look at ways to shift to a new perspective around what relationship could look like (and it is different every time, because YOU design it).

In its broadest sense, this is a book about evolution, but more specifically the evolution of romantic love, illuminated (especially in those dark corners) by the tribulations of my own personal evolution.

I'm just a regular guy, a nice guy even, although some of my exes will disagree with me on that last count. I had two actually tell me I wasn't as nice as I thought I was. That gave me pause; to have not just one (I could possibly have written that off) but two women I was close to tell me I wasn't all that nice. In retrospect I could have responded with, "Well, you are not vibrating at as high a frequency as you think you are," but I was not clever enough at the time. That evaluation was disconcerting for me, because even though being described as a nice guy to a potential blind date, for instance, is the kiss of death, I still saw that as part of my makeup.

American Heritage Dictionary defines "nice" as:

> 1. Pleasing and agreeable in nature.
>
> 2. Exhibiting politeness and courtesy.
>
> 3. Of good character and reputation.

OK; I'm good with all of that. But what did it mean to *me* to be THE NICE GUY?

It meant that I was considerate of others, that I would consider their needs as well as my own. A lofty proposition. Unfortunately, being a classic middle child from a dysfunctional family, when I got to young adulthood, I combined that consideration for others with an extreme aversion to conflict and became a placater and a doormat. Yes, it is possible to be too nice.

In retrospect, I suspect that the assessment as "notasnice-asyouthinkyouare" came from finally uttering the word "no" to partners whose needs I was continually trying to meet at the expense of my own. Really? How dare I? I had made the mistake of trying to continually please others as a relationship success strategy.

I'm obviously not alone. As I look around, I see that many others have experienced much of the frustration that I have. What has brought me to write about these experiences is a feeling that we can do better in how we relate to each other in the name of love. The more I investigate, the more evidence I get that human male/female interaction may not be congruent with mating for life.

And it's not just that relationships aren't lasting; it's that they aren't more fulfilling and satisfying to begin with and maybe that's WHY they are not lasting. We can (arguably) put a man on the moon, and this is the best we can do as men and women considering all of the information and freedoms we have? (Oh, what? You're going to take me to task over the man-on-the-moon thing? Don't take me so seriously; this is not a typical self-help book. While I do hope to affect some change, we are going to have some fun along the way...)

Part of the problem is that most of us were never taught how to effectively navigate the waters of romance: "effectively" being the operative word. We learned what relationship looked like from our parents, and unless you were one of the few who had a positive role model for that, you were doomed to repeat it until, by trial and error, you stumbled onto something that was maybe a little better.

Well, for me, "a little better" is not going to be good enough for what has become a lifelong endeavor. I want extraordinary, and not just for me and my partner, but for the rest of those who consider relationship a priority. Whether my reasons for being so enamored with romance have been environmental, genetic, karmic, astrological or merely random, interaction with the opposite sex has always been front and center throughout my life. That alchemy has brought me my greatest joys and has also precipitated my lowest depths of despair. And while those dark times were not very much fun, I wouldn't trade a moment of any of it because it has all brought me to the point I am now: certainly not fully enlightened, but farther along in understanding the glorious machinations that occur between men and women.

Unfortunately, it is harder now than ever to achieve that. We can be distracted in so many ways by information, media and just the frenetic pace of our everyday world that the interface of two humans can seem trivial. The silver lining is that we are experiencing a global shift in sensibilities around intimacy, domestic violence, gender roles, and personal consciousness so that there has never been a better time to devote to our partners than right now.

We just have to make a choice to do that.

So that is what I will set out to do: through the recounting of my experiences, both personal and professional, create a new paradigm for relationship based on conscious choices about what we want our love lives to look like through the creation of relationship agreements or contracts, very similar to marriage vows, only much more specific.

Let's get started.

WHY EVEN BOTHER?

Men and women together: what a glorious mess.

We are both a version of human being, so, the same, and yet, so very different. And in those differences we are drawn together in ways that have inspired inspirational stories of how exalted those unions can be. Still, I look around at my experiences and the experiences of others and see so many falling short of those lofty expectations.

Like, "Happily ever after."

How's that goin'?

It has become abundantly clear that in this day and age, the reality of humans mating for life is not working the way it's supposed to. Divorce rates have hovered around 50% since the lawmakers took away needing an actual reason to back out, which means that, as often as not, couples who promise to spend the rest of their lives together are opting to back out of that agreement. "Irreconcilable differences?" Really? That's supposed to cancel out "for better or for worse?"

Are we trying to fit a round peg into a square hole? Are humans meant to mate for life?

Considering my relationship history, it could be argued that I have been the poster boy for serial monogamy. If we look at that from the perspective of "happily ever after," I am an abject failure.

On the other hand, it could be argued that I have been lucky enough to have had a wonderful, full, splendid existence in the company of amazing women.

Nice reframe, huh?

It could be further argued that my creation of a new paradigm for relationship is a backdoor way to justify my pattern of behavior for my entire life as it relates to women.

Nah!

I just think our whole existence is a mystery and as human beings we try to attach some rhyme or reason to it. This is my attempt to make some sense out of what we do together as opposite (complementary) genders that applies to life as we know it today.

Both genders play an equal, though usually different, part in this relationship dysfunction.

We are not only going to look at what goes wrong but what goes right, and what can go differently, so that we can apply it to the present and future and make what we do as men and women more fulfilling and enjoyable.

On some level, it all seems like a lot of trouble, doesn't it?

Why DO we do it? Engage in relationship, that is?

I like Woody Allen's take on this in his soliloquy at the end of "Annie Hall" (Woody himself being a notorious example of someone who has been relationship challenged).

It helps to imagine this with his unique voice and mannerisms:

> "I, I thought of that old joke; you know, this guy goes to a psychiatrist and says, 'Doc, my brother's crazy! He thinks he's a chicken.' And uh, the doctor says, 'Well, why don't you turn him in?' And the guy says, 'I would but I need the

eggs.' Well, I guess that's pretty much now how I feel about relationships. You know, they're totally irrational and crazy and absurd, and, but uh, I guess we keep going through it because, uh, most of us, we need the eggs."

So, metaphorically anyway, we need the eggs. Yes, as humans, we are social. Some would say we do it to maximize pleasure. Tony Robbins, the peak performance strategist, would say we do it to "magnify the human experience." I love that perspective. Think about sharing a simple event: a sunset, say, and how much more profound it is to share that with someone. And sex! Although some of you may even argue with me about this one, depending on your experiences, both with others AND by yourself.

Then there is that perpetuation of the species thing in which we do need for men and women to come together (you decide if the pun was intentional) so that humans can continue to rule the world. But it can (and should) be argued that, as it is, the world population is expanding at too high a rate. The problem seems to not be one of attraction, procreation and any danger of becoming extinct, but of the quality of the relationships after our initial urges to couple begin to feel routine, humdrum. OK, commonplace and boring. Annoying, irritating and adversarial. Hell, we can do a full 180 and end up hating the person who not so long ago was The One.

Why *do* we bother?

EARLY RUMBLINGS

For many in our culture, identity and success are defined by careers or schooling. For me, it has always been about what relationship I was in. Being married and divorced twice, as well as being involved in numerous other long term relationships, that definition includes a long, sordid, glorious, frustrating, varied, rich and diverse history.

Not that I haven't engaged in wide-ranging livelihood and education. At various times I have been a clerk, a busboy, a doorman, a cook, a short (luckily untested) stint as a lifeguard, a pallet maker, a bouncer, a landscaper, (the world's worst) bartender, a woodworker, a carpenter, a construction worker, a painter, a manager, a jeweler, a salesperson (cars, even used ones, jewelry and advertising), a photographer, a delivery boy, a journalist, a life coach, and a hypnotherapist. One of my first jobs was helping my Dad in the summer with his milk route.

Yes, I was the son of a milkman. Remember milkmen? Guys in white trucks and white uniforms who not only delivered all sorts of dairy products right to your door but were also often implicated in cases of children not looking at all like their "fathers." But my birthright was not as ignoble as it sounds; the milkman in question was married to my mom and I was their legitimate child.

I can remember waking up at 3 AM during the summer of my thirteenth year to help my dad with his route. It was fun, but not in the way that had garnered milkmen the ribald reputation they had; I can't remember ever coming across a situation that was even remotely sexual, and believe me, when I was thirteen I had my eyes open for that kind of thing. My eyes had been open for "that kind of thing" for as long as I can remember; it does make a case for the "milkman gene," if such an entity exists.

"What Happened?"

How often have we heard that phrase uttered in response to a recent breakup?

We were together almost every day. She had dark, silky, superstraight shoulder length hair that she torturously tossed around just for me. I wanted Denise for my own, never recognizing that my yearning for her attention was going to start me on a journey that I would alternately savor and regret for many years to come.

That fateful day, she had congregated with her friends in the corner, whispering, tittering and mooning over another guy, and a much older guy at that. As confusing as relationships were to me then, that part was the most perplexing; what was the appeal of someone that old? In retrospect, she was obviously some sort of "Daddy's girl," but back then, that kind of thing was fairly common. Now she was flaunting her betrayal; she was passing around a picture of him! I knew she was doing it just to make me jealous.

She had even kissed it!

You would think she was seven years old.

Wait; she WAS seven.

So was I; we were in second grade, for crying out loud. And the picture was of Troy Donahue (go ahead; Google him. Actor, heartthrob, Corvette driver, competition for the woman of my dreams).

Seven years old; I should have been consumed with ideas of frogs and lizards and baseballs and comic books. But all of those took a back seat to the attention of my Denise.

That particular relationship was short-lived; after snatching the picture and tearing it into a thousand tiny pieces, I decided right then and there she must not be my soulmate (although that is probably not the term I used at that particular juncture). Besides; what was up with her? Why wasn't SHE paying more attention to ribbons and dresses and Barbie (not to mention ME) instead of imagining herself liplocked with a much older and obviously unavailable man?

That was an early start on that primrose path. Some theorists suggest that there should have been a latent period in there before adolescence where the opposite sex wasn't that important to me.

I apparently decided to forego that stage.

"What happened?" Why didn't Denise and I ride off into the sunset? (Or at least into 3rd grade?) How could a love that strong, that true, end so tragically to have her ripping his image out of Tiger Beat magazine and ripping my heart asunder?

"What happened?" indeed...

Denise betrayed me, yes. She would be both my first love and my first heartbreak.

But we would always have recess...

She would the first in a long series of relationships, none of which have lasted forever. And I look around and realize that I am not alone; most romantic relationships in our culture end prematurely and yet we still struggle to live up to the promise of the Faerietale and "happily ever after."

K-I-S-S-I-N-G

My first kiss was at a loosely supervised birthday party where the parents left a bunch of fledgling adolescents to their own devices. We ended up playing a game called "Seven Minutes in Heaven." It started out like "Spin the Bottle" but two people participated and got to spend seven minutes in a darkened closet with whomever else was spun-selected. I want to apologize to Beth publicly now for what had to be the worst kisses in history; I had no idea what I was doing. But hey, we all have to start somewhere, right? I mean these were lips pursed, dry, head-rolling, best-imitation-of-Hollywood we could muster. It was junior high and we were what? Eleven years old? Tongues? I didn't know tongues were supposed to be involved; that wouldn't happen 'til about a year later.

By then, Laura and I had been going "steady" for a while, which at that point meant holding hands and practicing still more bad kissing. We soon got tired of that and broke up. Suddenly free, hormonally driven and on the lookout for whatever was next, I got entangled under the stairwell at school by Valerie, who showed me what a French kiss was. Interestingly, as soon as she slipped me the tongue, it was like I had done it all my life; a lightbulb went on.

Not even an hour later walking to class like the BMOC I thought I was, I got accosted by Laura in the halls, "How come you never tongue-kissed me!!!???"

News traveled fast in middle school, I guess. I didn't have the stones to tell her I had just learned how not even an hour before.

The next fall, I started my freshman year of high school and at the end of a football game, not under the bleachers, but right in front of everyone, ending weeks of anticipation and angst, Caroline and I kissed the first of what must have been a million innocent adolescent kisses. My life took on a whole new meaning. We were inseparable for two years, making out in the halls before homeroom, Chemistry (we sure had plenty of that), study hall: every chance we got.

She was The One.

Then it ended. I seem to remember her dumping me for an upperclassman. What the hell happened there? That kind of love is supposed to last forever.

Isn't it?

Apparently not. But that was the start of a pattern of me dedicating my life to finding that partner, The One, my soulmate, that would fulfill the promise of every Faerietale, every song, every Hollywood movie.

We *are* supposed to mate for life, aren't we?

Maybe it's time to rethink that old axiom, because when I look around, I see a lot of people, the majority actually, who have had numerous relationships, like me, that haven't lasted for a lifetime. Is it because we are not really supposed to mate for life, or is it just that we suck at it? Or could it be both?

We will explore both possibilities in attempting to find a way to create extraordinary relationships that last not only because they are "supposed to," but because they are so fulfilling, joyful, fun, satisfying, supportive and passionate, we will *want* them to continue.

THE OLD WAY

Animals!

(Best if read with a stilted British accent, as if read for a segment of "Wild Kingdom").

For your anthropological consideration:

The male of the species is generally larger than the female, displaying varying degrees of hairiness usually concentrated on the head, face and genital area, but in some males this hirsutism manifests as a thick furry display across the entire body, especially across the back and chest. The female, smaller and less visibly muscular is generally less hairy, with (usually) no facial hair. Different from other animals in the wild, the female has the brighter plumage, but that is acquired in the form of copious accumulations of garments and footwear. The female especially will engage in physical embellishment to the point of caricature. Male apparel is generally based on whatever is cleanest and closest (not necessarily in the order). The males are largely less vocal, unless encouraged to speak to further their cause. The females of the species at times will chatter endlessly.

Being physically larger, and unfortunately endowed with what sometimes approaches toxic levels of testosterone, the males usually tend to exercise domination in getting their needs met. The females, having been subjugated, tend to get their needs met though deceit, coyness and withholding of sexual favors. Until fairly recently, this male domination has resulted in a general perception of the female being a somewhat "lesser" gender, often appearing as property or a lower class of humanity. While this perception changed radically in the 1960's, gender equality among the males of this species is still not an idea that is universally accepted.

Socially, they devise a complex hierarchy, based on physical attractiveness, intelligence, aggression and amount of stuff they can accumulate. They can be extremely social, and while some of the species choose to wander alone, most adopt a pack mentality. Within the pack, they form dyads, usually male/female but also to a lesser extent, male/male and female/female. The male/female dyads are necessary for perpetuation of the species and they have shown themselves to be quite prolific in this regard. They brood well whether in their natural habitat or in captivity, however, the offspring need to be nurtured for an inordinately long length of time, sometimes for life. The packs will form a social hierarchy and will often adopt a set of rules to govern themselves.

One of the prevailing mindsets is the notion of an ongoing harmonious existence in coupling based on the euphoria experienced in the mating process. Through folklore and perpetuation of this story through every medium available to them, they labor at attempting to prolong that rapture. Partners vow to mate for life, and while some are successful in this endeavor, as often as not these pairings end in drama, trauma and dismay. These disengaged individuals then look to reconnect with others of the opposite sex, mistaking the mating euphoria for other longer lasting bonds that would actually encourage lifelong union. Instead, they routinely go through the whole mating ritual time and time again, confusing the drive to procreate with companionship, perpetuating the cycle of anguish.

Of course, frustration and despair would not exist without the species' ability to think, and actually consider their futures, which is based on their unusually large cerebral cortexes. At the risk of oversimplifying, these oversized brains result in behavior that can sometimes be considered sentient, or even conscious, but most often resembles a much more reactionary, reptilian comportment. As a result, they can consider what future outcomes of their actions and decisions can be, but in some twisted cosmic joke, they are never guaranteed of an outcome. Psych!!

The good news is that as a species, they seem to be evolving, however slowly. The bad news is that as a result of the pervasive psycho-sexual intergenderal attraction that at one time was essential for their survival but is no longer necessary for perpetuation of their species, their population continues to expand exponentially (although they fuck like bunnies, unlike their leporine counterparts, they have no true predators, besides themselves) and their numbers will soon outweigh their environment's ability to sustain them, at which time they will be more occupied with mere survival than why their relationships are not more satisfying.

(OK, I think that is quite enough of "Wild Kingdom for now...)

That Armageddon is fodder for another book. Instead, let's examine potential ways to decrease that cycle of frustration and despair that seems to surround this species' coupling behavior. What about other species? How do they handle their relationships?

Zoologists claim that there are other animals that mate for life. I am curious about exactly what that looks like. Do they "date," and experiment with various potential partners or when they are of a certain age and proclivity, do they hook up with the first potential baby-maker that crosses their path? Which one ultimately chooses, male or female? Or is it mutual? Have you have ever seen the elaborate mating dance that albatrosses do? OK, maybe not; how about the pigeons down at the park? It's quite elaborate and somewhat amusing, not unlike the mating dance of us humans. By the way, albatrosses will fly over thousands of miles over the course of a year, doing what albatrosses do, but when it is time to breed, they always return to the same place and partner to do that wacky dance they do.

Swans, sandhill cranes, bald eagles and turtle doves are also known in the bird kingdom to spend most of their reproductive (love) lives together. "Most" is an operative word here though, because in 2006 there was a reported case of "extra-pair copulation" with one sandhill crane triangle (reports are sketchy on who it was that cheated though). The bald eagles will only search out another mate in cases of death or impotency (insert your own Viagara joke here).

Gibbons are the nearest primates to us in genetic makeup that mate for life. Males and females are roughly the same size and spend a lot of time hanging out together but scientists that monitor their behavior closely have found some evidence that when they are not together, there is some measure of monkey business going on. French angelfish form monogamous pairs that travel, feed and hunt together over a lifetime. In the termite kingdom, some species have a king and queen that literally give birth to the entire colony.

Despite those examples, if you think about the entire animal kingdom, it's a pretty small percentage of animals that spend their whole lives together. And even then, scientists have found cases of "philandering" in every species. David Barash, a psychology professor at the University of Washington claims that monogamy in the animal kingdom can be disputed across the board with both males and females being the errant party.

It can be argued that since we, as humans, are animals, having multiple partners in our lifetime is just hard-wired into our genetic structure. Barash acknowledges that but adds, "We are never so human as when we behave contrary to our natural inclinations."

The question becomes not only, "What are those natural inclinations," but as sentient Homo Sapiens with the ability to behave in ways that are beyond reaction to our singular and collective pasts, with the arguable potential to create an imagined future, what would a "happier humanity" look like? Is natural selection "natural" if we create it? Does it matter? Is it more "civilized" to create rules that go against our natural instincts just to be more evolved? Without getting too far off track, what "should" human romantic relationship look like?

A Little History

We exist in a modern world, far removed from an agrarian culture, living in the same village we grew up in, hunting and gathering, working on the farm, having babies at 13 years old, raising them, hoping to survive whatever life threatening challenges come our way and then dying at 45 years old. Medical advances have increased our lifespan immensely and our quality of life has evolved to a point where our survival needs, by and large, are taken care of fairly easily. That brings us to a point of having to deal with more "first world problems" which include our emotional health and relationships in particular.

The field of psychology has evolved to where we are not just animals in metaphorical cages, living our lives as just so much stimulus and response. If we are going to continue to evolve, we have to look at approaches to our existence that are working and those that are not.

One place to start is in examining the premise that humans are destined to couple and spend entire lives together. In their book, "Sex at Dawn," Christopher Ryan and Cacilda Jetha contend that, anthropologically speaking, we are NOT intended to mate for life. Instead:

> "We have good news and bad news. The good news is that the dismal version of human sexuality reflected in the standard narrative is mistaken. Men have not evolved to be deceitful cads, nor have millions of years shaped women into lying, two-timing gold diggers. But the bad news is that the amoral agencies of evolution have created in us a species with a secret it just can't keep. Homo Sapiens evolved to be shamelessly, undeniably, inescapably sexual. Lusty libertines. Rakes, rogues and roués. Tomcats and sex kittens. Horndogs. Bitches in heat."

So why have we adopted this limiting framework of sexual exclusivity, and stuck to it for such a long time if it goes against our very nature?

First of all, there are those who would deny the findings of Ryan and Jetha. Vehemently, especially as it promotes their own agenda. Secondly, that framework actually DID work for quite some time.

Nathaniel Branden, in his book "The Psychology of Romantic Love," does an excellent job of chronicling the history of mating since the time of primitive man:

> "Economics, not love, was the motivating force for union in primitive societies—indeed, in practically all hunting and agricultural societies. The family was a unit established for the purpose of optimizing the chances of physical survival. Man/woman relationships were conceived and defined not in terms of "love" or of psychological needs for 'emotional intimacy' but in terms of the practical needs associated with hunting, fighting, raising crops, child rearing and so forth...

> Man's superior strength and women's need of protection, especially during times of pregnancy and childbearing, were made a justification of the inequality of the sexes and woman's subordination to man."

He continues on through the cultures of the Roman and Greeks, medieval times and the Renaissance on up through just before the Industrial revolution and the advent of capitalism in the United States. Our country was still largely agrarian. Men were men, and women were women. And let's face it, one fact IS carved in stone: women bear the children, and back then, raising a family of six, eight, ten kids was a full-time, all-encompassing endeavor.

The Industrial Revolution is when the shift occurred from the needs of the "tribe" or the collective to the individual.

> "Industrialism and capitalism resulted in far more than an explosion of material well-being. For the first time in human history it was explicitly recognized that human beings should be free to choose their own commitments. Intellectual freedom and economic freedom rose and flourished together. Human beings had discovered the concept of individual rights."

One of those individual rights was the concept of romantic love being the basis for marriage. World wars and recessions notwithstanding, American life was marching along pretty smoothly (well, for the men, mostly. If you could talk to most of the women, somewhat less so, although there were rumblings of discontent among women that resulted in the suffragette movement and the right to vote).

Fast forward a few decades to the '60's. This is where, as a culture, we took individual rights to a whole new level. Women's Liberation and readily available birth control created an incredible paradigm shift. We have to consider first of all, the idea that women were now considering that they weren't just baby machines, that there was more to life than just being an accessory to perpetuating a bloodline. And of course, that decision didn't exist by itself. We were looking at a boom in prosperity, in quality of life, in convenience and an expansion of the media.

All of a sudden, gender roles changed. Women entered the workplace in droves and vied for men's jobs. Attitudes were shifting about men's roles in the home too. Part of the problem though was that while the roles were changing, the rules were lagging far behind. That kind of change comes slowly, especially in a situation where the ruling class (the men) were not willing to let go of their power: not without a fight anyway. Well, here we are, about 50 years on and a LOT has changed. Arguably, not enough, depending on who you talk to; some traditionalists would argue that too much has changed, and they will still try to hold on to the old way.

In a recent conversation with a teenage girl, she told me that she would never ask a boy out on a date. I was nonplussed (I had heard and read about being "nonplussed" but didn't think it could actually happen to me...) She mentioned that her friends wouldn't ask boys out either; it was "too forward." I said, "Do you realize how much pressure this puts on the boys to make this all happen? And that it makes the realization of whatever wants and desires she might have be completely contingent upon the actions of somebody else?" She considered that and agreed. I think I may have at least planted a seed.

Gender inequality and whether or not we are "supposed to mate for life" aside, we are doing a piss-poor job of getting along as men and women. At least some of that blame has to fall on the shoulders of our institutions, especially for those who don't like to think for themselves.

Church and State

I hesitate to get on either of these soapboxes, but hey: here goes...

If I google "matriarchy" or "patriarchy" I open up an informational can of worms that leads me to believe that men and women are mortal enemies. I don't get it. I mean, I get what women are so pissed off about in our culture: no equal pay, domestic violence, glass ceilings; "it's mans' world." And I get that men have had it their way for so long that they don't want to give up that control. I know that there are fundamental differences in who and how we are as humans and that being different is a valid reason for hating others in some circles, but shouldn't we be getting past that? To me, the advantages to harmony between the sexes far outweigh the disadvantages of all that enmity.

The internet is no help; for all the bad press around Constantine and the Council of Nicea in AD 325, and how that was the start of male dominance, there is conflicting information that says that he wasn't such a bad dude. Some will argue that the church has a lot to do with that male dominance and a lot of those arguments hold water: even the Eden story where Eve is created from Adam's rib and then she persuades him to eat the forbidden fruit smacks of misogyny. For every entry on the "divine" feminine, there is another one to debunk that and extol the virtues of the authoritarian male. Does that polarity exist? Sure it does, both in its extremes and all of the grey area in between. The question becomes, "How do you want that to show up in your life and more specifically, in your relationship?"

All that male/female conflict aside (and it's no small aside) what we really want to look at here is the "bond of holy matrimony" (cue heraldic trumpets and angels singing on high), which is supposed to be an exalted union. This hallowed tradition is the model for how we are supposed to partner in this modern day and age. It is "sanctioned" not only in the eyes of God, but also by the state. I am not here to marriage-bash. Not the institution, anyway, but more how we go into it, how we go about it once we are in it and how easily we can get out of it. There are rules of religion and government that dictate much of our behavior in that.

But what happens when church, state, and human nature are not in alignment? And then you throw a little bit of wine into the mix?

I met Jessie at a local watering hole and before too long, we were trading relationship stories. She was coming off of a 20 year marriage that had gotten physically abusive. She had a restraining order on her husband; his mug shot was even on the internet (what had she been doing with HIM?) and at that point, her freedom was just a matter of the divorce being finalized. We entertained a mutual attraction and dated a couple of times but then she decided that she wasn't ready to go any further at that point. A few months went by, our paths crossed again and she seemed much more open to the idea of us spending time together.

A lot more.

We went on a date, then ended up at my house. One thing led to another and before too long we made our way to the bedroom (somewhere in there is when "a little wine" might have made its way into the mix). At some point, although she was very enthusiastic about the proceedings in the beginning, I felt her interest start to wane. Clearly she was having some misgivings, and while they were not communicated verbally at the time, she was clearly conflicted about actually consummating our tryst. Disappointed, but understanding her reluctance based on information she had shared about her (still) impending divorce, we came up for air, untangled, got dressed and she went home. Everything seemed fine. The next day she came to my workplace very upset, pontificating that we were "going to Hell" and "had committed a mortal sin."

What??!! I tried my best to hearken back to Sunday school. (Why hadn't I paid better attention back then?) My mind raced through the Ten Commandments, sort of. Which of the "thou shalt nots" had we violated? There had certainly been some coveting involved, and technically, this could almost be considered adul... Wait... Really? Adultery? Why hadn't this come up at some point in the proceedings before "Ohh...Take me!"?

Did we commit adultery? How far did we have to go to make that "official?" We had certainly lusted in our hearts (Thanks, Jimmy) and shared some very "bad" intent, but without penetration or orgasm, were we destined for Hell?

Not so much to justify our actions, but to attempt to lessen her assurance of eternal damnation, I asked how her God was feeling about the physical abuse that had been inflicted upon her in her "holy matrimony" as opposed to the affection, tenderness and OK, passion that we had shared. Or was He more concerned about the legal contract between the two of them that was about to be rescinded soon anyway? And once those papers were signed, could we engage the same way, and not go straight to Hell?

Those arguments fell on deaf ears: in her heart and mind, she had sinned. And I guess, technically, I had too, but I was somewhat less concerned about my future in purgatory than she was. A question I didn't get to present was, "Did she feel she was being disloyal to her abusive husband, or to an idea, an institution?"

While my words here may seem sacrilegious to some, it is not my intent to judge religion and its rules, whatever they may be. Rather, my question is around incongruent behavior. I am not supporting infidelity; I am actually a fan of monogamy; anything else is simply too dramatic and energy consuming for me. Besides, unless it's an open relationship, cheating is lying. I can say that now, but at some point (as you will see later in the book), although I never thought I would cheat, I somehow found a way to justify it. No, this was more about a conscious decision between consenting adults.

With Jessie, clearly there was a conflict between our "nature," her matrimonial circumstance and subsequent legal availability. As civilized humans, perfidious behavior exists in practically every culture on the planet. Yet, the rules tell us that it is not OK to do that. What rules were we supposed to be following?

Infidelity used to be grounds for divorce. Now you don't even need that; irreconcilable differences will suffice. Could the state and the legal system be any more vague in dissolving a contract that was supposed to be "for life?" I have heard some relationship experts campaign for legal contracts between partners (like a prenup before the nup). I say the lawyers have their fingers in quite enough pies; let's have our contracts or agreements be between two hearts, and do the best we can with that.

We are dealing existing in a modern world. Bottom line? We are playing by some antiquated rules that may not apply anymore. Women are not just baby machines, mommies and homemakers anymore, and they haven't been for a while. Religion has gone a long way to control women and keep them under the thumbs of men. On a global level, we obviously still have even further to go before they are free of that yoke. Conversely, men are not just grunting Neanderthals, protectors, providers for their families and husbands to "their" wives.

I am not calling for the abolition of religion, government *or* belief systems: quite the contrary. As part of creating relationship contracts, belief systems are front and center. What I am suggesting first is a <u>conscious</u> examination of whatever the rules are that you are abiding by. Are those rules yours, or did you just adopt them from your family of origin? The same goes for social mores. Because of our virtual interconnectedness, etiquette and protocol exist now that weren't even part of the conversation not all that long ago. This is much more complicated now than it has ever been; the entire planet can be considered community.

MODERN LOVE

The World Wide Web

We can't talk about our modern world without mention of the internet and the way it has not only impacted not just our personal relationships but almost every aspect of our lives.

At this time in our culture and history, as men and women we have such incredible freedoms that we hardly know what to do with them. While there is not absolute freedom or equality for everyone (that would be chaos) and there are many injustices that still exist, there are innumerable opportunities for us, not only to consider differing points of view and new knowledge, but also how our behavior around that information is going to manifest. Much of this centers around the fact that our boundaries have been expanded, if not completely obliterated, by the internet.

Have you stopped to consider the ramifications of having the internet in our lives? We can "google" just about any question and get an answer. What is the gross national product of Uzbekistan? What does "chthonic" mean and how do you pronounce it, who was that actor in "Memento," what's killing all the bees, and while we're at it, what *are* the lyrics to "Smells Like Teen Spirit?" (not to mention "Louie, Louie.")

We now have the entire planet at our fingertips. What does this have to do with relationship, you ask? Consider what a distraction the internet is in terms of how it eats up portions of your 24 hour day. And not just the time that is spent in front of a computer screen, but what it can introduce into our lives that takes away from the amount and quality of time and energy spent with your partner.

Consider this: let's say one of the activities my sweetheart and I enjoy together is going out to eat. We make a reservation online at our favorite restaurant for a nice dinner, and through some random surfing, (while waiting for the order to arrive: how rude!) my dinner mate discovers that the Chilean Sea Bass on the menu is being unethically fished.

What?!!!

First of all, what does that even mean? Second of all....put the damn smart phone away! And third of all, I really LIKE Chilean Sea Bass; I don't want a reason not to eat it!! But now my partner has one, and not only that, but did you know that they cut the beaks off of baby chicks so that they don't peck each other in the prisons they call cages? What? This chicken is not free range? "Oh, waiter..."

The next thing you know, we are not only not going out to eat together, but are eating separate meals at home because I want Beef Stroganoff and she is not only lactose intolerant, but that cow was not grass fed! Or free range. Or contented. Or whatever it is cows need to be for it to be OK to eat them...

Don't get me wrong; I am not saying that all this information is a bad thing. What I AM saying is that all of this information gives us that many more areas to be distracted, to take on another cause, for there to be another place where we can disconnect.

Then there is the social aspect. Remember that old girlfriend who you broke up with all those years ago that you still think of whenever you hear "Total Eclipse of the Heart" in the elevator or at the supermarket or on the oldies station or remade as a tango on Dancing With the Stars? (Not that I watch that show...) (OK, my daughter and I watched it together, but I only watched it with her).

You can find her with a couple of clicks of a mouse. And, yeah, she married some dork, but they are divorced now and, whaddya know? She wonders too if she made the wrong choice way back then.

Wow, really? That's great, if you are both single and living in the same town. But what if she's single and you, well, you are having some problems with your current flame: she hates Bonnie Tyler (Total Eclipse of the Heart: try to keep up). And look at that picture of TheOneWhoGotAway on her Facebook page; she's still HOT! (Of course, you don't know that that photo was 10 years and 50 pounds ago...) And she is witty and nice and she "gets" you. And now you wait for her e-mail at work, or maybe a text. And the next thing you know, you are having an emotional affair.

An "emotional affair." You haven't seen this woman in 15 years, but you are telling her about how awful it is that your wife won't go down on you anymore. That and the whole Chilean Bass thing... What's that? She loves Chilean Sea Bass? Of course she does.

Virtual Greener Grass.

Let's talk about internet dating. I've done that. Numerous times. Yup.

There are some amazing women out there on the World Wide Web. Incredible. Hot. Smart. Funny. Fun. No, really... I mean, I'm pretty cool, and I'm on this dating site, so there must be my female equivalent out there too, right? Well, there is, but there is also a lot of deception and partial truths and untold stories as well. I think that internet dating sites have their place in our current culture. I have met wonderful women through the internet, had great first dates (dancing to a cheesy 80's pop band or hiking to a special place in the mountains overlooking the city) and even memorable first kisses (and handshakes). I like the idea that internet dating sites are a "clearinghouse" where everyone (for the most part) is available, as opposed to our regular moving-about-in-the-world interactions where if we are attracted to someone, chances are they are NOT available.

But the *promise* of internet dating makes existing relationship that much harder. Look at the alternatives! Whether they are "real" or not, they can be considered as such. One time, when I was "in-between-relationships," I went on a dating site and for my tagline I wrote, "If we are all so fucking wonderful, then what we are all doing on Match.com?" (I was feeling a little disenchanted with the process at the time, and thought I would go with a lead that was an attention grabber...) That headline was rejected in less than 5 seconds! Talk about a vigilant censor! I'm sure there was a computer filter in there that was going to reject any profanity, so I amended it to say something a bit kinder and gentler; "Darn," I believe. My (slightly bitter) point at the time was that if we were so wonderful, we would all be taken. Well, that is flawed logic, because our world is different now, remember?

The good news is that if you ARE "in-between" relationships and you are free to relocate, the possibilities are (virtually) endless. The relational playing field has changed; we are not limited to that circle of those that happen to physically cross our path. The internet has created a social network that arguably makes anyone with a computer fair game for engagement. It stands to reason that the larger the group you are choosing from, the better the chances that you are going to find someone suitable.

This is both a blessing and a curse. A blessing because we are not limited to prospective partners in our social sphere. Conversely, a curse because we may be supplanting perfectly good local human specimens with "faultless" virtual partners who may have attributes that don't really exist. In the 2014 movie, "Her," Joaquin Phoenix as Theodore ends up falling in love with a computer operating system. Ironically, "she" ends up falling out of love with him once she outgrows him and subsequently dumps him.

While operating systems have not evolved to this point in reality, there are aspects of this paradigm that DO exist today, that make human interaction that much more difficult. Horror stories abound about internet dating experiences that don't match up to the promise of those personal marketing campaigns disguised as Match.com profiles. Some people "internet" really well, since interaction is often not in real time (or space) and they are given the chance to deliberate over their responses, but as the technology advances, encounters become more real time (like Skype) and there isn't as much room for misrepresentation, like this:

Valerie's cover photo had a very bohemian, casual air to it: It was not a glamour shot, not hardly. There was a casualness, an openness: reclined on a couch, not suggestively, but with lots of leg showing in a pair of cut-off jeans. Her profile also suggested an articulate sensibility and once we started e-mailing, there was an instant rapport between us; we spoke the same language. It was the same on the phone; she knew how to talk. The problem was that she lived four hours away. Well, that wasn't going to stop me. After a couple of weeks of getting stirred up enough by our verbal intercourse, I decided I was going to hop into my car and make the drive so we could meet in the flesh. We decided to meet at a roller skating rink, of all places. What the hell, I thought, it's her turf; if she wants to be on wheels, I can roll with that (sorry...).

I arrived at the rink and hadn't even laced up my skates yet, looking around for the person I knew only by her photo, when I was approached by a complete stranger who somehow knew my name. Somehow, Valerie had aged and well, expanded, in the time it took me to drive 209.2 miles.

I know, I know; a relationship should not be based on physical appearance alone, but I felt that I was exercising a reasonable expectation about actually being able to recognize the person from their profile photo. She could have at least warned me. I tried not to let me disappointment show, but the reality was that there was absolutely zero chemistry in the meeting for me.

We ended up having a nice date, but the ride home seemed a hell of a lot longer than those 209.2 miles.

What was she thinking? Over subsequent bouts of internet dating, this scenario would repeat itself, not always but often enough that it would qualify as a phenomenon: people misrepresenting themselves on the internet. Why, I may have even been guilty of this myself; while I always tried to post the most recent photos I had, I was describing myself as "athletic and toned." At some point it was pointed out to me that it might be more accurate to describe myself as "slender."

Really? But, I've always been physical, I've always been athletic. OK, well, maybe not so much in this new job, and I haven't played basketball in a while, a couple of years actually. Hmmm... In defending myself and others in this position, I guess we see ourselves caught in a moment of time, regardless of how we look in the mirror every day, when we were at our "best."

Not that there aren't those out there who do endeavor to deceive. Why would they do that? Don't they know who at some point, they are going to have to physically make an appearance and their cover will be blown?

Yes, but before that meeting, there is another aspect of virtual approval in internet interaction that enters into all of this. I've heard stories from women about getting hundreds of responses in a week. Hundreds! How affirming of one's desirability is who? Regardless of whether it is based on a true representation or not. It's like playing a dating video game. It's not Fantasy Football, it's Digital Dating and you are controlling the joystick (sure, go ahead and insert your own double entendre here) There are some people out there for whom that is enough; they don't even have to actually meet.

Internet addiction exists. Why? In its simplest terms, anything we are addicted to is changing our state, that is, either bringing us pleasure, or numbing us to pain. As this relates to relationship, whether it is on a dating site or even on something as benign as Facebook or Twitter, our brains are lighting up, getting stimulated by the approval of others.

Whether we are getting "liked" or "poked" on FB for some pithy remark we made or winked at on Match, we are getting reinforced and validated for who we are as humans. While we may not actually be salivating, the pleasure centers in our brains are firing away, making us feel good.

In some ways, it beats the sloppy, messy, inexact, unpredictable real world of actually having to physically interact with other human beings.

Sort of.

There is another hierarchical aspect to internet dating in that we have the power to reject prospective suitors, gunning them down like some kind of Masters of Doom scenario, leaving a wake of jilted lovers. I WIN, finally, in the Game of Love!

Exaggerated? Maybe a little, but for some, this has become a part of personal interaction that is a substitute for actual human contact. The one area that the net hasn't broached yet is touch, but

I would be willing to bet it is not all that far away. As dire as this all sounds, I am a believer in internet dating. If you are looking for a partner, it makes sense to go to a place that is a clearinghouse for a potential mate.

OK, again, there are the deceivers out there who are really NOT available, but let's assume most people on a dating site are there because they want a relationship. That makes more sense than having to wade through our daily existence, being attracted to others that may or may not be available. Granted, it is not a perfect system but it beats sitting at home watching reruns of "Law and Order" (for instance...)

And while I have experienced that virtual chemistry online, there is no substitute for being in the same space as someone, breathing the same air, touching, sparks flying willy-nilly.

I have an internet success story to tell, but more on that later.

A NEW WAY

How about this for a premise: We don't mate for life, and that's OK.

Then, to start, we take away the assumption of "Happily Ever After." Now, all of you "Fairietalers" out there; just calm down. This is not to say that any relationship cannot last long term, even "forever;" we are simply taking away that *assumption*. The new model is to create relationship together, as a partnership, like an adventure, allowing for those parts that are planned and those others that come up, both positive and negative that you never saw coming, open–ended so that the relationship is allowed to evolve as the partners change and grow. Bear with me as I walk through this.

How about, instead of "happily ever after," the focus was more in the present (with an eye on the future): maybe "happily until?" Constantly, consciously evolving and possibly "ever after," but that not being the assumption, but the RESULT?

Or not...

Because, as is evidenced by divorce statistics and the litter of shorter term relationships scattered across the relational landscape, the reality is that some peoples' paths cross ours for short, finite periods of time and then we move on. I've seen too many relationships drag on merely because the parties said they would stay together: miserable, but together, dammit.

In a nutshell, here's the idea: instead of the focus being "Let's commit to spending the rest of our lives together," have it be "Let's devote ourselves to having the best relationship we can possibly create." Then, construct an agreement outlining each individuals accountabilities, (both to-do's and not-to-do's) with the idea being that first, each individual gets clear on what they do and don't want, and then, in the writing of the contract, they are communicating openly about what the union should look like. Under certain circumstances (most notably, a relationship on the rocks), you can even include a trial period. Let's say a couple is ready to call it quits, after a year, five years, even 20. Don't they owe it to each other and the relationship to commit for another, say, three months, and devote themselves to starting over, as a trial, to see if they can salvage it?

Included in that structure, I would recommend 'check-in" times to monitor how it's progressing. Too analytical? Not spontaneous or passionate enough? Too much work? I contend that the alternative—just allowing relationships to happen—is what makes them less than extraordinary.

As you "check in," (and it can even just be an annual event, like an anniversary) if necessary, you can renegotiate the agreement: the renegotiation allowing for changes in circumstance, personal growth or even whim. What I am suggesting is that arbitration can occur around a new idea, say, "Let's take the summer off and explore Tuscany. Is that something you might be interested in? Is there a way we can possibly do that?"

I'm asking you to put aside our old ideas about how we are going about relationship. We need to start doing things differently. I know this plan is not for everyone. There are those out there who "know" their love is true, who have met their "soulmate" and believe their love will last forever (Oh wait; isn't this nearly every couple in love or deciding to marry? Pardon my sarcasm, but really; who gets married thinking it's going to end, that they will end up despising, disrespecting, demeaning and even hating their beloved?)

But circumstances change, and people change. Yes, people DO change. Unfortunately (or maybe fortunately) they don't change because (or the way) WE want them to, but some of them do actually change. Hopefully, in YOUR own life, there has been growth and evolution so that you are not the same person you started out to be. What does that mean in terms of who you are in relationship NOW with as opposed to who you were previously? Let's dissect the equation a little more

THE MALE/FEMALE DYNAMIC

We have access to incredible freedoms and information these days: arguably TOO much. It's confusing out there, but I can't help but think that the time is ripe for us to create a new, more conscious paradigm for how we look at romantic relationship that is more in line with who we are inherently as human beings, not just at our primal core, but in our hearts and minds at this time in our evolution.

Why are we collectively experiencing such an inability to evolve in the quality of our relationships? Outside of arranged marriages, nobody goes into marriage in our culture thinking it's going to end. What happens?

Let's get this straight right from the getgo; I am not against marriage. And I am not necessarily promoting serial monogamy (although I think it gets a bad rap...) What I am against are relationships that are miserable, soul-sucking endeavors that continue for no other reason than that they have been started.

But when is it time to leave, or to cut a partner loose? Dan Savage has an acronym in his syndicated sex column "Savage Love": DTMFA, which stands for "dump the motherfucker already," which sounds like it applies to men only, but is non-gender specific. Let's face it; some partners simply need to be cut loose!

I'm also not saying "quit" as soon as things get hard, either. What I am advocating is conscious, deliberate, cooperative relationships of our own design, as opposed to reactive, combative, adversarial dyads (don't you love that word to describe the pairing of two humans?)

I mean, really... Don't you get to a point every now and then (usually when things are really going badly) when you say, "That's it; I'm DONE with relationship; this is not worth it!!! I'm better off by myself." For some, we get bucked off that horse, go into "never-again" mode, then dust ourselves off and get back on because, well, the ride just feels so damn good. For others though, that one surprise "dismount" and subsequent pain is enough for a lifetime.

Uncle Alex was my Dad's twin brother. They were estranged for over 30 years after WWII about some stupid money issue. I didn't get to really spend any time with him until I was an adult because, as it turned out, he was living basically as a hermit. In New York City. He was reunited with our family through some sleuthing done by my sister, who felt that it just wasn't right that my Dad and he be estranged. As it turned out, Uncle Alex was living just a couple of miles away from her. He looked like a street person, but had had a long standing job as an aeronautics engineer. Once, when I got him to sit down and tell me some of the stories of his life, he recounted that he had never married because the woman he was betrothed to ended up jilting him for somebody else before he came back from the war (sounds like the war was hell for him in more ways than one...)

Talk about a broken heart! He spent almost his entire adult life alone over what he perceived to be a couple of betrayals: my dad and his fiancé. His case is extreme; he attached so much pain to those treacheries that he was no longer willing to risk human contact, for fear that it would happen again. It took my sister an incredible amount of time and effort to even get him to answer his front door, but she persevered and eventually got him back into the fold as a participating relative.

A relater. Someone who would engage in at least some sort of relationship. Unfortunately, at that point in his life (he was around 70 years old) he no longer looking for a mate. But think about that; a whole adult life without intimacy. Over a broken heart.

What a waste.

He obviously made a conscious choice around that. In some ways, it seems easier to make that decision, when things are not going well, relationship-wise, to throw in the towel. "I can't take it anymore," "I quit," "You suck," "You are never going to change." The list is endless. But what if we took that "certainty" that "love stinks" and reversed it? You know; consider that the whole love thing could be really grand?

I'm sorry; too much optimism for you? Well, then put the book down and step away. Because this book is for those hopeful romantics out there, even though at times I may be exposing the seedy underbelly.

I personally bought into the Faerietale early and hard. I was undoubtedly influenced by actual fairytales; they always lived happily ever after. Then there was TV! Donna Reed, Leave it to Beaver, Lucy and Ricky, Father Knows Best.

And yet, despite those rosy models, life at home was not following that pattern. Not with two alcoholic parents: one a reluctant Mom, the other having no clue how to support a family of four kids, never mind how to parent them. They carved out a miserable existence for each other and created a model of how NOT to be. It was all very contrary: the conflicting information of a rosy family life on TV juxtaposed with the chaos and dysfunction when the TV was turned off.

I guess it didn't matter if I was confused; I jumped in anyway, always, maybe because I was chasing what I saw on TV but more likely because "love" just "happened." Or what I perceived as love, anyway; which was just attraction and infatuation.

And it has always ended, despite the warm and fuzzy memories of every girlfriend, wife and encounter; those first kisses, that best first date ever, love in a pup tent, "smuggling" Kauaian clay, getting caught under the boardwalk in Pt. Pleasant beach, Frankie's ('who IS this guy?"), leftovers left on my porch, riding the pony, long adolescent bike rides to Rovere's beach, lunches at Edie's, fireworks on the roof, cracksweat on the Kalalau trail, "I'm-the-only-one-of-the-Cinco-de-Mayo-who-can-do-this"   at Evangelo's, the Grinding Stone. My lovelives have been rich indeed. My adult life has been measured by the company of the wonderful women I have been lucky enough to call "mine" (Don't get all up in arms here... I was "theirs," too!)

Some of what I will propose will be scary, or at the very least, take you out of your comfort zone. But nothing ventured, nothing gained, no blood, no foul: whatever cliché you want to use, there are huge rewards at the end. Extraordinary relationship; why would you settle for anything less?

Most of what ends up holding us back from doing anything is fear: either real or imagined. Every one of us has been hurt, burned, betrayed, rejected, abused, deceived or otherwise wronged.

So, again, why bother?

When I look at the state of relationship in our culture, I see a general malaise, a lackadaisical, cavalier sense of entitlement. I'm not talking about the "honeymoon" phase of relationship, when we DO put our best foot forward in trying to impress a potential mate. I'm referring to that time when the chemistry disappears and the blinders come off and our perspective *changes*.

Suddenly, we are faced with not only presenting ourselves as we "really" are but also with the prospect of accepting our partners as THEY "really" are.

Yes, "really."

"Really" in quotes there because well, who ARE we really?

There's that internal version.

Then the external one.

Then other versions that only show up in certain situations.

Then there is the version of ourselves that is subject to change, either gradually or at a moment's notice, putting the entire relationship equation in a completely new perspective.

It's getting more complex by the moment, isn't it?

Factoring in those definitions from above, we go from having a relationship that is at once exciting, novel, and probably most of all, promising (which includes, but is not limited to, the highly promoted, nirvana-inducing *"everlasting"*) to a union easily taken for granted. Taking it to a more negative place, we cross over into boredom, tolerance, annoyance, disdain, dislike and in extreme circumstances, even hate.

"What happened?" indeed.

Most of us have heard that phrase in response to telling someone we know that we are no longer in our most recent relationship. The assumption is that it is supposed to last. And frankly, I'm sure you and your partner thought it would as well. And probably wanted it too. It's basic human nature that if something is good, we want more; we want it to keep on going.

But, as has been documented on bumper stickers and elsewhere: "Shit Happens." Even in the very most charmed life, there are going to be ebbs and flows and times when you simply are not getting the outcomes that you had anticipated. For many, this is when the relationship gets tested: when the challenges come up, when situations arise that were not part of the original equation. And that is part of the dilemma in this modern world: changes come more quickly in ways that we couldn't even have anticipated. Essentially, ebbing and flowing at a much faster rate. In a recent conversation about our changing world, a friend told me, "Yes, the grass is always greener on the other side of the fence. And now there are just so many more fences."

I am not promoting that we jump from relationship to relationship, especially when things get too tough. I'm all for couples staying together. But staying together in dynamic, loving, giving, joyful union, where both partners are getting their needs met, and ideally, the partnership is larger than the sum of the two parts. Together, you are more than, well, you get it...

We've all heard the phrase "opposites attract." Yes, in the world of physics, it is absolutely true and as physical human beings we are subject to the laws of physics.

Sort of.

The problem is that we are not taking about the poles of a magnet when we are looking at the hearts, minds and psyches of two human beings. Do they attract? Sure, it can be argued that we seek out that which we do not have or possess. And it can also be argued that that is how we grow, by having someone close to us who is challenging us on a daily basis. But there's the rub; that constant challenge. You may like the excitement and challenge of being with an extrovert, if you are not one, or an outdoor person or a foodie ("foodie": that concept didn't even exist a short while ago. I LOVE to eat, but I prefer not to dissect it as part of the enjoyment. Or "deconstruct," as the foodies would say). But once the novelty of those new experiences wears off, you may be faced with having to constantly participate in activities that you don't like.

I would contend that the more harmony there is in a relationship, the better the chance of it staying together.

So, when we ask, "What happened?," the answer is usually that once two people REALLY got to know each other, the places they didn't match up outweighed the ways they did, or one person changed (which brought about the same result) or often, in a new relationship, once the "honeymoon," the infatuation was over, there simply wasn't enough between the two parties to go forward.

But remember, we are changing the paradigm. Your intent may BE for the relationship to last "forever." That is still doable under this new paradigm; we are just going to go about it differently, in smaller increments, making it extraordinary again and again.

I would be remiss if I didn't include mention here of a basic aspect of human existence: selfishness.

From the time we are brought into the world until the time we leave, we have human needs that need to be met for us to survive, and even thrive. Throughout this book, I will be exhorting you to have your focus be on your partner's needs. That is correct; your partner's.

Isn't that what love is?

It sounds wonderful and lofty to do that, and at the same time, I know from personal experience that, if that is all you do, and your partner happens to be one of those blood-sucking, soul-stealing, emotion-draining relationship vampires, your needs are NOT going to be met by that kind of person, and either you go without or get them met someplace else.

I would consider that unproductive and less than extraordinary. Not that your partner should be responsible for meeting all of your needs: quite the contrary. But if all the need-meeting is going on by one party, it creates an unbalanced, unhealthy dynamic in the relationship.

And that is what we are looking to change.

But first, let's look at two sides that make up the whole.

Men and Misogyny

Men are half of the equation. They can certainly be assholes, right? Well, I guess that depends on your point of view or your history (whether or not you've ever been one, or with one... or more...) (Btw, men; stick with me here. We are going to look at both sides).

I'm a man; I've been around men, and the truth of it is, most of us ARE assholes. At this point in history, by and large, as a group, we have not figured out how to act, and I am talking specifically about how we act around, with, among and to, women. Why does misogyny exist? Somehow, as men, many of us have not evolved past the idea of physical dominance, that simply as a matter of size, what should be our complementary gender has become an adversarial one. Why do so many men consider women the enemy? We dominate them because we CAN?

"The Way of the Superior Man." There's a book title that is pretty much guaranteed to get chests puffing out and conversely, panties in a bunch, and that's before anyone even opens the cover. If the title isn't enough for you, how about the sub-title? "A Spiritual Guide to Mastering the Challenges of Women, Work and Sexual Desire." If you are not familiar with David Deida's work, prepare to get polarized, and Deida would love for just that to happen. In a nutshell, Deida feels that our culture has become too androgynous and that we would be more fulfilled as men and women if we returned to our polar positions. Men as men and women as women. At first glance, it might come off as a misogynist's handbook, but he has got some compelling arguments, and says them in a way that is passionate and articulate.

While I don't subscribe to everything he is saying, as I work with couples, I do find that some of what he is proposing is extremely applicable, and there are couples who can benefit highly from his teachings. Recommended reading, either way, and then throw some of it out at the water cooler and watch what ensues, because he DOES stir the pot.

In our culture, we consider 18 years old to be a passage into manhood for our males. I think it is safe to say I was a little behind the curve. I turned 18 right as I was graduating from high school. My Mom, a three pack a day smoker, would pass away that summer at age 52.

No one in my family had gone to college and I was to be the first. I had been a basketball star at a small high school in New Jersey with questionable guidance about what to do after that. A good student, I was even being considered for the US Naval Academy (until the recruiter came and I realized how early I was going to have to get up every morning. That, and it was right near the end of the Vietnam War and the military was not enjoying its highest approval rating ever).

All I wanted to do was play basketball, so when I took my SATs, I listed three universities with great basketball programs to have my scores sent to, with no consideration for academic rating, part of the country, how much they cost and certainly not whether or not I was qualified to play there.

The next thing I knew, I was on my first plane trip ever to Milwaukee, Wisconsin to play for Al McGuire's Marquette Warriors. Not that Al knew I was going to play for him. My grandiose plans included walking on, wowing them with my small town skills and having them roll out the red scholarship carpet. It was clueless on so many levels.

I walked into the archaic Marquette gym, all brick and meshed windows, with an elevated track around the perimeter and pictures going back to the 1920s of their basketball glory, and saw two seven foot players at the other end of the court playing one on one. They were Jimmy Chones and Maurice Lucas, both of whom would go on to play in the NBA.

I, however, would not.

We were to have a week of tryouts for the freshman team. Lucas was one of the freshman who had already been awarded a full scholarship. The school would grant two additional scholarships to players that earned them through their play. Among those in the running were student athletes that had been invited to attend Marquette, pay their own way and maybe qualify for the scholarship.

Invited, huh? You could get invited to <u>possibly</u> qualify for a scholarship?

Wuhl... wait... why didn't I get invited?

I had faith in my abilities anyway, although there was a little voice in the back of my head warning me that in was in WAY over my head.

I ignored that voice; I had skills...

The first day of tryouts, I was ready; I was in the best shape of my life. We were about ten minutes into some drills and I was up in the air, going full speed toward the basket and crashed into another player. When I hit the floor my ankle exploded, and through the searing pain, my basketball life flashed in front of me, like they say happens when you die: all of it, in about two seconds real time, but years in slow motion.

You may be wondering what this story is doing in a book about relationships. Well, I'm going to get to that, don't worry, but I am also telling you this to chronicle my deferred journey into manhood.

I was 18 years old and every bit a boy. There I was, a thousand miles from home in a strange city, my Mom had just passed away, I was attending a Jesuit university having no idea what a Jesuit even was and I was walking around on crutches for weeks. Hank Raymonds, the freshman coach, assured me that I would get a chance to make the team when I was ready to come back.

Three weeks later, with my ankle taped so tight I could barely move, I made it onto the court at practice for the last five minutes. I didn't even touch the ball. The next day I didn't even get onto the court.

Dejected, I went to Coach Raymonds and quit the team. Looking back, what would it have meant to be a "man" in that situation? To not quit, for one. Was I going to make the team? Possibly, as a benchwarmer. Was I in over my head? Absolutely. But I took what was the most important focus in my young life and let it slip away. I made a decision that would affect the rest of my life, based on a busted ankle, a bruised ego and no sense of the perseverance it took to be successful.

During my rehab, I remember being in my dorm room sprawled out on my bed. I was in serious pain; the staff was not prescribing anything more serious than aspirin for the pain, I hadn't showered for days (I was a college student the first time away from home...) and I heard a knock at my dorm room door. A couple of friends from my Psych I class had heard the news of my injury and had come up to give me some support.

Female friends, that is. One of them was Jessica. She and I had exchanged glances standing around before class but hadn't made any connection beyond that. And despite the fact that I don't think she said more than three words in the time she and her friend Nancy visited, I was smitten. What better way to soothe my damaged ego than to fall in love?

We became inseparable. That is until I had to drop out of college because I wasn't getting a scholarship (oh yeah: that...)

But, as luck would have it we were both from the East coast and got to spend time together over the summer. A lot of time. Which her dad was not so keen on. He was a pint-sized psychiatrist (not that his size had anything to do with anything, outside of a possible Napoleon complex) that once called me on the carpet for taking a shower at his house after Jessica and I had spent the day together. Oh, it was separate showers and all; he just didn't like my long-haired, draft-avoiding, dropping-out-of-college ways. He later sent me a letter to that effect, citing how he felt it was "countermaturational" for a young man to spend entire days with a young woman (especially his daughter).

What a dick.

Jessica went back to school in the fall.

I, however, did not; my walk-on scholarship dream had been dashed and I parlayed what was supposed to be a summer job as a doorman at an Upper Eastside of Manhattan apartment complex into a nine month career. I eventually moved back to Milwaukee to be near her: young love and all. I eventually wore out my welcome in Milwaukee during the next few years over a series of misguided decisions, including one during the last summer, when Jessica went back east, I did not, and her best friend and I got a little too friendly with each other.

So, yeah; I was an asshole, a guy, early on, through my adolescence and into my early adulthood. And then on into my middle age, at least some of the time. My transition into manhood would be slow indeed. What was I thinking?

That Jessica's feelings had no bearing on the matter?

That I could run roughshod over the emotional lives of others and expect to get away with it?

That there was some sense of entitlement that came along with being male?

As I look back on that now, I realize it was not so much about becoming a man as it was becoming an adult.

I got lucky, through serendipitous intervention, leaving Milwaukee when I was 21, hitchhiking across the country and ending up in New Mexico by way of Yellowstone Park in Wyoming. I met a wonderful woman who I ended up living with for a year. She was a radical feminist, and until I met her, I had adopted a very old-school traditional, patriarchal (on the surface) upbringing, which was basically: it's a man's world. Well, Alice read me the riot act, in her own very persuasive way. Did I mention she was 29 at the time? Gee, that seems like so young now, but back then, she was the first "woman" I had ever been with (the others seemed like "girls"). I was very aware of our age difference at the time, mostly due to the fact that I was a very, very, young, sheltered 21 year BOY. And while she taught me to be LESS of an asshole, I was still an asshole in ending that relationship (I moved out while she was away on a vacation with her daughter. I know, right?) I had a lot to learn, and really, my journey was just beginning. Through the miracle of Facebook, we have since reconnected and I have both apologized for my transgressions and thanked her profusely for the gifts and lessons that she gave me.

She taught me a lot of things, not the least of which was the concept of "women as fellow human beings." I don't know if that was her wording at the time, but it was what I came away with. It made perfect sense then, and it makes perfect sense now, and it just amazes me that we still have the separation of the sexes that we do.

Yeah, I get that men don't want to lose their "power." And generally, I think it is safe to say it is better to have power than not. What I question is wielding power in romantic relationship over a person that is supposed to be your ally. From that time back in the 60s and 70s when awareness shifted in terms of patriarchy and matriarchy, we have come a long way towards equality of the sexes in our culture. But not far enough.

As we get further into the nuts and bolts of co-creating your relationship agreement, if the two of you decide you want to have an "old-fashioned" "I'm the man of the house and what I say goes" coupled with "OK, honey; just keep that bacon rolling in" kind of relationship, that's great-- as long as that is your agreement and it really is how you both want things set up. But both of you need to be honest about it, because in our culture today, this is still a fundamental starting point in what the structure of the union could be.

Is it a man's world? I think it is safe to say, that, while I have seen a radical shift in the power structure between men and women in my lifetime, there is still not gender equality. I still find myself having to apologize for the actions of my "brothers" far too often.

That being said, there is a lot to be said for maleness. Those qualities that we associate with masculinity move this world forward and stand up for what's right and keep us safe. And most women (in my informal poll) want their man to be masculine in bed.

I believe, though, it is time to redefine what it is to be masculine that encompasses strength through giving and protecting, not taking at the expense of others. Men, if you find yourself making blanket statements about women that are derogatory, take some time to realize how inaccurate general statements like that can be. If there are women in your past who have mistreated you, forgive them, and move on. As a result, some of the justification for misogyny will disappear.

Fortunately, we are at a period of time in our culture where there is a radical shift occurring in this direction. (For more on this, go to LeanIn.org).

Women and Misandry

A misandrist is a woman who hates men. Unlike misogyny, it's not a term we hear that often. Let's face it; women have been oppressed in our culture for a long time and it is still a man's world. If I were a woman, I'd be pissed off about that, and believe me, I have run across a lot of women who carry that frustration and anger with them on a daily basis. And I have had some of them take it out on me, largely because they could (which is to say, I let them).

So, to be fair, if men are assholes, then women are bitches, right? (I should have your attention now! Relax, relax; I'm just trying to get some equal time in for those of you who bristled at the "men are assholes" position). Besides, it should be noted that there are some women out there for whom that designation is a badge of honor.

Barbara, for one, informed me early on that, in no uncertain terms, that she "wasn't nice." Wanting to see (and acknowledge and encourage) her softer side (which did exist), I argued that she was nicer than she thought.

I was wrong.

And once the initial infatuation was over, she showed me just how not nice she wasn't.

Barbara was carrying around a lot of anger. When she told me the stories of her past, I thought, "Damn, this woman SHOULD be angry"; raised in a very strict religious household that she left to be on the streets as a teenager, she faced not only fear but sexual and emotional abuse at the hands of boys and men. Though she had no reason to be angry with me, unfortunately, I was guilty by association; that is to say, I had a penis too.

Subconsciously donning my best "savior" hat, I put up with it for a while, I guess because I thought she would come around, and she would see that I was offering her something different.

Apparently not, and my tendency towards conflict avoidance just enabled her rages. The first couple of times did raise a flag over the inappropriateness of her reactions (bathroom privacy and spending time with my male best friend that was visiting), so we had conversations about her triggers and expressed anger over my perceived misdeeds.

But those conversations had no effect on her behavior; what I saw as rage she described as "just being upset."

So, she was right; she wasn't "nice," and ultimately, what I perceived as verbal abuse was an absolute dealbreaker.

For you guys out there, btw, if you haven't learned this lesson yet, here it is: If a woman tells you she isn't nice, regardless of whatever reason you have for not wanting to believe her, believe her and walk, no, RUN, the other way. Because at some point, it's gonna come up, and she'll be able to say "I told you so" and you won't have a leg to stand on. Of course, I am assuming here, that you are a guy who wants and values kindness and consideration for others in a mate. Maybe you don't. Maybe you want to be with a badass (If so, I've got someone I'd like to introduce you to).

But I am going to tell you, ladies, that if you take that resentment into your relationship because "all men suck," it's going to be less than extraordinary. If you are angry with the idea of being born female in our culture then you have a fundamental issue that is going to be a part of your everyday existence.

If the inequality is a core issue for you, then devote some time and effort to changing it: work for a women's group, work educating men. Become a part of the solution. If you are angry because you have no power, figure out where the power is that you want, and go after it. If it is in the workplace, there are avenues that are open for that.

If it is power in a relationship, and that is truly what you want, there are passive men out there that will let you be in charge. Believe me; I was one of them. But be clear that that is what you want, because at some point, you will probably lose respect for your partner (if you ever had any). If what you want is "your way," then find someone who is willing to accommodate that, but be prepared that at some point the relationship may not work for him because his needs are not being met. And if he grows a pair, the dynamic of your relationship will change drastically. You could probably prolong that relationship a bit longer if you don't take your anger for men out on him. He, after all, is giving you what you want; it's all the rest of those assholes who you are angry towards. Essentially though, no one wants to be dominated; some will accept it, but only because they see no alternative.

A third option is to find someone that will partner with you: see your strengths and assets, weaknesses and foibles and treat you as an equal. If you find this person, it is extremely important that your anger for other men does not get transferred to him just because of his gender.

Simply put; yes, women, you have "earned" your right to be angry. But direct your anger at those who deserve it, not just at anyone who, by virtue of his gender can be viewed as a surrogate to take on the brunt of your vitriol. I know this anger issue does not apply to all women, but if it is part of your psychological make-up, you will need to come to terms with how you want it to show up in your relationships.

As in the example in the last chapter with misogyny, if you find yourself making blanket negative statements about men, you will have a hard time creating extraordinary relationship. Try softening your stance; first, include the word "most" or even "some" when referring to an entire gender. Then, figure out what qualities you find so negative and go out and find someone who doesn't display those traits. See how easy this is?

Let's assume though, that you not only don't hate the opposite sex, but are a big fan.

Now what?

Men and Women Together

Men are like THIS.

And women are like THAT.

Simple, huh?

Well, it used to be. Now, not so much.

First of all, I don't believe in broad generalizations as they apply to individuals. If we are talking about sociological trends, fine, I'll listen to your statistics and trends. But if we are talking about the issues of an individual or a specific couple, all probability goes out the window. When we are talking about or dealing with an individual, we are talking about a unique human being, so don't talk to me about "men this" and "women that." Usually when others are speaking in those terms, they have an agenda to promote, and almost invariably, it's their own.

What seems to be an issue is that we get together as men and women, all fired up and passionate and stupid (that's "goodstupid," btw) and then the infatuated, in-love, googly-eyed period ends. Maybe we can morph that into something deeper and maybe not. And it seems that MORE often than not, we can't. It could be argued that this is just an evolutionary imperative; that in terms of diversity, we should have more and different partners. It would seem to me that the pairings should last longer than they do around the idea of family and how long it takes our offspring to run off on their own. Of course, we are not out on the Serengeti; though we have much less life threatening pitfalls than our wild kingdom counterparts, our world is in constant flux. What adjustments should we be making for the way our world is structured today, with constant and radical change a given?

Traditional gender roles were much more clearly defined 50 years ago, and it used to be that the assertive, fast, hard, solid and fiery were attributed to the male (yang in Eastern philosophy), while the slow, soft, yielding, diffuse and earthy (yin) were attributed to the female. Now, anything goes; you can have a woman that is all yang and a male vice-versa or you can have attributes of both in each. One question becomes, at the start of this reassessment, who are YOU on the male/female spectrum? It can be argued that we all have male and female attributes.

Are you a "man's man": all testosterone laden and ass-kicking, large and in charge, master of your domain (<u>not</u> the Seinfeld reference), a Type A doer and a fixer? Or are you more of a "gentle-man": sensitive, non-combative, accepting, slow moving and reflective?

Are you a girly-girl: estrogen receptive, nurturing, soft, more passive and allowing? Or are you a superwoman: career driven, baby-making', take-charge, bringhomethebaconandfryitupinapan do-it-all and ask what's next?

It's very confusing. Confusing, but RICH. There are so many more possibilities, but it also creates so may more ways that we can miss connecting because the question becomes not only who are you but who do you want in a mate? We've all heard the axiom "opposites attract." Is that what you want in a partner? Your polar opposite? Are you sure? Wouldn't you appreciate someone more like YOU? I'm just asking, because part of the idea behind this paradigm change is that we get really conscious about what that all looks like.

Heterosexually speaking, men are attracted to women and women are attracted to men, and there is a whole spectrum on which this occurs, from simply noticing another person as a member of the opposite sex, to arguably the most intimate, passionate exchanges that two people can share, and many, many points in between.

How aware are you of the opposite sex? When you are in a group, do you see "people?" Or "men" and "women" as separate very gender-specific individuals?

I don't believe either is a wrong approach, but your answer will give you some insight into how important the male/female dynamic is to your picture of the world. If you are seeing everyone as just people, then the differences between the sexes are not that important to you, or they may not be important until you get one on one.

If you distinctly see men and women separately, then other questions pop up. First, what is your general feeling about that? Does it make you excited? Apprehensive? Combative? Anticipatory? Are they the "enemy?" Or a source of potential pleasure? Do you prefer spending time with the opposite sex, or your own gender?

Because our species wants to perpetuate, to some degree we experience members of the opposite sex on a primal, cellular level as potential procreative partners. This does not happen (usually) on a conscious level, but it creates an undercurrent of attraction that is constantly in play. This attraction occurs on an extremely wide spectrum from feigned indifference to wanting to copulate with anything in a skirt or pants (based not so much on your apparel preference, but what's underneath).

This scale can be measured in levels of attention, both that we are giving and receiving. If there has been a pattern in our lives where we get a lot of attention from the opposite sex, this filter can be more "active." Conversely, if we very specifically don't get attention from the opposite sex, it can become a non-factor. If you are at either extreme (too much attention or not enough), focus on the opposite sex can become an obsession.

On what level does this impact your life? We all have filters in place for what we want to notice, like after we buy a new car, we tend to see that same car everywhere. Those cars were always there, but now we notice them. Some of us have a propensity for attraction, because it stimulates us, or we get fed by it.

Do you have a filter in place specifically for the opposite sex? Do you notice an attractive man or woman when they come into your field? That is the very first step in relationship: an awareness that another exists.

The second step is being noticed back. If we notice someone noticing us, there is a mutual awareness. If someone is watching us, and we are not aware, there is no connection. Same thing if we notice, but they are not aware.

For the sake of argument, let's assume that at least one of you is attempting to convey to the other a sense of interest, and let's assume that interest has to do with some kind of psycho-physio-cellular stimulation (let's call it the "Juice"). The next stage is the acknowledgement of the connection: a smile, or even just prolonged eye contact. This can be the most minimal of exchanges; it can last for a second, and never occur with that person again, as when we pass someone on the street.

From there, we might engage and attempt to communicate. This is usually where the trouble starts. It can be non-verbal, with body language or, if the opportunity presents itself, we open our mouths and do our best to verbalize. We have now entered another person's physical space and attempted to converse. There may be actual cause for conversation; there could be a legitimate curiosity, a burning question that needs answering, a comment that wants to be expressed, or it may be casual conversation for the sake of conversation.

But what I am talking about is intentional engagement for the purpose of letting another person of the opposite sex KNOW that you are attracted to them.

You are flirting!

Why do we do that?

It's fucking FUN, that's why! Our brains are firing away, sending signals to body parts to release chemicals and hormones, and it feels good, because dammit; our species IS going to be perpetuated. Woo-hoo! This is our version of that dance that the albatross does, and in many ways, it is just as comical, if not more so.

But not so fast; YOUR part is being expressed. What's happening across from you? If you are doing your job even halfway right, that person is aware that you have some interest in them. They have now sized you up, in much the same way that you have them, and they are deciding if they want to reciprocate. Here's the difference, though; you have initiated the contact. They may have been minding their own business and here you come with your agenda to perpetuate the species (or some modified version of that) and they may just not be interested.

But suppose they are...

And a few months later, the two of you are standing at the altar, professing your undying love for each other.

Oh, wait; did I skip a few steps?

Just because we want someone, that doesn't mean they are going to want US. (I've always wanted to create a bumper sticker that reads: "The Problem with Relationships is That There's Always That Other Person Involved"). There is wanting someone, and the "juice" we get from that, and there is wanting them to want us, and that is where we so often run into a snag; that whole requited/unrequited thing...

Based on an idealistic romantic shopping list of factors, the determination of whether or not we are a suitable match now gets extremely complex. Let's assume there IS a mutual connection; everybody's smiling, and laughing, you go out to dinner and neither one of you is lactose intolerant, ok, he's a dog person and she's cat, but the two of you gloss over that, you agree that Sean Connery was the best Bond, and you both voted for the same person for president. Every single one of those compatibilities is lighting your brain up like the score keeper on a pinball machine (dingdingdingding). End of date. Butterflies. Good kisser (and let's face it; this could have been a deal breaker. What is up with all the bad kissers out there? I don't think there is enough feedback on bad kissing).

Where was I?

Another date. Phone calls, e-mails: every day.

You are in a relationship! You are both feeling like this could be "it!"

It???!!!!

You mean, that mythical soul mate? The love to end all loves?

The ONE?

Whoa, Kimosabe... (For those of you old enough to remember the original Lone Ranger, you can also remember the sound of a record needle sliding abusively and discordantly across record vinyl. Insert that here).

This is where the paradigm shift has to start to occur. Hands down, the biggest obstacle we face, collectively, is that we mistake this beginning infatuation for love and a basis for long-term relationship. More on this very soon, but the gist of it is that you are both in a quasi-self-induced, chemically altered state. In the beginning everything is wonderful and harmonious, or at least the illusion of that, but then, as that self-induced "high" wears off, the "perfection" starts to become a bit less so and all of a sudden, she notices (and it's an issue) that he doesn't like her cat.

What??!! But it was all so ideal just a few weeks ago.

This first chink in the armor is when the blinders come off (I know it's a mixed metaphor; don't be so anal...)

As we set out to engage in relationship, we have a few broad directions in which we can head when such challenges arise.

We can totally accept the person as they are, warts and all. (And I say "accept," not "tolerate." The latter carries with it a judgment that starts to steer us away from a healthy and positive path).

We can embrace that which we admire in the other and hope that that which is less desirable will change. And that is a possibility; part of the premise of this new paradigm is that our world IS so changeable, so why wouldn't that apply to our partners?

We can set out to deliberately change them, which traditionally has had a dismal success rate.

We can change the way we ourselves view the situation. What is our belief system around their behavior? Is it truly our own belief system, or someone else's that has come before us, that we have just adopted as gospel? For instance, if you grew up around the idea that money is the root of all evil, does that mean you would not partner with someone prosperous, because it means they are somehow immoral?

Or if we find that our prospective (or current) partner's behavior is simply unacceptable, we can move on and find someone perfect.

Or, you can just run over the cat.

I'm kidding; I love cats. There is a dog story later, though.

Addicted to Love?

It's infatuation, folks. Hands down, my favorite state. What a wonderful existence it would be to live there all the time, right? Probably not; too much of anything gets to be mundane and boring. How about inducing the state whenever we want, like taking a drug?

As my high school friends who ostracized me for not partaking will tell you, drugs and I never got along. That being said, there is a little discussed natural amphetamine, phenylethylamine (PEA), that gets released in our bodies as a result of attraction to another human being. Those of you who have experienced this know just what I mean. Personally, it is my drug of choice, over oxytocin, endorphins, dopamine, adrenaline, norepinephrine, testosterone, estrogen or pheromones. But combine those with PEA and that is quite a potent cocktail we are talking about (it makes Sex on the Beach look like a Shirley Temple). Face it; we are love junkies.

Here's the problem with PEA, though: your body builds up a tolerance to it. But assuming the same stimulus is still there, you create more, and build up a tolerance to that until at some point the system says, "That's it; this lab is shutting down." ("Breaking Bad" anyone?).

That is the end of the infatuation phase, and you crash; the blinders come off, and your little snookums is now just another human being with pimples and cellulite, bad breath and nose hairs, issues and baggage.

When I was younger, I thought infatuation was "love." I mean, c'mon; every Faeriefuckingtale and movie and song told me so. I would fall in love, get all euphoric, blind and stupid and then when the crash came, I thought, "Well, this must not be *love, true love,* because it's supposed to last forever, and besides, I am not feeling nearly as good as I did last week. She must not be "The One." So I would go out and find my next soulmate. And then the next one after that.

I can honestly say that every relationship I have ever been in has started with infatuation. What better place to start?

The tricky part about infatuation is that is just happens. I was minding our own business, working on a construction project and going to the local diner every day for lunch when the sweaty waitress with the long braid running down to her waist started making sure that my lunch was "OK" a little more than was really necessary.

And then one day, as I was leaving said diner, out of some old movie from the fifties, without even thinking about it, I winked at her us I was leaving.

What? Winking? Really? Who does that?

After I went back in the next day and she took my order, she remarked, "You winked at me yesterday."

Blushing (yes, really, because as has been already established; who winks?) I said, "Yeah, I'm sorry; I don't know where that came from. It just slipped out."

"No, don't apologize. No one has ever winked at me before. It gave me butterflies."

The next thing I knew, I had made plans to meet her down at the dock after I was done at work.

She was already there, but she wasn't the sweaty, greasy, hair-braided hash-slinger who I was familiar with. The hair was now released to the breeze coming in off the ocean, the apron was gone and as she was leaning back with her elbows on the railing, she was sporting what to this day were the longest most beautiful summer-tanned legs I have ever seen.

I was toast.

There was just one problem; I was meeting her to tell her we couldn't get together anymore because I was in another relationship. I know, I know; believe me, I know. Why meet in the first place?

"Hey, how was work?" she asked.

"It looks like this project is going to drag on for a while; the owner keeps making changes."

"Well, that's good; that means I will get to see you more."

(So now my brain gets another shot of PEA, because not only am I hot for her, but she's indicating she is hot for me. But I am not totally oblivious yet. There is that part of me that is remembering my original mission to tell her we can't see each other).

"Yeah, well, umm, about that: I just wanted to be able to talk to you away from the diner. Look, we are obviously attracted to one another, but I am in a relationship with someone else."

"Fuck; I KNEW it!"

"I just wanted to be able to tell you face to face and to be honest about it."

"So why meet me here? Why get my hopes up?"

"I honestly don't know; it seemed like the right thing to do. I didn't want to blurt something out at the diner and I still want to be able to eat lunch there every day."

"Lunch? You're worried about where you are going to eat lunch?"

"I'm kidding (I wasn't really; I DID want to keep eating lunch there every day; it was the best in town, and right down the street from the project); I just... I don't know, I'm sorry; it seemed like the right thing to do. I'm sorry. I shouldn't have flirted with you in the first place. You just seemed nice and it starting turning into something more than it should, and so I just wanted to set the record straight."

She looked me right in the eye and we held that for I don't know how long. The wind was still blowing her hair. I could smell the salt coming off the water and the heat from the sun on our skin. That's right; I could smell the heat. My senses were overlapping, working overtime...

She shook her head and smiled this little smile, "Alright, whatever; go home to your girlfriend." And she turned away and started walking back to her car. I caught up to her and we walked in silence through the parking lot. She got in her ratty old car and rolled down the window.

I said, "So... see you tomorrow?"

"Yeah, see you tomorrow..." She lowered her head and smiled as I stood there like an idiot. Then she looked up and said, "You have the most incredible blue eyes."

And she rolled up her window and drove away.

And I am thinking, "Blue eyes? What blue eyes? My eyes are... what color ARE my eyes?" Hard to believe, but up until that moment, I had never consciously thought about my eyes. They were just my eyes. But "incredible?" I had "incredible blue" eyes!" So, the first thing I did when I got in my car was to look at my eyes in the rear-view mirror, and sure enough, there they were: my eyes. Incredible blue? Hardly. Certainly not PaulNewmanIncredibleBlue, but OK, I guess.

Of course, it didn't matter what I thought; Sally thought they were blue. And not just "blue," but "incredibleblue."

I drove home, which took almost an hour, and couldn't stop thinking about what had just happened. I did the right thing, didn't I? Of course, none of what transpired was communicated to my partner; we didn't talk about much of anything anymore. Not only that, we didn't <u>do</u> much of anything either. Sex was rare and perfunctory. We didn't go out. We did like some of the same TV shows though; we did have that. But the "juice" had long since left our relationship and we didn't replace it with very much outside of coexistence. We were an ongoing couple, like so many other couples, staying together primarily because we has said we would.

As I drove to work the next day, all I could think about was lunch.

I walked in, sat down, and there was apron-wearing, hair-braided, sweatygreasy Sally. She stopped in front of me, pen and pad poised, expressionless.

"I'll have the Denver Omelet with a side of home fries," I said.

"Coffee with that?"

"No, just a large lemonade."

She brought my order. "Anything else?"

"No, thanks." She stood there for a couple of seconds too long.

"I hadn't realized what was wrapped up in that braid," I said, wanting to break the tension.

She stared me down, thrust out her hip, shook her head, then smiled and turned away to tend to her other customers.

She made sure to be at the register when I got up to pay the check. I said, "Can you meet me by the dock again today?"

"Sure," she said, like the invitation was no surprise at all.

It was the same kind of breezy summer day, and while her outfit was different, it had the same effect; lots of bare arms and legs and shoulders. Skin.

I walked up to her, our eyes locked. When I got close enough, I took my hands and placed them at the back of her neck underneath all of that luscious hair and pulled her towards me and kissed her as if we had kissed a hundred times. She returned it the same way and then, hooked her left leg around the back of my right knee.

I don't know why I remember that move so distinctly, but it was the start of a love affair that lasted a thousand days. As you can well imagine, the rest of my life became very complicated, but we will return to consequences and outcomes later when I talk about jealousy, regret and karma.

Infatuated? Oh, yeah, you bet.

A wise decision? No, of course not; this had nothing to do with wisdom. I needed another "fix." I needed more "juice."

Yes, I was an addict.

"Hi, my name is Roman and I am a Juicejunkie." Addicted to "love?" Robert Palmer would have me thinking so (especially after his famous video), but I was not addicted to love; I was addicted to infatuation.

And here is where I would get into trouble. Time after time. I had been led to believe that that attraction, that euphoric, blinding, logic-killing sensation, was love.

But it's not.

And what I needed was not so much a 12-step program but information that would prove to me once and for all that this infatuation phenomenon existed and was indeed separate from deep, true lasting love.

Not that my legacy of serial monogamy wasn't evidence enough. But I needed facts. I needed science, I needed...

The Written Word.

This was before the internet, btw, so for me, in much the same way that we accept whatever we see on the internet, if I saw it in a book, it represented gospel to me.

Unless of course, I read it and just simply didn't pay any attention to it. Yeah, the old ignoring-the-wisdom-of-those-who-have-come-before-us-because-I-know-better approach.

I had been exposed to this information probably fifteen years prior. My older sister had handed me a copy of M. Scott Peck's "The Road Less Traveled." I thumbed through it, and wrote it off, basically being in my 20's and knowing everything, like every other twentysomething who has ever walked the planet. It wasn't until I picked up the book again in my early 40's and read his chapter on romantic love that the lesson sank in:

> "Of all the misconceptions about love the most powerful and pervasive is the belief that "falling in love" is love or at least one of the manifestations of love. But two problems are immediately apparent... The first is that the experience of falling in love is specifically a sex-linked erotic experience... We fall in love only when we are consciously or unconsciously sexually motivated. The second problem is that the experience of falling in love is invariably temporary. No matter whom we fall in love with, we sooner or later fall out of love if the relationship continues long enough. This is not to say that we invariably cease loving the person with whom we fell in love.

But it is to say that the feeling of ecstatic lovingness that characterizes falling in love always passes. The honeymoon always ends. The bloom of romance always fades."

(Can we just have quiet in the room for a few seconds? 1-2-3-4...)

WHAT???!!!!

What do you mean, "it always passes," "always ends," always fades?"

Not MY love, not OUR love. Not cluelessinyour20s (OK, 30s...) love.

OK, 40's...

But after a couple of failed marriages and numerous other relationships over my first 20+ adult years, I started thinking maybe this Peck guy is on to something. (By the way, if you haven't read "The Road Less Traveled," put it on your reading list for as soon as you are done with this one).

I started asking around, and sure enough, he was right. It always fades, it always passes, it always ends.

Always, always, always...

Always.

Oh, sure, we hear about the occasional outlier couple that have been together for 50 years and they're still going at each on the kitchen table 6 times a week. First of all, I don't want to think about that particular visual and second of all, they're lying. I'm not saying there are not happily married couples that have been together for a long time that still enjoy a healthy robust sex life. But it's not that same infatuation that they had in the beginning. The good news is that they have taken that initial feeling and allowed it to evolve into something much more meaningful.

I once did a presentation on this concept of fading infatuation in front of a college class on Human Sexual Behavior. At the very beginning, I apologized to anyone in the class who was currently in love, because, as I now knew (and was eager to impart to everyone), it was going to end. Needless to say, it was not well received. And you may be experiencing the very same skepticism.

I understand.

And I empathize.

You may be thinking, "Well that didn't happen when I was with so and so."

Perhaps not, but did it happen to them first? No? Really? Then why aren't you still together, experiencing all that euphoric bliss?

Start asking around; gather your own evidence, see what you come up with.

But do me a favor; don't stop reading the book here because you see me as some sort of heartless heretic. There are couples out there that are experiencing extraordinary relationship. We are going to take what I have learned from them and make adjustments for our life and times and do the very same thing ourselves.

There is hope! There can be love after infatuation.

(Wait. Did he just say the L-word?)

The L-Word

You know the one I'm talking about: L-O-V-E. Hopefully, in your life, you have had the occasion to utter the phrase "I love you" to someone.

What does it mean to you when you say that? If you are saying it early on in a relationship, it generally means something like, "With you now in my life, I am complete, I am euphoric." That's the infatuation talking, the chemicals. And don't get me wrong; I'm not knocking it; as we have previously established, nobody loves that feeling more than I do.

The problem enters when the chemicals wear off, when the "juice" is gone and it doesn't feel the same way; does that mean I don't love you anymore? For me, it used to, when I didn't know any better. But now, once I am past the honeymoon phase, I will use that same word to mean, "I want to fulfill your needs, I want to satisfy you, I want you to feel safe, and excited and connected and significant as a result of our being together."

I've always felt that the word "love" had too many meanings in the English language: you can "love" a movie, you can "love" your kids, you can "love" a friend, you can "love" your mother or father, you can even "love" your car.

One of my favorite progressions in a new relationship is when there is an obvious connection, but neither party has committed to the "L-word" yet. Then it starts: "I love your hair," "I love when you kiss me like that," "I love the way you dress," "I love your texts in the middle of the day," "I love how you love that I love your loving lovingness."

And then...

Someone gets up the cojones to say those three words, and just those three words, in that exact order: "I love you."

Hopefully they are not left hanging there, and get a "Thank you" or a "That's nice..." because anyone who has ever put an "I love you" out there is hoping to get one back.

Here is a humorous exchange from an episode of "Seinfeld:"

> George: "I might tell her that I love her."
>
> Jerry: "That's a big move, Georgie-boy. Are you confident in the 'I love you' return?"
>
> George: "50-50."
>
> Jerry: "'Cause if you don't get that return, that's a pretty big matzo ball hangin' out there."
>
> George: "I've just got to say it once; everybody else gets to say it. Why can't I say it?"
>
> Elaine: "What? You've never said it?"

George: "Once, to a dog. He licked himself and left the room."

Subsequently and unfortunately, George, does NOT get his "I love you" return, and hilarity ensues. In real life, that ain't funny. We want our "I love you's" reciprocated. We want to know that someone loves us back, or if we are fortunate enough, to hear those three words first.

Why? What's the big deal? In his book, "Perfect Love, Imperfect Relationships," John Welwood speaks not only about loving, but of the problems that come along with being *unloved:*

> "All the most intractable problems in human relationships can be traced back to what I call *the mood of unlove*—a deep-seated suspicion that most of us harbor that we cannot be loved, or that we are not truly lovable, *just as we are*. This basic insecurity makes it hard to trust in ourselves, in other people, or in life itself."

I do believe that as humans we have an innate need to be connected to others: to love. Very often, that first, "I love you" has more to do with a feeling than a way that you are committing to BE with someone. Moving from a passive verb: "it feels good to be around you," to an active one: "I want to give to you of myself."

So how do we transition from that feeling of intense infatuation, when everything is "perfect" to one (or both) of us now seeing a more realistic, vulnerable, imperfect but joyful, fulfilling union: to creating extraordinary relationship?

It helps to have a model for that kind of thing: either a couple you know that has been successful in that, or even better, you can have someone teach you.

As luck would have it, I met someone truly loving.

Eleanor, supported and encouraged, <u>loved</u> during her formative years, was someone who not only knew how to give, but was perfectly willing to do so. Ironically, she was much younger, and our relationship was "scandalous," but we didn't care. It was a truly eye (and heart) opening experience for me. For her, it was an opportunity to share what she had to give with someone old enough to appreciate it.

Not that that relationship was without its challenges (otherwise we would still be together, right?) Ultimately, the fact that we were at such different stages in our lives created a disconnect between us, not the least of which was a decision about whether or not we would have children together. Another ironic part of that disconnect was that, even though I was older, I was not mature enough for that kind of relationship at that point in my life; I still had a lot of work to do.

But a seed had been planted.

I believe that some people cross our paths as teachers, and that can probably be said for almost everyone we meet. She taught me the concept of being with another "giver," which came as an epiphany for me and was a great lesson to learn.

Until I forgot it.

Not right away, but eventually, temporarily, in a weakened, blind moment.

Like most addicts (and understand, this was not about sex as much as it was about the romance, the infatuation), I relapsed. I let myself be blissfully led astray. "Two givers? What?"

Eleanor and I had long since gone our separate ways. I had been working in a car dealership as the finance manager. Part of my duties there included arranging financing and vehicle registration for our customers.

A woman had called our dealership, temporarily staying in New Mexico, wanting to purchase a vehicle from us. Part of my job was trying to figure out the best way to register the vehicle: in her previous state, in New Mexico, or the state she was eventually moving to.

"When will you be moving to your final destination?"

"I am going from here to Arizona temporarily for a few months and then eventually moving to Idaho, so I need a sport utility vehicle."

I asked, "Do you have an address in Arizona or Idaho?"

"No, I haven't made those plans yet."

"Well, the best thing to do is to register your new vehicle in the state where you are licensed, since you have a corresponding physical address, and then when you finally land in Idaho, just switch it over."

"That's sounds logical."

She gave me her previous address and I contacted their MVD, and learned the charges that would be applicable, which included a $100 surcharge for registering a vehicle as a truck. When I informed Amanda of that surcharge she said, "But it's not a truck; it's an SUV, and I have registered SUVs there before and was never charged that."

"Well, I am just telling you what they told me. Let me contact them again and see if I can get it straightened out."

I never did get it straightened out with Florida MVD, and Amanda, thinking I was trying to fleece her, was refusing to pay it. We still hadn't met, but we kept talking on the phone until the day came when she was driving a rental car into the dealership and would drive away with her new FourRunner. She met with the salesperson first and then it became time for her meet with me to do her paperwork.

I emerged from my office to greet her and was met by one of the most stunningly beautiful women I have ever met: perfectly straight blond hair, blue eyes (WAY bluer than mine!), dressed in cargo pants and a simple, unassuming top. She took my breath away.

I said, "Hi Amanda; it's nice to finally meet you. I have still been going around with Florida MVD about this registration issue, but I haven't gotten the answer from them you were looking for."

I could see the immediate frustration in her face, as she prepared to dig her heels in and contest.

And then I uttered what surely sounded like a line, but was my actual heartfelt sentiment: "I've been trying to find a way to have you be right."

It got her attention. She visibly relaxed and we went into my office.

Ultimately, the dealership ended up absorbing the extra cost of the registration, but there were some other complications around her financing. Three hours later (yes, three hours), she emerged from my office, the proud owner of a new FourRunner, and she and I were mutually googly-eyed. In between fielding phone calls about her financing, we shared divorce stories and compared notes on relationships and psychology, which we were both interested in.

Needless to say, we were bonding all over the place. I knew she was going to be staying overnight in Santa Fe. As she was leaving, I walked her out to her new vehicle and I said, "I would love to have dinner with you, but of all nights, I have a date tonight. It's my first in months, but it's a first date and may not go too long. Can I call you if we get done early?"

I had good intentions, I really did. This was a prime example of my brutal honesty, combined with too much information, getting in the way. I didn't want to break the date; that would have been inconsiderate, but I also didn't really want to go. Oh, and also, as it turned out, this was not just any date; this was a date with Lily that had been postponed from two weeks earlier, and I had had the hots for Lily for years, but we had never been able to be single at the same time. Until now.

Lily showed up for the date in a spaghetti strap dress that was just a little too big for her, so she spent the better part of the night hiking it back up when she felt too much cleavage was being displayed, which was not only fun but endearing for me. This was all just the worst possible timing, though; literally years of missed opportunities to connect with this woman and here she was, sitting across from me with her perfectly disheveled curly red hair, freckled shoulders and British accent. I should have been enchanted.

And I wasn't present at all.

By the time the date was over, she nearly ran out of the restaurant. What's funny is that if we had met on the original date two weeks prior, there might have been a totally different story to tell. Interestingly, years later, I was able to tell Lily the story of why I was such a horrible date.

She was not amused or understanding.

Or forgiving.

But back to Amanda.

I called, she answered, and we went out for a glass of wine. Actually, we went out and I had a glass of wine; as it turned out, she did not drink. Amanda had a long list of foods and beverages she would not eat. No sugar, and I mean none, so at the supermarket, every label had to be checked. No, not just checked: scrutinized, analyzed. Do you realize how many food products have sugar in them?

I didn't.

But I do now...

But I am getting ahead of myself.

We just picked up where we had left off earlier: totally connected. We talked for hours, closed the bar, went back to her hotel room, connected still more until we giddily drove through a freak hailstorm at four in the morning looking for an all-night drugstore to get some condoms.

Amanda ended up moving to New Mexico and staying there with Skipper, her Shih Tzu. We were off and running. For a good while anyway, until the infatuation wore off and we were left confronted with our glaring incompatibilities, not the least of which was the dogperson/catperson debate.

I fell into the "catperson" camp, but y'know, we often make concessions in the name of "love." I had never been around a Shih Tzu before. I guess they are known to be a little high-strung. Skipper was the posterdog for high-strung. He had been a rescue dog and had been abused, so needless to say, Skipper had some issues above and beyond his ShihTzuness. When she brought him over to my house, I would have to put my cat outside. One time, the patio door was open and he got a running start at Sootie, my cat, who was sitting serenely in the middle of the yard. He sat there, watching this lunatic dog run at him at full speed and didn't move a muscle. Well, Skipper was not prepared for that; he was expecting Sootie to run. It was like a scene from a cartoon; Skipper screeched to a halt within inches of the cat, then turned around with his tail between his legs, questioning not only his supposed dog-dominance, but his whole world order. (Sootie took on the title of CatGhandi from that point forward).

At some point towards the end of my relationship with Amanda, Skipper would sit on the couch in between us while we were watching a movie, and invariably get the affection that should have been rightfully mine.

Yes, "rightfully mine." Yes, I was jealous of a dog.

I wasn't predisposed to be overly affectionate with him anyway. (OK, I never petted him, alright?) But somehow that didn't prepare me for our dramatic ending one night. Things had not been going well between Amanda and me at that point anyway. There were many ways beyond Skipper and the no-sugar and the no-wine where we didn't connect; the crystals, and the metaphysics and the assumption that my daughter and I were going to move into her place, just to name a few.

Yes, my daughter. Amanda didn't have any kids of her own, and I think she sorta felt about them the way I felt about dogs. But since my daughter already had a great (divorced from me) Mom, I wasn't looking for a replacement or even an adjunct, so my daughter wasn't really a big part of the picture in this relationship although she was in others that were more kid-friendly.

And never mind my daughter, but the assumption that I was going to move into her place was never discussed and I had a perfectly nice place of my own, thank you very much. Obviously, we were failing to communicate, and the infatuation bloom had long since left the rose of our relationship, although I have to say,

I never stopped finding her attractive. She had this one pair of yoga pants that had these lemon slices on them. If she was wearing the lemon pants, she could pretty much get me to do anything. She must not have been wearing them this particular night though, because Skipper was being especially Skipper-like, grooming his nether regions and then pushing his nose into my hand to share some of his doglickings.

"Skipper, that's disgusting," I said, wiping my hand off on the couch that had so many of his cooties on it that a few more weren't going to matter (granted, a regressive moment...)

Amanda took offense to the fact that I had not only wiped away his tainted canine spittle but had admonished him for sharing it with me:

"He's just being a dog. You know, you never liked him."

Despite the fact that that statement was absolutely true, I felt the need to defend my actions.

"Well, it doesn't help that you're more affectionate with him than you are with me."

"Well, maybe if you petted him once in a while, he wouldn't be quite so needy."

Looking at this in retrospect, this spat was not about Skipper sharing his asslickings with me or even that he was getting Amanda's misplaced affection. This was just the precipitating event about our larger, issues of incompatibility. But now we were off and running, and there was no turning back

Things had apparently degenerated beyond my apparent disdain for her pooch, but I wasn't prepared for her coup de gras,

"What if I felt about your daughter the way you feel about Skipper?"

Now, you have to understand, I have this very primal protective father bear thing that kicks in when there is even the remotest chance that my daughter is being threatened or maligned in any way.

"What did you say? Are you comparing my daughter to that mutt?"

She repeated, "Yes, what if I felt about your daughter the way you feel about Skipper?"

"That's what I thought you said. We're done."

I walked out, and it was the end of our relationship.

I got blinded by the lemon pants. And while my attraction to Amanda wasn't just about her body (she was also brilliant), this brings up an important point, which is how much of an emphasis we can place on physical appearance.

At the risk of oversimplifying, I chose the path that ignored the lesson learned. I went for the juice and ignored what I had learned about being with another giver. Knowing what I know now, would I have made a different decision?   Maybe.

But you know and I know, it doesn't work that way. Before we make a decision, we don't know what the outcome of the alternate path would have been.

I have come to a point in my life now where I understand that shortcoming in the decision-making process, and so take responsibility for my choices, not knowing, ever, truly, what our outcomes will be.

So, no regrets. And at the same time, that obsession on experiencing infatuation, succumbing to that mutual physical attraction, has perhaps led me into relationships that may have been shorter-lived and probably less extraordinary than had I followed the path of more commonality, creating a connection that was potentially more profound and deep.

Older and somewhat wiser now, my priorities have changed. Deep conversations about practically anything, laughing hysterically about something that used to seem so terribly important and serious, languishing in bed on days off with bodies intertwined and multiple cups of coffee, making soup, hiking and sharing favorite places and coming HOME to my best friend have moved up on my list, and "the Juice," while still somewhere on the list, is no longer at the top.

The Perfect Partner

I toiled as a woodworker for almost 20 years. I loved taking a pile of lumber and crafting it onto a functional article of furniture or cabinetry. One of the strongest joints I could craft was the dovetail that most are familiar with as the joinery in the drawer sides of most well-built antique furniture. Dovetailing has become a metaphor for anything that fits really well, and I know, having crafted them from piles of unworked wood, it is a painstaking process to get them to fit correctly. That fit becomes increasingly difficult the more dovetails there are, and if they don't all fit, the sides are not going to mesh.

I use this metaphor for relationship as we try to take all of the pieces of who we are as complex individuals and integrate them with another. As our worlds become increasingly more complicated, it becomes harder and harder for our relationships to integrate in ways that work for both individuals. Years ago, it was so much simpler: men were men and women were women. There was a yin-yang, female-male polarity. It can certainly be argued that our culture has gotten more androgynous and that that has taken some of the "juice" away.

At the risk of over simplifying, the yin-yang symbol represents a balance in the universe, but more specifically, two polar opposites that exist to complement each other. If those two opposites are unbalanced, then one side becomes dominant. In masculine/feminine terms, yang represents the male: active, assertive, open. Yin represents the female: passive, receiving and dark. (I know the concept is much more complex than I am making it out to be, so all you Taoists and Buddhists just calm down).

As humans, we possess both yin and yang qualities. Again, in years past, that was much more clearly defined; men were yang, women were yin. As we have become more androgynous, the act of men and women coupling has become much more complicated. And frankly, it doesn't matter what society is doing, what matters is *what that balance looks like in YOU and in the person you are partnered with.*

In my family of origin, my Mom was predominantly yang. Behind the scenes that is. We were just hitting the feminist revolution as I was growing up, but my Mom was ahead of the curve. She ran the family in every way except in the eyes of my Dad. He thought he was "the boss" but everyone else knew better. So I had that model of a strong woman in a relationship as I ventured forth into the morass of adult relationship. Without consciously thinking about it, I was attracted to strong women; *this is what relationship looks like.* Then when I met Alice that all got reinforced. I decided that I liked the idea of having a strong woman in my life: someone I could respect and look up to. Early in, I still wasn't sure what to do with that and I was too passive in who I was, and so a lot of those relationships ended up being disharmonious because there was too much female yang to my overabundant male yin.

My suggestion is that you start with yourself and figure out what you want that balance to look like in yourself. Then, decide what that balance would look like in (and with) a partner, and let that be front and center as you go about choosing who to be with.

There are a million ways for all of this to manifest. One word of caution, especially for you women out there that think you want a masculine man, a *"real"* man so that you can be *in your feminine.* While that may be true in certain areas, it can also mean putting yourself in a subservient position, living someone else's life where you are just an adjunct. A lot of women have fought long and hard to get closer to gender equality in our culture. If you are deciding to go that old school route, be conscious about it, and don't complain when you realize you are have become a secondary citizen in your relationship.

With that in mind, how do we decide who to partner with? How conscious of a process is that? These days, with internet dating sites and social media, it is much more conscious than it used to be. It used to be that we would sort through whomever was in our social circles, get attracted to some aspect of them (usually their physical appearance) and then hope that that attraction was mutual. As often as not, that other person was not available (married, in a relationship with someone else or simply not interested in you) and we would go on our merry way until we found someone willing to engage.

It's a wonder anyone ever gets together, it's so random. But there are a lot of people in the world and somehow, the numbers work out, as well as the chemistry equation.

Or does it?

It does in terms of *getting* men and women together, but how about *keeping* them together, because that seems to be the problem, doesn't it? We are supposed to stay bonded for life, and somehow, that bonds breaks down.

Maybe it's because we settle.

Oh, sure, we don't think that in the beginning, when we don't know the other person. They are "perfect," well, the promise of perfect anyway. Why not? In the beginning, it's all fantasy anyway, so why not just assume they are perfect until they prove otherwise, which is inevitable. But in the beginning, we hold on to that image for as long as we possibly can, ignoring the flags that come up during the infatuation stage (this is Mother Nature, keeping us together long enough to procreate). And then when the crash comes, all the warts get exposed and we realize that our "perfect" partner is somewhat less so. But we are supposed to stay together, so we settle.

It sounds terrible, doesn't it? Would you prefer for me to sugarcoat it? OK, we "accept the other person for who they are." There, that's so much better isn't it?

But indulge me for a moment; wouldn't it be great to find the perfect partner? Someone that fits all the parameters of who you want in a partner, including them thinking that YOU are the perfect partner. How cool would that be? Most of us have an image of that in our minds, and as we get older, and have had some "practice" in terms of what we want and don't want in a mate, can consider aspects of certain partners and combine them; gee, wouldn't it be great to find someone with Rita's body, and Dawn's kindness, sense of humor, hair and mind and Maria's face and Bernadette's cooking and somebody-I've-never-met's love of basketball and Barbara's success and drive and Sally's family too, let's not forget them and Eleanor's love for children, or Lucy's penchant for fun? Huh? Wouldn't that be great?

No wonder relationships are getting harder as we get older; we can make these odious comparisons and indulge ourselves in frivolous, unrealistic exercises like this that make real human beings pale in comparison. I can hear the platitude-writers in the background already: "I love you just the way you are" (or is that Billy Joel singing?) Maybe the perfect person for you does exist and maybe, just maybe, you could be lucky enough to find that person. But then what are the odds that you would end up being the perfect person for them?

Let's assume that you have not found your perfect partner (otherwise you wouldn't be reading this book, right?) and let's assume that you are not a puppy-loved (or puppy-loving) adolescent and this is not your first rodeo and you have been around the block a few times (can I mix any more metaphors in there?) and you are getting a sense of what you want and don't want in relationship.

What makes the whole equation even harder is, there are a lot of fucked up people out there. Alright, that is a little harsh; let's call them imperfect humans. That way, we ALL fall into that category; none of us is perfect. But, let's face it, there are some who are a lot more imperfect than others. Don't misunderstand me; there is no one on the planet that has more compassion for how much evolving we still have to do. And I would like to think that we *are* evolving, and I would also like to think that the pace of that has accelerated since the advent of computers and the internet, not to mention the billions of interactions and our cumulative experience on the planet as Homo Sapiens. When I put on that compassionate hat, I see all of us struggling as humans to get our needs met, and I can explain "bad behavior" as actions by those attempting to meet those needs in ways that are counterproductive or worse, destructive.

Collectively, are we more evolved now than we were fifty years ago? If I put on my somewhat rose-colored glasses and say "yes," I look at how I was raised and the rules and sensibilities that were in place and current times seem like a quantum leap forward. So, collectively, (though arguably), we have a "better" pool from which to choose a partner.

But then to muddy up the waters again, there are lots of different versions of what "perfect" would be. What one person would see as greed could be interpreted as drive in another, and if you want fancy cars and houses and big bank accounts, running roughshod over others to achieve that might be perfectly okay. Another person's kindness might be construed as weakness, or a lithe body seen as "slight."

So we have our version of perfect that we try to meld with someone else's version of perfect and try to forge some sort of reasonable union. That is, until someone "perfecter" comes along. Shit; no wonder it's such a mess out there. So, forget "perfect." You will make yourself crazy pursuing that elusive apparition, not to mention probably ending up horribly alone with eleven cats or that one dog that you reallyreallylovemorethananyhumanbeing (however true it is that that dog will never leave you... well, until it dies and shatters your life for years afterwards...)

Chances are, you are NOT going to find the perfect partner. But at some point, you are going to pick SOMEONE, and then it should be your task (and that is the collective "your": the two of you together) to create the best union you can within your collective human imperfections (Geez, doesn't THAT sound exciting?)

So, yes, Virginia, we DO settle. Or "accept," because what we are being presented with in our reality is the person in front of us. This imperfect human, just like you in their imperfection. And I am going to officially sanction that we do just that and hope like the Dickens that they are willing to do the same.

"I'm Not Brad"

How do we go about choosing?

Like in any other animal kingdom, there is a hierarchy. Attempting to find an easily recognized example, at the top of our cultural hierarchy, Brad gets Angelina. Or vice versa, depending on your celebrity preference and who you think wooed whom. The universally attractive, smart, funny, rich and sometimes just plain lucky can get anyone they want. The rest of us exist somewhere below them on the hierarchy of desirability and qualification. (And at the risk of lumping Jennifer Aniston in with the rest of us, somehow even she got demoted).

Interestingly, that relationship at the top of the relational foodchain (celebrity-wise) has dissolved. It seems that none of us are immune to the challenges of maintaining extraordinary relationship, although, it can certainly be argued that those at the top experience their own unique set of problems, however enviable.

How is it that it carries more weight to be desired by someone who is higher on the scale? Have you ever been told after you broke up with someone that you were "out of your league?" Yes, the "league" exists, although it is very subjective, not talked about openly and is subject to interpretation. Placement in the league is not a science, and is subject to not only *your* interpretation, but the evaluation of others.

Rita had a thing for guitar players, a group of which, unfortunately, I was not a member. One of Rita's aspirations in life had been to be an "a-list" rock 'n' roll groupie. Early on in our relationship, she had disclosed to me that she had slept with over 200 men. When you do the math, male or female; that's a lot of "partnering." Undoubtedly, "auditioning" with roadies and such is where some of her "200" came in. I think she might have even made it up the ladder to sleeping with the bass player from Megadeth, but I may be remembering that wrong.

In our relationship, it was primarily her need for male attention, but also a "better" situation, combined with my insecurities, that made us a very toxic and dysfunctional combination. So, we had a problem on our hands. Our solution? Don't go out in public together, don't communicate about others in our lives and let her find her way to feed her need for attention without my knowing it. As the hierarchy goes, I think she felt like she could do a lot better than me and ultimately, after many tries to make it work between us, we split.

If you choose someone below you (by your estimation) you have "settled." Not only will you be probably always looking to upgrade, but you won't respect your partner. On the other hand, being above your partner on the hierarchy has its advantages: you are in a "one-up" position, and if that is important to you; that makes you feel important. And there is something to be said for having someone look up to you and respect, even revere, you.

Warren Zevon wrote in "My Dirty Life and Times" that he was "looking for a woman with low self-esteem."

This is where it gets a little convoluted: "looking for a woman with low self-esteem" connotes wanting someone who might be above you in the hierarchy, but SHE doesn't think so. Basically, "I'm looking for someone who is willing to settle." It also begs the question, "Do you want to be looking up to your partner, or down at them?"

The "hierarchy" doesn't really exist, except in our own minds, and it is different for everyone. Where I put myself on the hierarchy will probably be different from where others put me, and where I put others will vary as well. And that relative position is subject to change. Most of these evaluations do not occur on a conscious basis; it is more of a subconscious calculation, sometimes in the moment, sometimes long term.

We don't talk about the League, except vaguely in passing. I had a client who was reporting his latest "success" to me in his Match.com searches.

"Look at this one," he said, showing me the profile of a striking blond who her friends described as easy-going and was newly available and had a great sense of humor and would never smoke, but was a social drinker (although we would later find out that she grossly understated her affinity for alcohol).

"I'll probably only have one date with her, but that's OK."

'Wow. There's some low self-esteem displaying itself,' I thought to myself. So I challenged him: "Don't you think you 'qualify' for this woman?"

He hesitated and then summoned up his best bluster, "Of course I do!"

Now, I am NOT the arbiter of who-qualifies-for-whom (although it's sometimes an amusing game to play), but whether or not he "qualified" for this woman depended entirely on which version of him showed up at any given moment. That hesitant, insecure version of him absolutely did not qualify for her (and granted, I am basing this strictly on her physical appearance and her loving-long-walks-on-the-beach profile). My point here is that there IS a hierarchy, just like in the animal kingdom, but obviously with humans, there is a lot more to the equation than which guy wins in a mountaingoat-head-butting competition.

Interestingly, in our culture, there are factors that determine our positions on the hierarchy, including (but certainly not limited to) physical attractiveness, social status, financial security, intelligence and personality traits. Some fortunate individuals seem to have it all (sometimes the result of being an offspring of two individuals who also "had it all") and they get a leg up on the rest of us as to their position on the scale. Then there are the others at the lower end of the spectrum: not blessed with physical attractiveness, intelligence OR personality. Most of us fall somewhere in between, and it is our perception of ourselves, and the other's perceptions of us, that makes the hierarchy a somewhat inexact equation. It could also be argued that there is an evolutionary component to hooking up with someone above you on the scale. Not consciously, but if there is a drive for that, then collectively, the whole mess arguably moves forward.

Is this how we collectively evolve? And do we evolve (produce offspring) just once (that is, with one partner) over the course of our lifetimes or are we supposed to experience numerous evolutions in our lifetime, that is, produce offspring not only with another partner that has different (and arguably "better" genes than our last one), but also a different set of circumstances? Of course, as we established before, our coupling has gone far beyond mere perpetuation of the species. I am just suggesting that that evolutionary thread is still seething constantly, stealthily below the surface, those salacious gene pools lusting to comingle.

Sex

Yeah, we had to get around to it at some point. Why is this so hard to talk about? I mean REALLY talk about: not "kiss and tell" nonsense, but parents initially talking to kids and ultimately (and intimately) partners talking to partners.

There are the obvious religious taboos that have been set in place over the years, but bottom line is that sex, one of the most fundamental human endeavors that runs through ALL of our existence on a cellular level, has gotten terribly distorted underneath layers of cultural, social and psychological (on no! not that!) bullshit.

SEX: it's not just for procreation anymore...

I was in an airport not too long ago, and they had the covers of the Sports Illustrated swimsuit issue covered over. I know: scandalous. And at the same time anyone can go on the internet and see unimaginable sexual acts and images. (That is, what *I* imagine to be "unimaginable." Somebody is obviously not only imagining these things but engaging in them as well... Btw, I do not endorse, engage in or otherwise support the multibillion dollar porn industry, but somebody must be, for it to be a multibillion dollar industry). Covering up that magazine cover addresses issues of female exploitation (there were no pictures of men in Speedos), and respecting certain people's sensibilities. But it points out how Puritanical we are as a culture, STILL, around issues of the human body.

And it just carries over into the bedroom.

Are you a good lover? Really? How do you know? Oh, she said so... Right...

I thought so too until I discovered I had been seemingly sending Rita into the throes of ecstasy for three years before she confided to me that she had never actually experienced an orgasm.

Never.

I would have been willing to do whatever it took to send her to that place, and thought I was, through our conversations and her responses, but for her, it was easier to pretend.

What the fuck? (If ever that phrase [WTF} should be uttered, it should be in this context). So, while I thought I was doing everything right, apparently I wasn't, and what disturbed me more than that was she chose to hide it from me. And not just hide it, but totally misrepresent it (Cue the "I'll-have-what-she's-having" scene from "When Harry Met Sally").

It begs the question, "Why would she (or anyone) do that?" I understand too, in this issue, which is widespread, there are many layers to the inability of anyone to achieve orgasm, and it is not just about what I was or was not doing "right." I didn't make this an issue about my proficiency or take her to task for her "dishonesty." I was actually thankful to her for disclosing that, especially after three years. I should have known that something was amiss; in a way, she had been the perfect lover. She had told me that it turned her on so much when I climaxed, it made her come. Perfect, right? Apparently the reality was less perfect than the concept. Unfortunately, with Rita, there were communication and trust issues anyway, so this particular challenge never did get resolved before we went our separate ways.

Why do some women fake orgasms? I've gotten lots of different answers to that question, including "Sometimes I just want to get it over with," "It boosts his ego," "I'm tired," "He doesn't know how to make me come," "I've never had an orgasm and don't want to have to admit that" and "It's just easier than talking about it." I understand there are men who fake orgasm too. That is a bit trickier because of the equipment involved and the end result (or lack thereof) but I have heard that it happens.

This question of pleasing your lover goes out to women too. Are YOU a good lover? Why, because he always gets off? Ladies, it's easy for men. They can stick that thang into just about any receptacle, wiggle it around a little bit and usually get the desired result.

Nobody is born a good lover; we all have to learn, somehow. Some of that education comes from experience, but it can also come from educational materials, and there are plenty of them out there.

This book is not a sex manual. You will not learn a single sexual technique here, outside of this; if you want to know how to please your partner, ask them. I will give that advice, and what percentage will actually take the advice and initiate that conversation? I will guess about ten percent.

Why so few?

I've always thought it was interesting that, innately, animals, wild and domestic, know how to copulate. I guess, so do we, but I would suggest that our efforts as evolved humans and extraordinary partners should go way beyond knowing what to stick where.

Do you remember your first time? Of course you do: bumbling, fumbling, inept, guessing... If it didn't feel so good, or have so much hype and expectation around it, we'd probably never want to that again. And all the while, it is "assumed" that we know what we are doing, despite how it's all coming across. I had one early partner tell me, "Umm, I'm feeling a little like Mrs. Robinson here" (and she was NOT that much older). Hey, we all have to start somewhere, right? Right, but we don't have to end there.

Angie made it her business to be a good lover (let me rephrase that. She didn't make it her "business." She made it a priority to be engaged, creative, intimate, passionate and fun). She was well-versed in the subject, so much so that she would hold seminars for women and teach them not only technique, but how to be more comfortable with their bodies and their sexuality in general.

Despite her sexual expertise and familiarity, I once went into a book store with her and pulled a copy of "The Art of Sexual Ecstasy" by Margo Anand off the shelf. As I began thumbing through it, at some point she clapped the pages shut.

"It's got pictures in it!" she said.

And my inside voice was saying, Why yes; yes it does.

Apparently, unbeknownst to me at the time, looking at pictures of naked people (and in this particular book, there are drawings, not photographs) to her was tantamount to cheating. Nude scenes in movies were also bones of contention (pun really not intended). I was expected to avert my eyes.

Interestingly, once she and I got under the sheets, everything was fine, but she struggled with ideas about fidelity and relationship in general, which led me to wonder, how much of this controlling, contradictory, crazy shit was I willing to put with for good sex?

This points out the mixed messages we often have around sexuality. We all have our ways of doing each other, which usually means "doing" for ourselves. And while what we are doing may be pleasurable to our partners, it could probably be more so. We almost always have to find out about that THE HARD WAY, that is, by doing something "wrong."

One of the most insulting things we can say to another human being is that they suck in bed (alright, let me rephrase that...) Let's say they are "sexually inadequate" (Although, if you were to use those words: "sexually inadequate," I can't help but think that the result would be equally, if not even more, rejecting). For most people, even the idea of suggestions about technique, position, frequency, timing, place, how hard, how soft, which orifice, how many times or where to put or not put your tongue, fingers or appendage of choice is absolutely intimidating. Because the implication, when we offer suggestions is "You are not doing it right," which translates to "You suck in bed."

And who wants to hear that?

What does it mean to you to be a good lover? In its purest form, it *should* mean, "Is lovemaking with you a pleasurable experience for your partner?" But lovemaking for many couples is an intimate minefield.

Let's face it, most people engage in sex to get off. Wait, that is WAY too simplistic. Let me make a few broad sweeping generalizations, OK? First, most MEN engage in sex to get off. As for the women, do the majority of women actually experience orgasm? (I'm afraid to look this up on the internet for fear of where it will lead me; I don't want my computer to "catch" anything). Alright; I did a "clinical" search at www.abcnews:

> "Current studies bear this out, according to the researchers: 98 percent of men say they "always" reach orgasm during sex, while women are "evenly distributed" between "always and never."

But before I get WAY off in left field on this tangent, let's not talk just about orgasm (not that you and your partner shouldn't, if that is what you choose), but about the concept of pleasure and connection around sex.

If your partner says you are the best they've ever had (and you are inclined to believe them) good for you. If not, then run out and get some books, or go to a clinic, and above all, start talking to your partner about it. If it used to be great and it has waned, no big deal. That waning is a natural occurrence and part of a chemical reaction in our bodies. The good news is, we can get that back, but the concept of "good sex" doesn't exist apart from all of the other parts of our relationships. And if the relationship has been going on for a while, there may be need of major repair in other areas before the sex gets better. The good news is, it's all doable. And then you can both be, for each other (I couldn't resist).

There is probably more deceit, disinformation, misinformation and outright lies around sex than any other subject. How could something so simple, so pure, so fundamental, so basic, so wonderful, pleasurable, blissful, engaging and just plain juicy get so terribly complicated?

Yes, there was the whole "Garden of Eden" thing, but that is just a little too metaphorical for me; I want to know what happened. How did we get to this place now, in our culture, where, if you are to believe the media and the marketing, everybody should be getting some, with whomever they want and a lot of people aren't getting any actual sex at all? Not that I think it should be a sexual free-for-all; that would be chaos. We'd never get anything done, outside of each other (sorry; that's the last time; I promise).

I am all for having had multiple sex partners in your lifetime; it just seems like that is what we were designed as humans to do, but let's have it be more conscious. Power struggles and hierarchies and rejection aside, when we DO get to that point of consenting adults consenting, I AM advocating for there to be more openness and freedom around what actually happens when the clothes hit the floor.

Finally, we can't talk about sex without mentioning and lamenting how that initial charge in the beginning of a relationship wanes over time. We want that to last forever, and it doesn't. It is part of a phenomenon known as habituation. Habituation is a psychological learning process wherein there is a decrease in response to a stimulus after being repeatedly exposed to it: an animal or a human may learn to ignore a stimulus because of repeated exposure to it. There seems to be a component to this that explains the eventual dissatisfaction with our partners who seemed so exciting, wonderful and "perfect" in the beginning. As much as I love Cherry Garcia ice cream (or Sea Bass), if I had to eat it every night, I'd get so familiar with it that I wouldn't appreciate it as much as I do having it every so often. Very often, in relationship, we do take the gifts that others give us for granted because they are always there. So, it might be time to mix things up a little: if you have gotten away from giving those things that you did in the beginning, start them up again, if that is indeed what your partner would like. But check in; maybe it would be something else now that would light their fire.

It's hard to imagine Brad and Angelina suffering from this, but we have to remember that they are human beings too. The challenge then becomes; what do we do to combat that? Do we wander, and cheat? Do we find new ways to rekindle our passion? What is important to remember here is what your priorities are and what the priorities of your partner are. Is sex that important? And I am not asking that as a rhetorical question. Is it? Because if it is, as a partner, you had better find a way for it to have that same charge once habituation sets in, because it will.

It's a hard issue to talk about, because basically, you are saying to your partner. "I've gotten used to you." And nobody wants to hear that. Actually, that's not true. There are some people to whom that phrase, "I've gotten used to you," would be a comfort, like that old pair of jeans that you don't want to ever get rid of because they are so familiar.

This addresses a certain personality type, and it's good to know where you are on this spectrum. If the excitement and novelty of infatuation is important to you, you could be a long-term relationship risk. Or, your potential partner could be. This is also subject to change later in life, as we go through stages of development and growth.

We will discuss personal growth later in the chapter, "Who are you?" but the awareness of self and being able to communicate about it can be an important step towards extraordinary relationship. Communication? Yeah, we had to get around to talking about it at some point.

COMMUNICATION

Think for a moment about how incredible it is that we can have a thought, and then, if we so choose, have the ability to take that thought and articulate it to another human being. What a gift. And by and large, we squander it, now possibly in more ways than ever with e-mails, texting and tweeting regarded as viable alternatives to actual conversation.

As humans, we have had this ability for a long time, just how long is hard to say. There is no universally accepted theory for how long man has been able to speak and converse and it would seem to be one of those unanswerable questions. The point is that, now, in our culture, we have the ability to reach more people more quickly than at any time in our history.

Are you able to effectively utilize that gift of speech to communicate when your needs are not being met? Are you even able to articulate to yourself what they are?

I was personally brought up as a member of the children-are-to-be-seen-and-not-heard generation (would that be GenCATBSANH?) It took me a long time to recover from that dubious gem of parenting acumen, and find my voice, but, I am proud to say, I was described fairly recently as a "talker!" So, despite growing up "knowing" that no one was going to listen to what I had to say, or if I said something, it was going to be met with scorn and derision, I have learned how to take my thoughts and feelings and convey them to others.

We learn to converse by parroting our early caregivers. Why we don't end up speaking goo-goo and gah-gah for the rest of our lives, I'm not sure, but we do learn those language patterns from what we are exposed to as infants and toddlers. Along the way, we are given some rules of conversation, sometimes as direct instruction, sometimes not. For instance, "Don't' talk with your mouth full." That's more of a manners lesson than a conversational one, but fairly universal and practical.

"Wait until the other person is done speaking before you speak." Less universal, but even those of us who have been exposed to this teaching often ignore it.

"Be honest." Maybe not universally taught and probably even less universally followed. These and others are rules that we learn by participating in conversation.

Unfortunately, in our culture, there are also gender-specific rules (and rules) that are assigned to men and women around not just how they communicate, but even more so, IF they communicate. Whether this is actually "true" or not is certainly up for debate; the "Men are from Mars, Women are from Venus" paradigm has become almost universally accepted as gospel. Broken down to it's most simplistic concept, men and women communicate differently. In very broad applications, that theory has a lot of merit, especially if you apply it to 1950s America: post war, Eisenhower, The American Dream, white picket fences and all that. But to me it seems overly simplistic and like so many other aspects of our culture, it has changed and is changing now even more rapidly. There seem to be men from Venus and women from Mars now too. Unfortunately, it doesn't help me to generalize when I am trying to relate in a healthy and positive way with the person in front of me.

We can be so much better at being able to communicate, but we are never really taught. Some of us learn, because there are books and programs that will teach us how to be better communicators, but most of us just get by on whatever has worked (or not) in the past.

Why don't we communicate more effectively? We learn early on in childhood, when we are totally vulnerable, generally powerless and without verbal skills that it's often to our advantage to withhold information or to flat out LIE. As we get a bit older and are surrounded by siblings or others our age, sometimes we learn that we can get our needs met by using our language skills to beguile, persuade, convince, bully, coerce or trick others so that we alone will benefit. It can be a valuable tool.

Don't Ask, Don't Tell?

I'm not referring here to the military application of "don't ask, don't tell," but a more general DADT about what of your private inside world gets related to others; what does get communicated in your relationship? True communication in relationship takes TWO. As an individual, your intent may be to be an open book; you may be fully willing for your partner to know EVERYTHING about you.

On the other hand, your partner may not want you to know *everything*. Let's face it, some people are more verbal than others. Some people are TOO verbal; they never shut up. At the other end or the spectrum there are those who hardly ever speak. Where are you on this continuum? Where is your partner? There are plenty of approaches that will tell you that communication is the key to happy relationship. I am going to agree. BUT, if you and your partner are on different ends of the spectrum on this issue, your path will have more challenges to it.

Personally, I am for full disclosure, but there is a down side to that, as lofty as the idea sounds. Full disclosure is often not pretty, or for the thin-skinned. If you are easily triggered or hurt by things that get said that might not be complimentary, full disclosure may not be for you. And, the truth is, we can never know the full extent of another person's internal experience. Through verbal communication, we can try to express that, but it is literally impossible unless you have perfected Spock's Vulcan mind-meld.

So, what DOES get communicated? Well, how about asking? For me, all questions get considered. With Barbara, because sex was an area of focus for us, when I suggested a full mutual disclosure of our sexual pasts, she said that that might be both painful and embarrassing. When I considered that, I realized and expressed to her that I didn't need to know all of those stories: that I didn't want to put her through painful and embarrassing disclosure just to satisfy my curiosity. Did I get most of those stories anyway? Yes,

I did, at her pace, and I hope that on some level it was cathartic for her, because many of the stories rang of insecurity, exploitation, dominance, cruelty, lack of consideration, ignorance and recklessness on the part of others. It was a wonder that this woman would ever want to have sex again, but through a lot of personal work, she was very comfortable in bed. But this was the same Barbara who couldn't look at a picture in a sex manual (or didn't want ME to) and would want me to avert my eyes while Sharon Stone was crossing her legs in "Basic Instinct." It was like she had reconciled her sexuality in her body, but not in her mind and heart, and certainly not in *my* mind and heart. I know it took a lot of courage for her to disclose her stories to me.

But what comes across as one person's courage can be another person's invasion of privacy. In my on-again/off-again relationship with Rita, once we were on-again (again), I had questions for her about one of her "off-again" experiences. She replied that it was "none of my fucking business." I can hear some of you thinking, *She's right; it wasn't any of his fucking business.*

But it wasn't that simple. She had mentioned to me when we got back together that she had been with someone else. And in the telling of that, she mentioned that it was "awful" and "I ended up sobbing" and that, not wanting to press her, I dropped it until later that night, when, at home in my own bed I wondered, *Did she get raped?* Early the next morning I went to her house to comfort her, wondering if indeed that had been the case. And she said "No, I wasn't raped." And relieved I had said, "Well, what happened? Why won't you tell me?" *That's* when she informed me in no uncertain terms whose business it wasn't.

Part of me agrees; we were broken up and she didn't have to tell me anything. But on top of so many other aspects of our incompatibility that led to our repeated "off-agains," that became a deal breaker for me. I didn't want to be part of a relationship where my partner felt that there was something that was "none of my business" ("fucking" or otherwise). It wasn't just that one incident that led to our (final) breakup; there were numerous reasons that we were on again-off again, not the least of which was a pattern of non-communicative behavior on her part. That's right; it's not always the men that don't want to talk.

This brings up the subject of secrets. For me, extraordinary relationship means full disclosure: that means there are no secrets. We can never disclose everything we are thinking and feeling; it is just impossible in terms of time and content. So, what and how and when it gets said is the essence of communication in a relationship.

"Talking on Eggshells" is a great program on communication created by Susie and Otto Collins dealing with being afraid to say what's on your mind for a variety of reasons, whether it's fear of judgment, reprisal or a blow to self-esteem. Imagine being afraid to say something to your partner. Yeah, imagine that... What kind of timid, beaten down, subjugated, dominated, defeated milquetoast would do that?

Right...

OK, maybe that's a little harsh; sometimes you just don't want to stir things up, and you just know, you just KNOW, that if you ask a certain question it's gonna start up the shitstorm. Sometimes it's not even a question; it's a response, and you know that if you respond truthfully, the evening will be shot, and you're not going to get to watch the second half of the Spurs/Cavaliers game in peace.

If full disclosure is one of your relationship goals, then it's important that all questions get answered, or at the very least, actually heard and acknowledged. The answer may be, "I don't want to answer that right now" or "Can I get back to you on that?" Those are not to be used as ultimate avoidance techniques, but perhaps just to wait for a more appropriate time or to fashion a response that is commensurate with the question.

The bottom line is that you can't make someone talk (waterboarding notwithstanding) and once you DO get them talking, you may not get the answers you wanted. So, if you are asking the hard questions, you'd better be prepared to hear the hard answers. Interestingly, in all honesty, in Rita's NOYFB example above, she could have told me ANYTHING. And I do mean anything. I was so wanting some disclosure, some secret, that I would have accepted any answer without judgment. This was the same Rita who had once "bragged" to me that she had been with over 200 men. Bear in mind that I have a vivid imagination, and in all the possibilities that I came up with, I would have been willing to accept even the most heinous.

Why was the disclosure so important to me? Because I realized at some point that I didn't trust her, and her confession would have bridged that gap for me. As it turns out, her response showed me that she was not willing to engage in the type of partnership that I was looking for. (Interestingly, in her subsequent online dating profile, she was looking for "true partnership." Obviously her definition of that was different from mine).

Communication Styles

What is your communication style? Avoidant? Expulsive? Too many words? No filters? Secretive? Raging? Defensive?

I dislike classifying ways of being into categories and dysfunctions, but it is one of the drawbacks of language that, at some point, if we want to talk about something, we have to identify it.

For instance, alexithymia is the inability to put emotions and feelings into words. While psychologists have not labeled this as a disorder, but a personality trait, I know numerous women that would be willing to attribute this trait to an entire gender (that would be us guys). We've all experienced people that have put up emotional "walls," and are seemingly not able to discuss their emotional world. Are they alexithymic? Or have they just been taught by mimicking those around them to not express themselves? Or have they decided, from their own experience, that they are not going to be heard anyway? While that is not a discussion to be decided here, what I am suggesting, to be able to create the most extraordinary relationship possible, it is best to know your level of comfort in communicating your feelings and also your skill level in being able to do that.

Which also brings us around to saying nothing. I know, I know; this goes against the idea of full disclosure. But, let's face it; there are times when you just KNOW that if you open your mouth, you are just going to bring on the aforementioned shitstorm. And, at this particular time and place, you don't WANT a shitstorm. So, my rule around that is that if you decide to say nothing and whatever it is comes up again, either in context or, oh, I don't know, waking you up in the middle of the night at 3:00 AM, then it needs to be addressed.

What? An example? God, there are so many... Well, there ARE so many because over the years, that was my default: say nothing. Say nothing, avoid the conflict, even if it did come up again, because conflict was to be avoided at all costs. See? I'm doing it again. Avoiding the issue. Alright, let me rummage around in the recesses of that dark closet for a moment...

Ah, here's one that's fairly benign.

Angie and I were getting dressed in the morning, and in putting on her belt, she remarked, "This is a great belt, because it's got all these holes in it, which makes it so much more efficient if I was wanting to spank someone."

I know, right? WHAT DID SHE MEAN BY THAT? Was it a playful invitation? Was she evoking a memory of some past S&M episode? Was she wanting to express some repressed anger as she brought the belt down with considerable force on the bathroom counter? Personally, I had experienced enough lashings early on during Mom's misguided attempts at effective parenting that I never have felt comfortable with the idea of associating spanking with pleasure. Ang and I had already discussed this, along with my assertion that this didn't belong as part of our lovemaking.

So, again; WHAT DID SHE MEAN BY THAT? I was curious, yes, and yet, that little voice in my head was saying, no, shouting, "DUDE, say nothing!"

And that's what I did.

The resulting silence was awkward, because the situation was begging for a response, but I said nothing. Right choice in the moment? As with any choice, I don't know what a response would have elicited, but I did make that choice. I don't know if my silence kept nagging at her like it did me, but it just didn't feel right to have what was increasingly feeling like a request for my submission out there, unanswered.

So a day or so later, I asked, "Remember the other day when you slapped the counter with your belt and talked about spanking someone with it?"

"Yeah."

"What did you mean by that? Are you looking to revisit the idea of some S&M stuff?"

"Oh, I was just playing."

"So, you mean you don't have a desire to make me cower to your whims and run screaming through the house saying 'Mommy, please, don't; I'll be good'?"

"No, I was just playing."

See? Sometimes you get lucky, and those hard questions get answered the way you want them to be. Or maybe Angie was just giving me a pat answer. Looking at it in retrospect, I think it WAS a request, a test, considering her past experiences, but I was willing to accept her answer at face value.

So, when is it best to say nothing? Usually you say nothing when you don't want to trigger an argument. But, I can say from experience, if you make a habit out of not communicating, resentments build and eventually you can get to a place where you have a silent (albeit conflict free) relationship. If that is what you want, fine, but if that is not your idea of extraordinary, you have to allow room for disagreement. Let's face it, it would be wonderful if our relationships were blissful all the time, but even the most harmonious couplings have their challenges. So, pick your moment; if you really think you are going to trigger a conflict, allow time for it (traditionally, those knock-down-drag-outs last about an hour or so, but some have been known to linger for days...)

(OK, forever...)

Sometimes my silence is not so much avoidance as me just trying to process whether or not this is MY own stuff that I need to deal with, that I am being poked by old proddings that don't apply anymore. I've been told that sometimes in response to a situation I would get "quiet." "Quiet" later got further defined as "moody," at which point I felt like it was time to explain my inner workings. To me, there is a huge chasm between "quiet" and "moody" and this is a good example of a couple sitting down and going over semantics.

"Moody" to me is kneeling drunk in the chamisa bushes with a butcher knife wondering if life is even worth living (that could be slight hyperbole). Getting "quiet" is just being introspective, checking in about whether or not I was being oversensitive or if this is something that needs to be brought out into the open. (What? Me? Oversensitive? Oh, yes, early on, Laura had brought it to my attention that I might be "too fucking sensitive." I sure could pick 'em, couldn't I?)

Whether or not we choose to speak is an ongoing decision, from minute to minute. Some of us have multiple filters around that, some of us have very few. The biggest downside of saying nothing in relationship is that your partner is left to assume what you are thinking and feeling. In the on-again/off-again situation with Rita, I was left to fill in the blanks, and interestingly, I suspect that what actually happened to her and with whom was far less heinous than what I imagined, but I will never know, and not knowing is not part of extraordinary relationship for me.

A great guide in figuring out your communication style is the book by Tim and Joy Downs, "One of Us Must be Crazy... and I'm Pretty Sure It's YOU." (One of my all-time favorite book titles, btw). They go over some very specific personality types, how it applies to you and your partner, and how you can make adjustments that make the whole thing flow more smoothly, without giving up too much ground.

Tips on Communicating

We've got rules for everything else, why not communication?

Here's one of my least favorite: "Don't go to bed mad." While I understand the premise behind this, what it comes down to is that you are putting a time limit on a resolution, at a time when both parties are at the end of their days, tired, ready for that time when our minds and bodies are getting ready to recharge, and what inevitably happens is that someone relents, just to end it. My solution? Just go to bed; tomorrow is another day. Maybe it's because I have the exasperating (to others) ability to not only go to bed mad, but once I'm there, to fall asleep like a baby then wake up like it never happened. I'm a big fan of a "time-out" when things get too heated, and to me a good night's sleep is the perfect break.

It has been pointed out to me by one of my partners that while I may be sawing logs and processing all of that angst through dreams I barely ever remember, my partner is lying awake all night, rehashing it all without my input. Well, that doesn't seem very fair, does it? So, as much as I don't like succumbing to that (what I feel is a rather arbitrary) rule, we decided that we will indeed, NOT go to bed angry with one another. Here, her not staying-awake-all-night-fretting trumped my "I'm-tired-and-I-want-to-go-to-bed."

That being said, problems and challenges don't get resolved just because we want them to by a specific, often arbitrary deadline. There are times when we have enacted a bit of a truce, allowing for us to get some rest and come back at the problem the next day with a fresh, rested perspective.

Speaking of when things get heated; often when a disagreement escalates, words slip out that might not have under ordinary circumstances. The ordinary filters that might be in place are not there because we get defensive, frustrated, hurt or angry. Anger is OK; it is a normal healthy human response to a real or potential negative outcome. It's when our responses or behavior around anger get inappropriate or extreme that it gets unhealthy. What is inappropriate or extreme? Different things to different people. One of the negative consequences of open communication can be that something you say triggers an unwelcome response in the other person. So, what do we do when that other gets triggered? I've known couples that, to me, were incredibly verbally abusive to one another. When questioned about it, the woman said, "Oh, we yell at each other like that all the time." Sometimes that can be cultural, or simply from someone's family background. If you grew up with that, that becomes a communication style. Wow, really? "Fuck you" is OK to say to your partner? Well, is it? Ask them. Or, if it's not, say so.

With numerous partners, if I brought up something even remotely negative about their behavior or our relationship, they would immediately go on the defensive, into "absolute" mode ("you never" or "you always.") What? Absolutes never exist. ;)

As I learned the hard way, someone in absolute mode usually doesn't want a lesson in semantics or sarcasm at that point in time. However, if this is a pattern, it bears being brought up at a later date.

"Tell me more." Three little words that can be life altering. Those three words essentially say, "I care about what is going on inside you, what I am hearing is getting through, but I need more clarification to fully understand it." But even more than that is the idea that you have heard and considered what the other person has to say and are willing to accept that as a valid part of whatever the two of you are discussing. How many people are there out there who have NEVER been listened to? Quite simply, this is one of the most powerful phrases you can use in getting another person to open up.

Communication in relationship gets a lot of lip service. Many experts will talk about communication, and tell you it is essential for a quality relationship. So, yeah, "communicate more." "Communicate better. Listen. Mirror. Paraphrase." I came across an excellent source that outlines exactly how to incorporate those strategies into your communication, and I will probably give this book to every new married couple as a gift: "Fight Less, Love More" by Laurie Puhn, JD.

She talks about those four words that nobody EVER wants to hear in a relationship...

"We Have to Talk"

How many of us have cringed at the phrase? You know when you hear those four words that nothing is going to follow that you want to hear. When you say, "We have to talk," you are demanding the other person's time. AND, more likely than not, you are wanting to initiate a conversation that could go on for hours, that, more likely than not, the other person is unprepared to handle.

What Puhn suggests are these words instead: "Can we have a five minute conversation?"

To begin with, you are now *asking* for some of your partner's time. Second of all, it's only five minutes. This is not to say that the problem is going to be resolved in five minutes. But it gives you a chance to express what you want to say, and to have them hear it, and if there is a negative reaction, time to process it without the conversation spiraling down into a quagmire of frustration, anger and miscommunication.

Once this method becomes part of the way the two of you communicate on a regular basis, it opens up a forum for respectful listening and resolving of problems.

Take a moment and think about a situation where you had to talk to someone about something difficult, and you were met with openness and compassion, with an open heart and an open ear. (What??!!! Never? Then this whole extraordinary relationship thing could be right up your alley...)

I highly recommend the experience. Wouldn't you want to provide that for the person you love too?

I have been accused of "not listening," and the follow-up to that often was, "That makes me feel invalidated." Now, if that was TRUE, if I actually wasn't listening, that would be a perfectly valid statement, and she SHOULD have felt invalidated. But a more accurate description of what was really happening there was,

"If you don't agree with what I say, or give me what I want, you must not be listening."

Ooo... very important distinction. I heard a story about a man who for godonlyknowswhatreason purchased for his partner's birthday a gleaming new red washer and dryer after she specifically told him how much she loved the washer and dryer she had. Now he *clearly* wasn't listening, by either definition.

On the other hand, if someone said to me, "I think you are over indulging your daughter because you never say 'no' to her" and I continue to treat my daughter the same way, that doesn't necessarily mean that I didn't hear her, or even consider her advice. It could mean a number of things: I don't agree with her, or, I DO agree with her, but I haven't figured out a way to change my behavior.

Could my partner feel invalidated by this? Absolutely; she can feel whatever she wants. SHOULD she feel invalidated by this? If this is an isolated incident, no. If this is part of a pattern of ignoring her advice, maybe. The point here is just because you are not agreed with or your suggestions, desires or wants are not acted upon, does not mean you are not heard.

Are you one of those people who has to be right all the time? If your answer is, "Well, I AM right all the time," then I would say yes, you ARE one of those people. And you probably don't have any idea how annoying it is to be around *you* in social situations. But is that who you want to be with your partner? Does it make you feel superior to know you are smarter than they are? Are you sure you are?

There is a whole lot that goes into that equation from a personal development standpoint, some of which has to do with self-esteem. Or maybe you were brought up in a household run by someone else who was "all-knowing." First of all, it became learned behavior (it's "normal" to be a pompous, pedantic ass) and then second of all, once you become an adult, and away from that influence, now YOU can be the one that's right! Woo-hoo! The only reason I am mentioning this here is that it relates to listening, and hearing, and having your partner feel like they have not just a voice, but an intellect, an opinion: that they are a part of a union.

How often do you say these words: "You're right"?

You may have to do this in front of a mirror, to practice, and actually take your hands and help your lips and mouth form the words. Still having trouble? Well, since you are in front of a mirror, and it is your very own image reflecting back at you, recite something you are right about; it shouldn't be hard. Then, say to that visage, "You're right."

Wow, doesn't it feel great to hear that? We all love to hear those words. Now for the hard part; go out and say them to *someone else*. I know it's not always easy; there are a lot of people out there that are just WRONG a large portion of the time. But wait for that moment when you truly, genuinely agree with someone, and let them know it.

Go ahead; make their day.

Want to take it to an even higher level?

Allow someone to convince you that their viewpoint is as valid or even more valid than your own. And then, let them know, "Wow, I never looked at it that way."

You may have to practice this with co-workers and possibly even complete strangers before you can actually try it on your partner, but it is an experiment that can yield wonderful rewards.

In considering the "information age," we think of the data that is floating around in the ether, available to all with a computer or a smartphone. What about the information inside? How well do you know your partner? How well do you want them to know you?

I wrote earlier about times when I would be "quiet." Normally, I am a "talker." That is, much of what is on the inside ends up being expressed, not to everyone, but certainly to someone I am very close to.

How safe is that in your relationship? How safe do you want it to be? Can you say anything to your mate? Now when I hear, "I have a question for you," my reply is invariably, "Oh good."

I want that sense of inquiry, of curiosity, of interest. I want to get it, and I want to give it.

Honesty

"You can't handle the truth!"

Remember that line from delivered by Jack Nicholson in "A Few Good Men"?

That retort applies in many of our everyday situations; most people don't want to hear the truth. The reality though is that the "truth" is a subjective, ephemeral interpretation of information, constructed from events, shaped by beliefs, usually communicated with an agenda and then finally, heard through very personal filters.

In communicating a "truth," it helps to consider your intent. Is it honest?

First of all, if honesty is not your usual default in terms of how you communicate, you are in for a constant internal struggle around what comes out of your mouth and HOW it comes out of your mouth. I have known pathological liars in the past, and they have no idea what lies they are spewing half the time. So, if you are a liar (c'mon, 'fess up... are you? Hah; I don't believe you! Liar!), you are going to be required to experience a huge shift just in terms of how you conduct yourself within this new perspective. And while I allow for extraordinary relationship to encompass many different "looks," I find it hard to imagine dishonesty being part of extraordinary.

Lucy actually once said to me "I find it easy to lie to people but I would never lie to you." (Wait; I'm having a flashback to Logic 101; If A is true, then B has to be false, right? Actually, I think A makes B invalid or inconclusive. Either way, a red flag shot up immediately, but I was still too clueless (or infatuated) at that point for her redflaggedness to register on the turn-around-and-RUN-as-fast-as-you-can-ometer).

We all lie, it's just a matter of big and how often. And if you think you don't, I'd be willing to bet there are extreme, life-or-death circumstances where you would. How about those lies of omission? And answers to the "unquestions?" (More on "unquestions" very soon). For me, extraordinary relationship means total honesty. Period. And that means that sometimes my partner is going to hear things she doesn't want to. My job is to do that in a way that is gentle, respectful and considerate. And well-timed, if the subject is delicate. For someone like me, who has been conflict avoidant in the past, this has been a challenge, "knowing" that something I am going to say will stir up the hornet's nest, but I consider it part of my personal responsibility in the relationship to make this the default way we communicate.

Conversely, I'm going to hear things that I don't want to hear. Either way, there are going to be times when it ain't pretty. There are reasons why we shy away from this, but the biggest is that we haven't learned how to do it effectively. There are no longer excuses for this, people; WE ARE IN THE INFORMATION AGE! Granted, we may not know how to spell because of texting, but there are books and programs out there that will teach you how to be more effective communicators.

Another reason, certainly more well-intentioned, but equally ineffective, is that we lie because we don't want to hurt the other person's feelings. Now this is at least an idea that has some merit. A perfect example of this could be receiving a gift that has your inside voice saying, "What could they possibly have been thinking when they chose this for me?"

Jamie went on a safari to Africa and visited the primitive Masai tribe. As a souvenir, she brought me back a ceremonial leather I-don't-know-what-it-was, like some kind of skirt or loincloth or something that had been soaked in blood. Yes, blood. I am assuming deliberately, but we never got around to those questions.

"You won't believe what I got for you!"

She was right about that. I would have never guessed that she had brought me back some smelly, sticky sacrificial garb that I can't imagine how she got through customs...

I don't even remember what I said, but I'm sure it was a lie. What could I have said? "Thanks, this is the most unusual gift I have ever received"?

I don't know what her association with this item was, but she was clearly very excited about presenting it to me. It was not unlike a cat presenting an owner with a dead bird it had caught. Later, in a probably misguided effort towards being extremely honest, and feeling that she had been so excited the item that she might want it herself, I return that smelly, sticky gift to her. She was not happy. My best move would have been to graciously accept the gift and let it rot and decompose in some decrepit corner of the basement.

But no; I had to be honest.

And while I am advocating total honesty as a part of extraordinary relationship, I would imagine there are some tenuous arrangements around circumstances that work, but I would hardly consider them extraordinary.

I have a client who is in a 20+ year marriage. He is having an affair that is not terribly discreet and there are circumstances where the wife and mistress are "required' to interact. The paramour knows he is married, and the "belief" is that the wife doesn't know about the affair. He says he loves both women, but under my definition of love, which includes a certain modicum of respect for the other person, he is not treating his wife very respectfully.

Are there agreements in place here? Absolutely. Does the wife know? I'm not sure. I suspect *she* suspects, but is willing to turn a blind eye and maybe there is an unspoken agreement. The spoken agreement between him and the mistress is that he will never leave his wife. I suspect she desires otherwise. So, agreements? Yes. Extraordinary? What do you think?

Honest? Well, with his mistress, yes. With his wife, absolutely not. Congruent with his image of himself ("man of his word")?

Ummm, well, sorta...

The "Unquestion"

By definition, a question is: A sentence, phrase, or gesture that seeks information through a reply.

But what happens when a question is not really meant to illicit the information that is expressed in its wording? These fall into the category that I like to call "The Unquestion." Simply put, unquestions are thinly veiled, difficult-to-answer, no-win solicitations of reassurance.

The classic clichéd unquestion is "Do these pants make my butt look big?"

Let's take a closer look at how to respond to that query. First of all, if you're lucky and the pants don't make her butt look big, you can be honest and gratefully tell the truth. You could even take the opportunity to take it a magnanimous step further: "Baby, I love your ass."

Where it gets tricky is when the truth is they DO make her butt look big and it has nothing to do with the pants; it is her big butt. (This is of course assuming that neither of you wants her butt to look bigger. Thanks to J Lo and Kim K, this particular unquestion is taking on a whole different perspective. Maybe now the new Unquestion would be, "Honey do these pants make my butt look big <u>enough</u>?")

There is less than a 5 percent chance that she is asking for input based on your fashion acumen. Generally speaking, that is not the real question; the real question is something more like, "Do you still find me attractive?"

There are different strategies for responding to an unquestion, depending on the situation, the relationship and the context. For instance, if you are getting ready to go out to the movies and you are already 15 minutes late, which means missing the previews (that you really look forward to, by the way), one strategy is to lie. OK, it's not really lying: it's stalling, it's denial, it's politics. It's a pat answer, an obsequious response.

Your best bet in this situation is a one-word response: "No." Do not embellish, do not go into detail; you are just asking for trouble if you do.

If it's an established relationship, and you are committed to honesty, and you have the time and cojones to risk a negative consequence (such as missing the aforementioned previews), you could go for a humorous response:

"Honey, do these pants make my butt look big?"

"Do you *want* your butt to look bigger?"

"No"

"Then you may want to consider another pair, but really honey; it'll be dark in the theater; who's gonna see?"

Technically, the blame is being put on the pants, not on you and your response. Dishonest, you say? Marginally. And, I only recommend that response if you really don't care that your partner is putting on weight (and possibly not care about getting any that night).

The success of this response will depend somewhat on your relationship history, somewhat on your delivery, somewhat on your partner's sense of humor, her mood in the moment, what kind of day she has had and how the planets are aligned. This approach has been known to backfire; you are living life on the edge, and unless you are feeling extremely lucky, I would not recommend it.

Or, you can answer the unquestion as if it were an actual question. This is where the dance begins. This approach entails setting aside the questioner's need for reassurance and making it about you and your obsessive quest for honesty. Are you prepared to do that? It can be argued that they opened the door, so let's forge ahead and say, "Yes, now that this is out in the open, let's talk about it."

Before proceeding, you have to decide how important this issue is and if this is the appropriate time to open that can o' worms. Is it worth hurting the others persons feelings? You may want to consider bringing it up at a later time when there is time for a "five minute conversation" session. And of course, all this evaluation is occurring in a moment's time.

I was unquestioned once (I love using this as a verb) on that exact topic, about a butt, and I tried to deflect it, joking, "Oh, this is a trick question, isn't it? Danger, Will Robinson, danger!" Google "Lost in Space.")

But her question was much more direct. It was not, "Do these pants make my butt look big," it was "Do you think my ass is too fat?"

She knew she was carrying a lot of junk in the trunk. What she was trying to find out was, "Is it OK?"

Oh, I was being unquestioned, without a doubt. And honestly, while I would have preferred for her butt to be smaller, it wasn't at the top of my priority list with her. At the same time, I was dedicated to honest, open communication and replied, "Well, it could be tighter."

I know, I know; you women are groaning, saying, "Really? How could you?" and the men are saying, "Wuhl... he was just being honest." Clearly, this was not the answer she was looking for; she wanted the pat answer.

How do I know that?

Her reply was, "Don't ever break up with me, because I will go out there and get buns of steel."

Which of course begs the question, "Well, if you can get buns of steel later, why wouldn't you just get them now?" (Luckily for me, that was inside voice). But, truly, if this was important for me, it would have warranted another conversation, along the lines of "Hey honey; remember that time you made that joke about buns of steel if we ever broke up? I would LOVE it if you had buns of steel."

Another classic unquestion is, "Do you think that woman is hot?" when she clearly is. If you have to answer the "hot woman unquestion," I am suggesting that you look at what the REAL question is. It could be a request for your consideration "Will you pay more attention to me as opposed to ogling her?" And if you are honest with yourself, and could have been paying more attention to your mate, and she is asking for it, DO IT!

 It could be more serious: if the hot woman is a friend or co-worker, it might be a question about whether your relationship with her is a threat. Is it? There are two important perspectives to look at here: yours and hers. You may look at this and say some version of "No, she is not a threat."

But is that true? Instead of giving *yourself* the pat answer, treat it as if it might be a threat, because it is being perceived by your partner that way, and who knows? She may actually have a valid point. Yes, it's fun to be around so and so at the office; she "gets" me, she laughs at my jokes, we have common interests, she appreciates me. And yeah, she's fuckin' hot, but... well, I can't admit THAT!! If I admit THAT, there is gonna be all kinds of shit to pay; first of all, it's going to validate my partner's suspicions. Second, I'm probably going to be asked to curtail that contact, and I don't want to do THAT and besides, I don't WANT her; I just want her to want ME, because well, that FEELS good, and that's something my partner can't give me: THE ATTENTION OF SOMEBODY ELSE. And it's not that I actually NEED that, but it feels GOOD. (Again, you are processing all of this in a split second).

But it's harmless, you think. Is it? Ask yourself this question: "Is this person getting attention, time, energy and/or affection that my partner could or should be getting?" If the answer is "Yes," then it may not be as harmless as you think. There are three ways to go forward.

You can deny any wrongdoing and continue on in the same way you have been.

You can realize it _is_ a threat and deny any wrongdoing but refocus your energy on your partner and curtail the distracting and potentially destructive behavior.

Or you could opt for the straight and narrow, hitch-up-my-big-boy-pants, "I'm-goin'-in" response: THE TRUTH.

The first path: denial and business as usual will obviously not lead to extraordinary relationship with your current partner. You may be thinking that it could lead to that with your dalliance, but that is flawed thinking.

The second path: denial and behavior modification, is at least honest with yourself and shows an effort towards congruent behavior, but it's mostly conflict avoidant.

The third: THE TRUTH, while the most difficult, is the most adult, most congruent of the three and can lead to not only personal growth, but a newfound honesty in your relationship.

I see some of you shaking your heads out there, thinking, _This guy has his Pollyanna head up his ass if he thinks this is possible._ But two reminders: we can make choices around all of this, AND, we are shooting for extraordinary here.

Generally, on the surface, unquestions are benign sounding forays into serious "issue" territory. Recognize them as such and proceed carefully. Again, the timing is important. It is often wise to delay the actual response, but to give it the attention it deserves at a time when the two of you can honestly dialogue about it.

Here's another example, of a possible unquestion, "Are you having an emotional affair?"

Well, no, of course you aren't; who in their right mind would answer this question in the affirmative? What good can possibly come out of an affirmative response to this question (well outside of true, honest, genuine transparent communication? And validation of the person asking the question, so that their feelings of jealousy are not just perceived as the twisted product of their low self-esteem and dysfunctional upbringing... for instance...)

As you may have derived from that last aside, I myself have not only fielded but asked some unquestions myself. I had numerous opportunities to employ this strategy to try and get to the bottom of suspicious behavior. Rita, who hardly ever wore make-up to work, would spend extra time getting gussied up on the days when the telephone guy at her workplace was scheduled to do some maintenance. It got to a point where I knew which days he was going to be there by what she how much extra time it took her to get ready. Sally had an ongoing flirtatious e-mail correspondence going with the IT guy and started staying after work to finish projects.

Did I end up unquestioning them? Undoubtedly. Was I needing reassurance?

Yes.

Did I get it? Hardly ever. What I got was the standard denial, even when I knew others were getting more than appropriate attention.

There were two factors in this that I needed to face up to. First, I had no control over their behavior. Secondly, I had too many eggs in their baskets, and back then I was not confident enough in *who I was* to allow them to get whatever it was they were getting from others. One of the biggest pitfalls that we run into in relationship is trying to get everything we need, psychologically and emotionally, from our mates. Personally, I've never been successful with that type of arrangement; I've attempted to get all of my needs met by my partner in almost every relationship I have ever been in, and it is a recipe for disaster. This became part of a downward negative spiral and a self-fulfilling prophecy; invariably, those insecurities painted a less than flattering picture of ME, and were a contributing factor in them looking to get their needs met elsewhere.

In my highest place, I wanted the entire world to see these incredible women the same way that I saw them, and to celebrate that. And in my highest place, I should have been celebrating that they were with ME, and not those other clowns. But that is not the way it usually played out.

Because I didn't spend nearly enough time in my highest place.

Too often, I placed the "solution" in the other person being able or willing to own up to or alter their behavior instead of me being able to accept it or at least change my perception.

In most cases of "unquestions," the unquestioner is just looking for some approval or reinforcement. But(t), what if the unquestion IS a real issue to the questionee? (Stay with me here). What if the unquestioner has gained 50 pounds and this is an issue in terms of attractiveness, and subsequent interest in the bedroom? And this is not just men about women; I look at some couples and (reluctantly) consider (however briefly to avoid emotional scarring) does she really allow that turkey-leg-wielding, overweight, potbellied dude to get on top of her? (And then I have to turn away from that imaginary screen: the visual equivalent of fingersintheearslalalalalala...)

Where was I? (THAT was not pretty...)

For Tom and Betty, clients of mine, this was an actual issue. But it was much more serious than just the-butt-looking-too-big-in-these-pants. When they married, in their 30s, she was working out, slim and fit. Three years (and about 75 pounds) later, she not only "unquestioned" him about her appearance, but she was also badgering him because now she wanted a baby. When they first married, they were both non-committal on the subject of parenthood. Now, he was even more non-committal because he no longer found her sexually attractive and because of that wasn't even sure he wanted to continue the marriage, never mind have children. When I asked how he responded to her questions about her appearance ("Honey, do you think I am getting too fat?"), he would say "No, not at all."

So, mostly to avoid conflict, and not hurt her feelings, he was outright lying.

He explained that she had gone on all kinds of diets but wasn't able to lose the weight. When I asked him about his body, he remarked that he hadn't gained any weight, that he could eat anything, including all the pastries and sweets he would bring into the house.

I said, "Wait. You're bringing sweets into the house when your wife is trying to lose weight? That doesn't seem fair for you to have them and her not."

"Well, she eats them too, but now we have decided not to buy any store bought desserts. She bakes and uses all natural ingredients."

"OK... So, how often does she bake?"

"Every night."

She is baking every night.

Every night. Is this the Pillsbury Poppin' Fresh Dough gluten-ful diet?

Can you see on how many levels there are conflicting priorities here?

Back to their "unquestion," "Honey, do you think I am getting too fat?"

Let's try to look at this situation from the widest (sorry...) perspective.

Point #1; her "diet" includes her baking (and the two of them eating) an entire dessert a night. One does not have to have a degree in nutrition or health to realize why she is not losing weight.

Point #2; why has she gotten overweight? Is it just laziness, family patterns or something more? Maybe she doesn't want to be attractive for him anymore. Maybe Tom's not spending the time with her in bed that he did in the beginning and *she's* the one not wanting sex.

Point #3: There has been a major change in the "blueprint" of their marriage; they went from the two of them not being sure about having a child to her demanding one, and him still being non-committal. That is a huge shift.

Point #4: he could probably be convinced to come around to having a child (he works with children, he likes children), but he is not sure he even wants to stay in the marriage because he is no longer sexually attracted to his wife.

So why does he lie to her when she asks the unquestion?

Tom doesn't want to hurt her feelings. There are other issues here, of course, too: honesty, masculinity, polarity, power, maturity. He is being conflict avoidant in an area that is important to him; his wife's appearance and their subsequent sex life. And while it runs deeper than what is described here, he needs to proactively step into his masculine presence and be honest with her.

If her appearance is so important, as part of this union, he needs to make it easier for her to achieve her goals of getting back to her optimum weight by not exhibiting behavior (his pastry addiction) that is counterproductive to what it is he wants. Which is more important: brown betty or healthy sexy Betty? (For those of you who don't know, brown betty is a dessert. Geez; I'm having to explain my jokes now...)

Betty wants a baby and doesn't really know why Tom is dragging his feet; she thinks he is just still unsure. Tom is exhibiting behavior that is inconsistent with how he wants Betty to look. Is his sugar addiction so strong that it takes precedence over his wife's appearance? That is a possibility. Maybe he is just being selfish; he wants to have his cake and well, you know...

Betty has threatened to leave if he doesn't man up as a sperm donor. They are at a stalemate and neither one really knows why, because while they are clear on what their individual priorities are, Tom has not communicated his to Betty or has not been willing to accept the change in their relationship as "what is." This is a common problem in relationships. Our bodies change as we get older. However, there are people, both men and women, who are in better physical shape in their 50s and 60s than they were when they were younger. It becomes a question of priorities.

What are some of the ways this could unravel? They will have a child. She will make it happen because he doesn't have the stones to NOT allow it to happen, and they will divorce, and that child will be the product of a divisive, then divided, home. Or worse, they stay together, miserable, and create a model of dysfunctional relationship for their child.

Can those negative scenarios be avoided? There certainly are steps that can be taken to prevent them. Not easy steps. Hard steps, but kind, loving, honest, communicative steps that could have this couple not only together as a family, but healthier, more satisfied and fulfilled. This is a difficult but workable problem, if both parties are willing to get clear about what their priorities are and be able to work together to give their partners what they want.

This all started with an unquestion. They are often not as benign as they seem.

Arguably

Ultimately, unless you end up being the last person on the planet, you are going to be at odds with another human being; there is bound to be some area of your life where the fulfilment of your needs is going to be in direct conflict with the needs of another. It stands to reason that these differences are going to come up around those that you spend the most time with. Some of these show up as mere differences of opinion, others are potentially life altering perspectives.

How do we most effectively negotiate these dialogues? In their book, "Crucial Conversations: Tools for talking when the stakes are high," Kerry Patterson, Joseph Grenny, Ron McMillan and Al Switzler present a method for resolving verbal conflict. The very first premise is that in a verbal exchange that has potential danger, whether perceived or real, we go into "fight or flight" mode. What this translates to verbally is a response that is either "violence or silence," out of a need to protect ourselves. Once we enter this state, our physiology changes and our rational minds tend to not work as efficiently because our bodies need blood and energy for other priorities.

This book will teach you how to handle those situations. It's not simple and it's not easy, but the potential rewards in every area of your life are tremendous. Read this book, and then apply what you've learned.

Perhaps arguably, nowhere in your life is the resolution of conflict more important than with your partner. Still, I hear time and again from my clients, "We fight all the time."

Welcome to the world of relationship. If you didn't want to have any conflict, you should have stayed single when you had the chance. There is going to be conflict in any relationship, but when does it cross over into "fighting" and how much of that is too much? That is a different point for every individual; as we've seen, one person's "verbal abuse" is just another person's "getting upset." Some of that is cultural, some of it comes from your family of origin's communication style, some of it is personality.

In her book, "How to Argue So Your Spouse Will Listen," psychologist Sharon Morris May writes,

> "All couples argue. Arguing in and of itself is not dangerous to a marriage. What is dangerous is *how a couple argues.*"

I cannot agree more. Differences are going to crop up, and of course, if you are right, your partner has to be wrong and after a few rounds of that disharmony, patterns get set and it all starts to look a bit bleaker than it did in the beginning.

But wait; is that true? If you are defending a position, does that necessarily mean that the person who is defending their position is necessarily wrong?

We ended up going to mediation to determine custody of our young daughter. In the very first meeting, the mediator took us through Mediation 101: "You (pointing to me) are going to state your case for ten minutes and you (pointing to my adversary [ex]) are going to be quiet and listen. Then you will reverse the roles."

We had very different ideas about what the outcome of this meeting should be. I wanted what I wanted and she wanted what she wanted. When we got done with our presentations, the mediator looked at us both and said,

"You're both right."

For some reason, those three words hit me like a ton of bricks. How could we both be right when we were so opposed in terms of the outcome? But it was one of those epiphanies for me; of course we were both right, in our own minds and in our heart of hearts, but I had not been able to see that before. Before, if I had a point of view, and your point of view was different, especially if it was going to prevent me from getting my way, you were WRONG! It changed the way I saw her perspective, and the perspective of all others going forward (Ok, ok, most of the time...) She was wanting to meet her needs as passionately and as ardently as I was.

She was right.

And so was I.

The next question was "So now what do we do?"

Had we both had the same epiphany, the solution probably would have been different, but as it was, I was able to deal with any concessions I made in a more peaceful way, both inwardly and outwardly.

Prior to that, like most people, my model for conflict resolution came from my parents. They'd get drunk every Saturday and Sunday night and go 'til all hours of the morning ranting and raving about the same shit over and over. And nothing ever changed. I looked at that terribly dysfunctional example and said, "I'm never doing THAT!" Which meant, early on in my adult life that I wasn't going to argue at all. I realized at some point as I was trying to negotiate my way through my own relationships that that paradigm wasn't working for me, that I had to not only learn <u>how</u> to argue, I had to learn that it was OK <u>to</u> argue.

In her book, Dr. Morris May covers the types of arguments, and the actual physiology of argument. What is probably most useful is her suggestions of actual language, because some of us know what we shouldn't say, but what do we say instead? Let's face it; most of us have not been taught how to effectively disagree. Well, you can't use that as an excuse anymore.

Here's one tip: know when to disengage. Sometimes there are situations when we are confronted and it is inappropriate or unwise to argue: a social setting, a time constraint, attempting to keep the situation from escalating to a point where some damage can be done or even just to get your thoughts together. Often, in a situation like that, discretion becomes the better part of valor and it is wiser to back away from the fray. However, in the interest of validating the other person's position and letting them know that they are being heard, my rule is if you are going to back away, you need to set a time and place to pick up the conversation again.

This isn't always as easy as it sounds. If you are dealing with a volatile type, they are not going to want to disengage; they want their pound of flesh, dammit, and they want it NOW! This is where it becomes an important part of your relationship agreement to decide how you are going to argue. I have found this to be an effective strategy if used honestly, and not just as an avoidance technique. And by honestly, I mean, set a time and a place to take it up again and then abide by that.

Who knows? It may even give you time to think about your partner's point of view and realize that you have been less than the perfect partner and you need to a...

Ap...

Apol...

Oh, go on, spit it out!

...Apologize

"I'm sorry."

For some, one of the hardest sentences to utter.

Part of the problem is that there is an awful lot rolled up into those two simple words. If we are truly "sorry," what that means is that we have put ourselves in the place of someone else, realized that we have caused them discomfort or pain, then are not only willing to admit that but express it and feel remorse around the whole event. And how can you possibly do that when you KNOW you didn't do anything wrong? You KNOW that everything that is going wrong in this moment is the result of a distorted perspective on the part of your partner. Furthermore, you KNOW where this argument is heading and dammit you are NOT giving in.

That's right, and on top of that, you KNOW she is going to demand an apology and no-way, no-how is THAT going to happen.

And yet, there is that person across from you, that person so important to you, possibly the most important person in your life:

upset, hurt, angry, or generally experiencing some sort of negative emotion as a result of an interaction with YOU.

Now, I know that there are those of you out there that simply ARE right all of the time. What a gift and yet what a burden to have to carry around. But c'mon, you can't be the only one, right? There have to be a least a few others that are right at least *some* of the time, don't you think?

This is where I'm going to refer you back to that Mediation 101 lesson from the last chapter. But wait, what if (and I know this is hard to imagine) what if some drastic anomaly has occurred in the universe and you realize, *Maybe she's right, maybe I made a mistake, maybe the pain and discomfort she is feeling is a direct result of my behavior.*

And it's time to apologize.

> "Now, an apology isn't an apology unless you experience a change of heart. To offer a sincere apology, your motives have to change. You have to give up saving face, being right or winning in order to focus on what you *really* want. You have to sacrifice a bit of your ego by admitting your error. But like many sacrifices, when you give up something you value, you're rewarded with something even more valuable—healthy dialogue and better results."
>
> From "Crucial Conversations"

I've been with more than one woman that would never apologize. One explained to me that if she did or said something, it was already out there and there was no taking it back, so what was the sense in apologizing? If I didn't like it, too fucking bad.

On the other hand, we have all known people who will apologize for the weather being bad or some other aspect of life they have absolutely no control over.

None of us is perfect; sometimes in relationship, despite our best intentions, we conduct ourselves in a way that doesn't consider the needs of our partner.

What??!!

I know, hard to imagine, but true. Sometimes this behavior is inadvertent and we don't know that our actions will bring about a negative reaction, sometimes we do it thinking we won't get caught, sometimes we are just looking to get our needs met and in the moment, that is our only agenda. But it happens and then it is time to own up and admit we were wrong.

Some of us are perfectly willing to make that concession, to join the ranks of "We the Imperfect," but aren't sure how to go about expressing it.

A true apology is going to require some listening, a bit of empathy and a desire to heal what has happened. Again, from Dr. Morris May's book:

> "The sentences you use when you apologize are really very simple, but you'll need a large heart with a desire to love deeply. When apologizing, be specific. Mention the event. Also include the hurt that your spouse felt. Be genuine."

"I'm sorry I spent an hour and a half talking to that woman at the party and it made you feel left out. I know parties are not your thing and it made you feel uncomfortable." (There; that wasn't so hard, was it?)

There are many layers to apology. Referencing back to those that are "always right,", there is also a power piece to the equation, a level of one-ups-manship that they are not willing to concede.

Upon hearing someone's complaint, responding with "I'm sorry you feel that way," is NOT an apology. Yes, it does contain those two crucial words, but it does not express any remorse for your actions or even admit any wrongdoing. I know a couple that had a wide disparity in education; she has a couple of college degrees, he barely made it out of high school. She would correct his grammar and vocabulary in public. I know: *ouch.*

I know they fought about this afterwards.

"You humiliated me in front of my friends."

"Well I'm sorry that you were humiliating yourself."

Apology? I don't think so.

Someone once asked me, "Do you want to be right, or do you want to be loved?" Interesting question, and while most situations cannot be distilled down into that simple of a choice, it can address the role of power in your relationship. In both of those relationships, there was a huge power differential, and those in power would have been served by considering how important that power was when it came at the expense of their partner's feelings.

If we go back to one of the premises of this new paradigm that we go into relationship to give, then in true heartfelt apology, you are giving your partner the benefit of the doubt. You are letting them know they are heard. You are validating that you may have made a mistake and hurt their feelings or caused them pain.

Another type of apology is the token apology, the pat apology: those where an "I'm sorry" gets thrown out just to placate the other, to smooth over potential troubled waters. These are very familiar waters for me; I was the poster boy for the Pat Apology. I've not only admitted my guilt for lots of my transgressions over the years that warranted apology; on top of that is all the shit I took the blame for that I never *did*, but apologized for just so we wouldn't fight. While I'm not handing out any pat apologies these days, I am doing my best to humbly admit those times when I fall short of being an extraordinary partner.

The bottom line is, we are imperfect. While I don't ever want to consciously do anything that is going to cause my partner any pain, there may be a gesture I forget, a date I miss, an inadvertent unkind word in a vulnerable moment that creates a disconnect. A sincere "I'm sorry" goes a long way towards healing that.

If apology is hard for you, go outside your comfort zone. Practice. Remember; we are going for extraordinary here.

POSSIBILITIES

So, what could go *right*?

This is the fun part: where you get to consider the new fairytale (or as Greg Brown would put it: The Humantale) about what you would want an extraordinary relationship to look like. And not to think about it in terms of what you *don't* want, but in terms of what you *do*. What is most important to you? And what is most important to your mate?

I love having my head rubbed. I must have extra nerve endings up there or something, but for me a good headrub is right up there with good sex; I'm not kidding. I love getting a massage and the head rub at the end (Ok, yes; it's like a happy ending for my head) or a shampoo at a hair salon: tugging gently on my hair, fingers gliding over every hair follicle, plying my scalp, gently probing the shape of my skull, kneading against the extremity of my very soul. Yes, yes, YES! If there were still practicing phrenologists, I would be there for a weekly session.

I used to ask Rita to rub my head. For some reason, she didn't want to, and at some point I just stopped asking (it's not like I was asking her to lick my feet or stick her tongue somewhere she didn't want to, for cryin' out loud...) Barbara, on the other hand, would *volunteer* to rub my head. We would sit and watch a movie at home, and usually, first, I would massage her feet, which she loved, and they we would switch. At the end, I would always tell her it was the best headrub ever (even if technically speaking it wasn't), but it really meant, "Thank you for wanting to and offering to please me. Again."

How did we come around to that simple exchange, that agreement? (That agreement being; I love headrubs, therefor you will provide them for me and you love footrubs and therefor I will provide them for you).

That's right; we told each other. She didn't have to guess, or intuit or pick up on signals I was giving; all she had to do was ask and listen. Well, and then *do*. That's the other part; your partner may not want to do what you are asking. You may want something put (use your imaginations here) where she doesn't want it put or vice versa, and that has to be OK too.

It ain't rocket science, folks, but there can be a method to it all. In "The Five Love Languages" by Gary Chapman, he explains that there are different ways that individuals give and receive love. His book is a great place to start for couples that have been together for a long time and they no longer "get" each other. How often have we heard this, sometimes in our own relationships, "I gave her everything, but she still wasn't satisfied?"

And that's probably true because you didn't give her what she needed, you gave her what you wanted to give, OR what you knew how to give or maybe even thought she would want to get. That sounds complicated, and it is, but it doesn't have to be.

Very simply, Chapman describes that there are five ways (love languages) to *give* that show that (and how) you *love*: Words of Affirmation, Quality Time, Receiving Gifts, Acts of Service and Physical Touch. For example, you may have given your valentine flowers, chocolates and jewelry every year and thought you were just the most attentive man on the planet. But if her top "love language" is Words of Affirmation, those gifts were probably unappreciated. And the opposite is true; if she wanted gifts and you were telling her how wonderful she is, she's thinking, "Fine, now whip out the American Express card." Not that the gifts have to be monetary either, but some people just like stuff, and when you give them stuff, they feel loved. Brilliant book: simple yet profound, and a great place to start to rekindle a spark, not to mention a great way to begin to expand your communication skills in a way that doesn't involve conflict.

Yes and No

As human beings, we love yesses. And for those of us who value harmony in a relationship, "yes" becomes even more valuable. Some of us like to dispense "no's" because of the feeling of control it engenders (remember being two years old? Me neither, but supposedly, that's when saying "no" starts and it can be very affirming creating that boundary for ourselves).

I remember this poem from high school. Although I am not a fan of poetry in general this stuck with me because of the tone of it. Bear with me...

Excerpt from The Ending of *Ulysses*

the watchman going about serene with his lamp
and O that awful deep down torrent
O and the sea the sea crimson
sometimes like fire and the glorious sunsets
and the fig trees in the Alameda gardens yes
and all the queer little streets
and the pink and blue and yellow houses
and the rose gardens and the jessamine
and geraniums and cactuses and Gibraltar
as a girl where I was a Flower
of the mountain yes

(Stay with me, here; stay with me!)

when I put the rose in my hair
like the Andalusian girls used
or shall I wear a red yes
and how he kissed me
under the Moorish wall
and I thought well
as well him as another
and then I asked him
with my eyes to ask again yes
and then he asked me would I yes

to say yes my mountain flower
and first I put my arms around
him yes and drew him down to me
so he could feel my breasts all perfume yes
and his heart was going like mad
and yes I said yes I will Yes

— James Joyce (1882-1941), *Ulysses*, (1st edition, 1922)
   Random House, New York (1946)

Yes, indeed...

Yeah, who wouldn't want that? And by "that," I mean the "yes," the affirmation, the positivity, the passion. You can fill in whatever you want in between the "yesses" there (probably not as eloquently as Joyce; I mean, c'mon... Andalusian girls, the sea crimson sometimes like fire and breasts all perfume?), but the point is that we want more "yesses" than "no's."

Could it be said that extraordinary relationship encourages more "yesses"? Discourages more "no's?"

Well, yes.

And no.

While our brains love "yes," "no" is important tool in establishing personal boundaries in our relationships. Whether it is to avoid conflict, to win the approval of the other or the pursuit of indulgence, too many "yesses" can be an unhealthy equation.

But let's get away from "yes" for a moment, and look at "no." In an article from Psychology Today by Judith Sills, Ph. D., "The Power of No," she states,

> "Wielded wisely, "no" is an instrument of integrity and a
> shield against exploitation. It often takes courage to
> say it. It is hard to receive. But setting limits sets us free."

Later on in this book, I will talk about the best version of you, but it bears reflecting upon as you take a look at your relationship to consider how often you are saying no. Can you say "no" at all? If not, that's a problem; you are too much of a pleaser and not getting enough of your own needs met or you are being controlled.

If you are a doormat, eventually, the resentment built up around that is going to manifest in some sort of negative behavior.

Where are your "no's" going? Where are your "yeses" going? The question is, "How many are there and are they being directed at the right people and circumstances?" If your relationship has been together for a while, some things may have gotten stale (sex, for instance), but it could also be that your priorities have changed around a particular interest (sex, for instance).

Alright, let's take sex! While this could have been terribly important in your 20s or 30s, it may be less so now in your 50s. Or vice versa! The list of what we have to say "yes" or "no" to is literally endless, now more than ever. So maybe it's "yes" to healthy eating now, and "no" to smoking. "Yes" to travel, "no" to PTA. "Yes" to relationship, "no" to weekends on the couch watching the games.

So, while extraordinary relationship, indeed, yes, has "yes" as a symbol of positivity and affirmation woven, yes, permeating, all through it, there has to be room for "no." Yes?

What we are really talking about here is conflict and harmony. If you are conflict avoidant, and you are "yessing" to constantly maintain the peace, there will probably be a loss of self-esteem as a result.

Ultimately, it comes down to the relationship equation: are there more "yesses" than "no's?" Which are YOU providing?

Givers and Takers

Very few selfish people will describe themselves as selfish but that comes along with the territory; selfishness is a perspective that is not conducive to being compassionate, empathetic or even aware of what others are thinking or feeling. Laura told me when we were first dating, "This time it's MY turn." Being early on in my relationship development, I had no idea of the far reaching ramifications of that statement, but I was about to find out. This was simply more evidence of that ongoing cluelessness that I had alluded to before. Seven long years later I would start to get a clearer perspective on givers and takers.

There's no mystery about what my role was in that relationship: right: total giver (could/should also be interpreted as "doormat"). Yes, some of my needs ended up being met by that selflessness, but ultimately, the rest of my needs were NOT being met, and that was a recipe for disaster.

Sometimes two takers will get together. Those taker/taker relationships don't usually last very long, for obvious reasons. One date, one night, maybe a little longer, but for those whose priority is meeting their own needs, if it's not being met, they move on. Not that there is anything wrong with that. Well, actually, that's kind of fucked up; if you are a narcissist, there are other books you should be reading in addition to this one!

In most relationships there is a give and take dynamic, an ebb and flow, around how individual needs get met. How and when this occurs determines the quality of the relationship over time. Often, when the ebb becomes ongoing for one, it can signal the end of the relationship. Ultimately, as humans, we have needs and we get them met, ideally in ways that are productive and fulfilling, but sometimes, in ways that can be counterproductive or even destructive. General rule of thumb for me is, ongoing ebb: bad.

If you have an extreme giver/taker scenario, at some point it will reach a "natural" end because there is nothing left to give. Let me rephrase that; there is always more one can give, but the energy to give it and the desire to do so wanes or disappears completely. There is a realization that it doesn't matter how much you give, IT IS NEVER GOING TO BE ENOUGH. There are those takers who are just black holes of consumption, emotional vampires, the Hoover vacuums of relationship. Their mantra is "What have you done for me lately?" Does any of this sound familiar? Could this be YOU? Don't just give me a pat "no" here, because if you have a history of casting others aside, of relationship after relationship constantly waning, you may be guilty here. When your relationship has the potential to evolve into truly *loving* someone, truly giving of yourself, do you have it within your capacity to do that, or do you turn and run off, to find the next fulfiller of your needs?

Sometimes, there can be a relationship between two givers. In some ways this can be ideal, but it can have its drawbacks too; if one giver is not expressing what they need, those needs can go unmet, simply out of ignorance of what that need is. OR, their partner can be a giver who is not a good listener, and only ends up "giving" what they think the other person needs or wants (like a surprise birthday party for someone who hates surprise birthday parties, for example).

This ties in with power struggles in that very often those with the power in a relationship are the takers. How does this work? I should know; I've been with more than my share of them. In a way, around a polarity model, it makes sense; one gives, the other takes. And for true givers, since they have that need to give, it satisfies one of their basic needs. But if it gets too one-sided, it's easy to see how the giver will end up not getting some (or any) of their needs met. It's easy to "blame" the taker here as being selfish, and that is true up to a point. But it is also the responsibility of the giver to realize what their own needs are and to express them to their partner so that that person at least has been exposed to what those needs are, even if they are not prepared to meet them.

Often, for givers though, that is not so easy. Without getting into too much psychomumbojumbo around self-esteem, very often givers have a hard time receiving: "No, it's OK, you come first" (and you can interpret that however you want...) Consequently, their needs are not getting met, they don't know how to ask for what they need, they will resent their partners for not satisfying them and will often go to extremes then to get them met elsewhere.

Yeah, welcome to my former life as a doormat. Where everything I was doing was for others and that allowed me to mistakenly justify getting my needs met elsewhere and in ways that were destructive. Like having an affair (I know, I know...I was young and clueless, remember? And, yes; I will tell that story. Just not yet...)

But back to givers and takers. This ties into aggression and passivity and general yin/yang tendencies that are all part of the make-up of our world. Ideally, there is enough balance in the personality makeup of each partner that it all meshes together in a way that works for both of you. But this is one of the places where it gets so complex. Where are you on that spectrum of giving/taking, where is your partner, and more importantly, how does that all manifest in the daily workings of your relationship?

Are you willing to accept your role, as it stands now? Are you willing to accept your partner's role? I hope so, because it's not gonna change. That is, it's not gonna change because (or when) YOU want it to. It just doesn't work that way. People change all the time, but we can't expect them to; that is just a blueprint for frustration.

If you are a taker, you probably don't even know it; you're too wrapped up in your own little world to see how much you suck the life out of others (OK, that was a little bitter... not that I was thinking about anybody in particular...) But really, I know (and we all know) people who think they are loving and generous and have no idea how much the world revolves around them. (Sort of the opposite of Carly Simon's "You're So Vain"; it's more like,

> "You're so egocentric, you have no idea this song is about you."

If you match this description, I can't help you, as much as I have futilely tried to in the past. And stay away from me! (Insert crossed forefingers here).

And apologies to Carly, btw...

If you *think* you might be a taker, there could be hope for you. Try this: go to your partner and ask them what you can do for them that you don't usually. After they give you a quizzical look followed by, "Who are you and what have you done with my husband?" listen to them and then, if it is in your power and inclination to give them what they ask for, give it to them!

See? That wasn't so hard, was it? Uncomfortable maybe, but wait until you reap the benefits of that. And can you think what the biggest benefit is?

Wrong! You're thinking about what you will get in return.

Let me help you here; it's that you GAVE, and it was appreciated.

I love getting stories from individuals and couples about aspects of their relationships that worked and those that didn't. One woman, that had been happily married for a long time explained that she thought their "secret" was appreciating little gestures, like her husband bringing her a glass of water in bed (aaawww, right?) Conversely, she told a story about her ungrateful (and unhappily married) sister who was constantly complaining that her husband wouldn't take her to Tahiti.

Obviously, we have two women here with grossly different value systems, and it could be argued that the first woman was setting the bar far too low. But who's to say? It wouldn't surprise me if wife #2 did make it to Tahiti and never even thanked her husband ("It's about damn time..."), whereas I would bet cash money that wife #1 thanked her husband for that glass of water.

In general, I don't think we are verbally appreciative enough in our culture. I think part of the reason for that is that complimenting someone or thanking them puts us in a one-down position, and most people are not comfortable there.

The other reason, and again, this has to do with power, if we compliment someone or thank them for their efforts, it is so often viewed as sucking up or kissing ass, especially if it is done in a setting where there is a power hierarchy.

For you givers out there; bless you. I know if it is in your nature to give, you are never going to stop.

So don't.

But what I did, since I was taking care of others (and often non-deserving others), I PUT MYSELF ON THE LIST OF THOSE I TAKE CARE OF.

Which includes the concept that it is OK to receive.

Ready for another story? This one is less relationship oriented, but taught me one of my most valuable lessons.

When I was 20 years old, I left my friends in Milwaukee and started hitchhiking west across the country. One day I was in Deadwood, South Dakota, which at the time was a small old west town that had western museums and recreated saloons. Growing up, my family had watched every western show on TV and now here I was, this kid from Brooklyn actually out west. I loved it. At the end of the day, I was walking out of town on the left hand side of the road looking for a place to pitch my tent. A Country Squire station wagon pulled over with the Mom, Dad and two kids. The dad rolled down the (crank) window and asked me if I wanted a ride.

"No, I'm just looking for a place to pitch my tent," I said.

"Well, come on out to our place. You can pitch your tent there."

I was a little wary (my cynical East coast upbringing) but I figured it was safe and so I went. I ended up spending two days with them. They fed me, washed my clothes, the Dad took me trout fishing in the stream behind their cabin, we grilled the thickest steaks I have ever seen on their barbecue.

After two days though, I was starting to get a bit uncomfortable with their generosity. On the third day, it was raining cats and dogs but I said that I wanted to hike to the lake at the end of Spearfish Canyon. Despite their protests about the weather, off I went.

I got drenched. To the bone. I was miserable. I hiked the 12 miles or so to the lake, looked at it forlornly in the rain, somehow found a reasonably dry spot to unroll my wet sleeping bag and spent a fitful night trying to sleep.

When I woke up the next day, the sun was out, the birds were chirping, the August flowers were in full bloom. I spread my stuff out to dry, repacked it and started my hike out of the canyon, back the way I came, which incidentally was going to take me back past the Moore's cabin. It was one of the most scenic and beautiful hikes I have ever had: the road followed the stream, the weather was perfect and it is one of the truly most beautiful places I have ever been.

When I was about 2 miles from the cabin, I saw a car approaching and sure enough, it was the Country Squire station wagon with Mrs. Moore behind the wheel.

"We were so worried about you. I was coming to look for you to make sure you were OK."

So, I went back to the cabin, spent another night with them and the next day I was ready to continue my journey further west. Mr. Moore offered to give me a ride out to the interstate.

"No, that's OK; I'll just hike."

Into the car I went.

By then, I was feeling REALLY uncomfortable, and my East Coast skeptic radar was fully extended. I started to think, This guy is going to pull off on the side of the road and try to molest me. Because CLEARLY, he had to have an agenda.

But no; he took me straight out to the interstate ramp.

Then, he reached for his wallet and took out a $20 bill.

Here it comes now... Here's where I get propositioned, *I thought.*

But no, he just wanted to give me some money to help me on my way.

"Mr. Moore," I said. "I have to tell you. I am really uncomfortable with all that you have done for me. Nobody, nobody has ever shown me this kind of generosity."

He considered that, chuckled, then turned to me and replied, "The good Lord has provided us with more than most, and sometimes when we get a chance, we like to share it with others."

Being the agnostic I was, I wasn't really sure what to do with that statement.

And then he added, "And you shouldn't feel uncomfortable with that. Rather, you should receive it in the spirit that it is given."

And with that, he offered me the $20 bill again.

You have to understand that first of all, I was fairly anti-religion, having been raised Russian Orthodox and forced to stand for 2 hour masses in Russian (that's right: we didn't need no stinkin' PEWS).

So, I was trying to process all of this, and came to the realization that the Moore's were just giving for the sake of giving. That's all.

Regardless of whatever lessons there were to be learned, I refused the twenty dollars but thanked him profusely for his generosity and went on my way. Later that day, I reached in the outer pocket of my backpack for my journal.

And a $20 bill fell out.

I don't know when or how he put it in there, but there it was. When I got to the next town, I went straight to the post office.

I wrote him a note that said,

"Thank you for everything, including the $20. I'm keeping it, in the spirit that it was given."

So, for all you givers out there, you also have to make room in your hearts to receive. It's OK, really. And also recognize the difference between receiving and taking.

Which brings us around to relationships with two givers.

Ideally, I believe that one should go into relationship to give. To me, that is what love IS.

That is what love DOES.

And if you do that with someone else that has the same mindset, you will have an experience of relationship like no other. It is very common for givers to hook up with takers. It's that stupid polarity thing.

But I am here to tell you; find another giver. Try it and see what happens.

It's not as easy as it sounds. At the risk of stereotyping, givers are not so easily recognized, while takers are often charming, charismatic, bright, shiny, sparkly individuals that are fun to be around. They are front and center commanding our attention luring the givers into their magnetic black hole of attraction. And who are we to resist?

Think about people who you have engaged with that are like this. And ask yourself, "How could I have fallen for that? What did I see in her? What was I THINKING?" Well, we weren't thinking; we just got charmed, and then at some point realized that nothing we ever do for these people will EVER be enough, and they cast us aside once they have sucked the very essence out of us and we are just a withered husk of a human being cast to the gutter saying, "What happened?"

Was that melodramatic enough for you?

Just say "NO," unless of course, you are into that kind of thing, the drama, the angst, the "passion" of it all. Yes, I have heard it referred to as "passion;" "I'm just a passionate person; that's how I live my life!"

"Well, you can live it someplace else."

Don't get me wrong; I am all for passion, but passion directed in a positive manner: creativity, a lust for life, dedication to a cause. But when your "passion" habitually crosses over into a negative downward spiral revolving around your unresolved shit, it's about creating some excitement in your life using the innocent lives of those around you because you're bored. You want adrenaline? Take up sky-diving, and let that satisfy your lust for drama.

I am obviously over-generalizing, but it is part of human nature for us to strive to get our needs met for as individuals and while there does seem to be a drive for some of us to take care of the "tribe" as a whole, that impetus seems to be secondary for many.

So, I'll admit it; I'm not Gandhi; I like to get my needs met as much as the next person. But I know from personal experience that while I am usually happy as a clam meeting someone else's need, it can be a fine line between acceding to most of your partner's needs and giving too much. I cringe when I hear stories about women who for their entire marriages have not wanted to have sex with their husbands, but do because it was their "duty." When does it cross over from giving, to giving too much, to being controlled and living a life of subservience?

I love to give. But at some point, if I am not getting MY needs met, at least on some level, my giving is going to stop and I am going to look to get my needs met elsewhere.

And that is an important part of this new paradigm: you have to get clear on what your needs are and then you have to express them to your partner. Oh, and then there is a third part to the process; be prepared to accept the fact that your partner is probably not going to meet all of those needs. Then the challenge is getting clear on what you are willing to accept as unfulfilled through them, and also whether or not those needs can be met elsewhere.

This is where compromise comes in and in compromise we are faced again with not only each individual's role as a giver and taker, but how effective each is in conflict and negotiation. We will discuss that more once we get into actually constructing your agreement.

Familiarity

Do you fart? Of course you do; everybody farts. But do you fart in front of your boyfriend or girlfriend, your date, your spouse? If you do, are they the infamous silent-but-deadly variety that are acknowledged by an opening of the car window a crack and nothing else? Or do you have the freedom within your relationship to just let 'em rip at whatever velocity and decibel level you can possibly muster? From Dan DiSorbo, who wrote "The Fart Tootorial: Farting Fundamentals, Master Blaster Techniques, and the Complete Toot Taxonomy,"

> "Farting is part of the universal human experience. Farting knows no borders: every person from every corner of the globe breaks wind. (The average person toots 14 times per day, in case you were wondering). But most importantly, farting is just funny."

Rita had a very neurotic cat that she had rescued from the shelter. To say that this cat was skittish was putting it mildly; she lived in her own little world that was inhabited by numerous unseen entities (to us two-leggeds, anyway) that seemed to make her world a constant adventure. Humans were to be avoided at all costs, that is, as long as they were vertical. Once they became horizontal, however, they became safe enough to interact with: to play, to sleep with, or attack while they were sleeping.

One night, Rita and I were reading before going to sleep, and Fluffy was just settling in with us and starting to nod off when there was a sudden flatulent explosion from an "undisclosed" source underneath the covers. That cat propelled herself straight up in the air about two and a half feet from almost a dead sleep.

Apparently she had never been fartled before. (Yes, it is a new word, a hybrid, if you will, of "farted" and "startled" and I want credit for introducing it into the vernacular...) As much as she might have needed a cat whisperer before that, she was definitely going to need one after.

Hopefully I won't have the animal rights people after me. This is not about Fluffy. She survived. The relationship with Rita did not, despite our olfactory familiarity.

Why am I telling this story? Stay with me; we are coming around to rediscovering the simple appreciation of familiarity.

So farting can be funny, yes. Conversely, not farting can be painful, in numerous ways.

Elizabeth was an apartment neighbor of mine that I think had a bit of a crush on me. She invited me over once and we were playing cards around her coffee table. All of a sudden she ripped what to this day is I think the longest and loudest fart I have ever been witness to. She immediately got up and left the room, and stayed away for a long time. At some point I heard her voice from the other room, "I can't come out; I'm too embarrassed."

I tried to convince her otherwise, but she was steadfast. I let myself out and was never invited back.

I am not striving to repeal social mores around flatulence. I do believe there is a time for retention and a time for expulsion, but I do want to talk about comfort levels, both physical and social.

In your relationship, do you have to leave the room to "take Donald out for a walk?" (All euphemisms courtesy of DiSorbo). Do you find it disgusting when your mate "answers the call of the wild burrito?" I have heard men say that they don't want to think about their lover cutting one: "It's not sexy." How you view your partner's poofs can be a barometer for your overall feelings towards them. While that may sound extreme, think about it; maybe the fun has left your relationship and it's time to get it back. What? *Too* familiar? I will contend that if you feel any emotion besides mirth around your partner's buttnoise (thanks to Zascha at 5 years old for this one), it may be time to reexamine how you relate to each other. And if that emotion reaches contempt, a complete overhaul may be in order.

I have been in entirely non-flatulent relationships. That is, farting was not "sanctioned" in front of the partner. Yes, anal retentive, and at times, physically uncomfortable and inconvenient. I don't think it's healthy, on numerous levels. So I am campaigning for, in the privacy of your own homes, for it to be flatulence free, which does NOT mean NO farting, but just the opposite: freely flatulent.

But someone has to be the first, to open the door, if you will, to this new-found freedom. So here is a potential dialogue after an SBD (the recommended ice breaker):

You (the courageous, trend setting pioneer/perpetrator), "Did you just fart?"

"No, I didn't fart."

"Well then; it must have been me..."

And off you go.

Another ice breaker could be, upon having cut one, is, "Is somebody baking bread?" which gets the other party to inhale deeply. A little cruel? Yes, and sophomoric. But funny (and effective) nonetheless. Have some fun, people!

Obviously, all of this entails one going outside of their comfort zone. One last warning: if you decide to experiment with this in bed, and upon your release, are so embarrassed that you decide to hide your head under the covers... you may want to rethink that. Unless you are one of those people that loves the smell of their own flatulence, in which case, hide away.

Where else are you going to find this kind of ground-breaking (I could have said "wind-breaking," but that would have been too obvious) advice?

It may seem odd to be reading about farting in a book about creating extraordinary relationship. But c'mon; this isn't about farting. It's about your level of comfort and familiarity with the person in your world who you want to be closest to. So, get closer! And one way to get closer is to share those activities that you have in common.

Children

We can't talk about giving and taking without talking about our progeny. Raising kids takes a lot of time and attention. These are our offspring, they are our babies and they are our future. The BIG "our," the collective "our," the it-takes-a-village "our." And raising children is hard because there is no prescribed way to get a set result. You can be the best parent in the world and have a child that you (and others) are convinced is the demon seed.

From the instant children come into this world, they are totally dependent upon others to meet their needs, and go about very quickly figuring out ways to make that happen. Those early needs are very fundamental: comfort and sustenance. As they get older, those needs become more complex, not to mention individual. And there is an extremely wide range of parental effectiveness in how those needs are addressed, from abuse and absolute neglect to ultimate love and support. Couple that with the fact that there is no failsafe way to raise a child and you basically have parenthood as a crapshoot.

I had a hummingbird nest near my back door one year. It started out about the size of a large walnut, and the mama came and laid two little Tic-Tac eggs in it. I was able to watch her sit on those eggs and eventually see them hatch. I monitored their growth every day for a couple of weeks. The adults actually incorporate spiderweb silk into their nests so they will expand as the little ones get larger. Then one day, I was watching those two little guys hanging out like they had for last 20-30 days and one of them just lifted up and took off, flitting those tiny wings a mile a minute like he had been doing it all his life. He never came back, and the other one left a day or two later.

That's quite a bit different from the process we have as humans. No, we've got to be nurtured and taken care of and fed for a long time, and traditionally, it is the female of our species that has done that. As women have entered the workforce in larger numbers, that role has changed quite a bit. And depending on which theory of psychology you subscribe to, to some degree, those early parent/child relationships set the tone for all subsequent relationships, which is problematic because most parents know very little about how to effectively parent, despite all the information that is available about different approaches. We are far better, collectively, than we used to be, but there is still a lot to be desired in terms of parenting in ways that will result in a healthy functioning adult. In the span of my lifetime I have seen a shift in male and female roles so that fathers are now much more involved in parenting than they were in generations past. While this is usually a positive development in terms of the children's ultimate growth, it makes for yet another (very important) area that partners can disagree on. That being said, it is a worthy pursuit, perhaps beyond any other that we undertake. So, hard, yes; and worth every bit of effort.

But let me get on another soapbox, if I may, for a moment.

First of all, too many kids just "happen," which, to me, in inexcusable with readily available birth control. I know, I know; we have a primal drive to procreate and it feels oh, so good to do that, and consequently the population of the world continues to expand exponentially. On top of that, there are belief systems in place that decry the use of any birth control.

If Mother Nature were smart(er), she would somehow make the act of procreation unpleasant and then we would have to consciously consider creating children rather than just having them happen. Perhaps Mother Nature is going to go about solving this problem her own way, or not, in which case we are going to have to figure something else out. But that is the subject for another day and another book.

Let's scale the conversation way back to individual families; are there enough resources to effectively feed, clothe, shelter and LOVE all of the children in any given family? Obviously, that has to be looked at in a case by case study. What if there aren't? Is it in the belief system of that family to curtail their baby-making? Ummm, often not; China has had to have the government step in and make that decision, and in part of their belief systems (the Chinese culture), a male child is "worth" more than a female child.

How fucked up is that? What do you think are the individual and collective long term ramifications of THAT brilliant belief system?

(I can see a scenario of resentful female Chinese women rising up to overthrow the current system).

But again, let's scale that decision to have a child or not back to an individual. I know of a woman who wanted a daughter. She was not married, but arranged to be impregnated with a little girl.

Yes, I know and you know, that, at this time in our procreational evolution, it is not possible to choose the sex of your child. Nevertheless, this woman was going to "manifest" a daughter.

Well, she didn't.

She had a son.

That she didn't want, and reluctantly raised by herself.

Any ideas about how that particular child-rearing went?

That's right; contentious, resentful and guaranteed years of therapy up the road for that unfortunate kid.

I have a daughter. Actually, of course, it is "our" daughter; I couldn't have done it without her mom.

(Let's take a look at that statement, "I couldn't have done it without her." I was referring to having our daughter together, but doesn't that refer to any relationship? We are so unique, any relationship we have with anyone else is going to be different than any other relationship. "I couldn't have done it without her." "She couldn't have done it without me." Interesting).

Our daughter was the glorious product of my relationship with my second wife when we were both 44 years old. Yep, 44. And our decision to have a child at that age was not without its challenges. But once we decided to marry, even though we were "older," a child was always a part of the plan.

Shortly after we had just met, I asked the future mother of our child to accompany me on a cross country move from New Jersey to New Mexico in the largest rental truck Ryder had to offer.

Somehow convinced I was not an ax murderer, she consented. We took the longer southern route, stopping first at Graceland and later a diamond field in Arkansas, which is a farmland that gets plowed regularly, and when it does, diamonds occasionally come to the surface. Yes, real diamonds. She was a jeweler, so we made sure to make this a part of the trip. There we were in a huge open field, looking for diamonds. In Arkansas. And then it rained, and I mean rained, and we got drenched, with no cover.

Muddy, laughing, soaking wet and without even a single diamond, we made it back to the truck. That truck was a two week rental and we made sure to use every day of that two weeks.

I proposed to her six months later.

We had a wonderful wedding, complete with a mariachi band marching us through the streets of Santa Fe and a reception at the Fine Arts Museum. We were off and running.

While a child was always a part of the plan, despite our ages, real life asserted itself, it all became a lot less fun, and we set our plans for parenthood aside and got some outside help to help us cope with the pressures of trying to make a marriage work.

A lot of help; we went through four counselors before we found someone that was a good fit for us. And boy, did we need help, especially me. I had done some self-help tinkering in the past, but I needed some serious intervention, and it was forthcoming. Something had to change, and it was going to be me. I had an immense amount of growing to do, and that was one of the decisions that came out of our joint therapy; it was time for me to examine what was working in my life and what was not. I couldn't expect her to change, but I could put that expectation on myself, and that's just what I set out to do. I also realized that I needed to do something for myself, instead of just always doing for others, so I went back to college to get my Bachelor's degree in Psychology and remembered how much I loved an academic environment, not just for the learning and the sharing of ideas but also for my sense of identity. Once I started classes, I was being exposed to even more information about just how much room there was for growth potential in me. It was classic midlife crisis. The good thing was that I was attacking it in a way that was productive: education.

And things seemed to even out between us. Then one day, I heard a disembodied voice coming through me, saying to my wife, "Maybe we should try again to have a baby."

As I remember it, I looked around to see where the voice had come from, and found no one. I don't profess to know how our world works, but I am convinced that our daughter was saying to us from some other dimension, in essence, "Look, you two; I'm coming down, and I am coming down through the two of you. So get it together long enough for me to get there and we'll figure out the rest as we go."

And come into our lives she did, and despite her presence, her Mom and I separated a year later, which was the hardest decision I have ever had to make. Even after all that counseling, from my perspective, we just were not a good couple together, and I moved out. The therapy just pointed out in more detail, how incompatible we were, not to mention how much more personal work I had to do. As in most real life decisions, there were far reaching ramifications of that choice, many of which I will never know, but can only surmise.

All that being said, having and raising a child has been one of the most fulfilling, meaningful and emotionally healing endeavors I have ever engaged in. Period. At the same time, I ignored the advice I would give to any couple that is not sure about whether or not to parent; "If you are not sure, don't do it. Children deserve to be wanted."

What I didn't know at the time was how wanted she would be, and it would become one of the constants in my life for the next seventeen years, as well as teaching me the true meaning of commitment. Prior to that, "commitment' was a promise that could be broken. As her Dad, I realized that once I decided to commit to co-parent (albeit not in the same household), I was going to be there for her no matter what.

As for the co-parenting part of the equation, while we have had our challenges along the way, we have set common goals and rules for raising our daughter and I am convinced that her having grown up in two households has been preferable to what it would have been like had we all stayed under the same roof. No, we don't know what that co-habitation would have been like had we continued it, but that is the nature of decision.

Along the way we evolved and ended up bringing another amazing person into this world. Evolutionarily speaking, our daughter is so far ahead of where I was in her path' I love that...

In retrospect, I believe growing up in two households has served our daughter in her upbringing. One aspect of children growing up in non-nuclear homes is that they can experience other examples of how adult relationships are conducted. First is the relationship between the parents. If that continues to be adversarial, it sets an example of conflict. Then there are the influences of other men and women coming into that child's life and how THEY relate to both of the parents. This can be positive or negative or both. I have had relationships where my partner was very involved in my daughter's life and others where they hardly knew her at all, and I was always very conscious about the role they would play.

I hate to think about any child being unwanted. My mother used to say, "I never wanted to have any of you kids." (so quotable, that woman...) In a perfect world, no child would ever have to hear that again.

Parenting done right SHOULD be conscious and it will be time consuming, but it doesn't have to be all-encompassing. Part of a child's upbringing should be your example of how to conduct a loving, affectionate, passionate relationship in their midst.

One perspective I have about children is that they are little people making their way in a world of giants and we should always be cognizant of what that must be like for them, which is generally powerless. Because of that, they should be loved and supported. Period. But I am not Dr. Spock, and this is a book about adult relationships.

What I am going to suggest is that you and your partner not get lost in the shuffle. Quite the contrary; your partner should be loved and supported as well as the children. If there are children in your household, whether they are "yours," your partner's, somebody else's, hell, they could be walking in off the street; you are a model for them. The way you are conducting your relationship with your partner is setting an example for those kids about what relationship looks like, and more likely than not, they are going to go out when they are adults and repeat it, because that is what they have seen on a daily basis; your actions daily are teaching them how to move about in the world.

Be the best parent you can; it's the most important job you will ever have.

Compatibility

Do you remember your best first date ever? There you were, probably with a perfect stranger and the more you disclosed about each other, the more you realized you had in common. How affirming was that??!! "I am not alone!" Music, politics, food, dogs, cats, literature, movies: it didn't matter, you agreed on everything. Click, click, click: all the tallies in the positive column. That's what *made* it the greatest first date ever.

How about your worst date ever? That may be just as memorable. Showed up late with no excuse, talked about himself all night, different politics, boring, bad manners, mean to the waiter, crappy car and bad kisser.

We are going to get along better with people who are more like us; it's that simple.

At one point, I was looking for the female version of myself. I found someone pretty damn close, except I could never beat her at Scrabble (and I mean never; Maggie knew all those stupid two and three letter words that aren't real words) and so I dumped her.

It wasn't just the Scrabble (I might have squeezed a win in there eventually if I plied her with enough wine, although that probably wouldn't have done the trick either; she just got smarter the more wine she drank) and I didn't really dump her (although she may tell a different version of that story...) There was someone else I was interested in at the same time (alright, alright, it was Rita, OK?) Rita and I had some serious "juice" between us and I went for the juice. (Are you starting to see a pattern here?) I have wondered what that other path would have looked like, because Maggie and I REALLY got along, like best-friend getting along, and I believe that is a key component in creating an extraordinary relationship. It just makes sense; the more areas you have in common, the less there is to argue about. The less there is to argue about, the more harmonious the relationship is going to be.

Often though, when you think you have found the perfect, compatible mate, they change. Some of this will depend on your stage of life. Let's face it, if you are in your twenties, as much as you may think you know who you are and how the world works, you don't. And this is a bigger problem in our culture than ever before, because we are no longer confined to the geographical boundaries that we were in the middle of the last century; the entire world is in our backyard.

 I know of a couple that married and then the husband joined a cult, and there were suddenly a lot of new rules to follow, including sexual abstinence. I remember the wife saying, "I did NOT sign up for THAT!" But they had promised to stay together: " 'til death do us part." They eventually divorced; I guess somewhere in the fine print of the marriage contract there was the "unless-you-join-a-cult-and-decide-you-no-longer-want-to-do-me" disclaimer.

As you are considering your beliefs, interests, values, and propensities, which are most important to you? Which are essential in a partner? A long list of compatibilities can lead to a very harmonious existence together. There are certainly no guarantees that they will stay that way, but it's a good place to start.

Have you seen those couples that describe themselves as "best friends?" What do you think that characterization comes from? They not only like the same activities, they like doing them together. I spoke with a gentleman recently: forty one years married, and HAPPY! I asked his secret. He had given it some prior thought, and said that he actually thought there was a little bit of luck involved, because he had found someone that he was compatible with. He felt that that was the biggest key to longevity in relationship. But he also said that they keep creating new ways to engage. When he retired, he wanted to take up golf and thought that it would be fun for him and his wife to do together. Now she's more of a golf nut than he is.

So, there is a lot to be said for compatibility and harmony in a relationship. But what about when the opposite is true? What happens when we get presented with our partner's Dark side? (cue ominous organ music from a b-grade horror movie...)

CHALLENGES

The Shadow

Too often, what began as euphoria and passion, laughter, support, alignment and bliss turns into vitriol, disagreement, disdain and even hatred. What happens?

If you are in the very beginning of a relationship, in the throes of the infatuation experience, very simply, no negativity is going to be recognized for what it is. Your altered state is going to take those red flags and disguise them as so many roses.

But once that rapture fades, the warts are going to come to the surface. Some of the time this happens in one big crash, other times it is a gradual process.

This is when the real work begins as part of the process to decide whether or not the relationship has potential for the long term.

Let's take a moment to describe "darkness" as it applies to personality and how we confront, negotiate, embrace, even define it. Words like hatred, aggression, sadism, selfishness, jealousy, resentment, violence, prejudice come to mind. But what about a more general brushstroke?

How about, "that which is interpreted as undesirable?" First of all, who is doing the interpreting? Is it constructive or destructive? To the self? How about to others? How about specifically the one Important Other? For instance, a compulsion to work, for the self (and arguably for the union) could be viewed as a valuable trait. But are all of those late nights at the office conducive to the intimacy and closeness that the partner might be needing?

At the extreme end of the spectrum, we look at darkness as "evil." From "Meeting the Shadow: the Hidden Power of the Dark Side of Human Nature," Connie Zweig and Jeremiah Abrams, pull together essays of great thinkers and philosophers to discuss the shadow side of human nature, from Jung and Campbell to Peck and Wilbur. "Many anthropologists and sociobiologists believe that human evil is a result of curbing our animal aggression, of choosing culture over nature and losing contact with our primitive wildness." I guess it could also be argued that some of what we interpret as evil is not so much the curbing of those wild tendencies but surrendering to them. Infidelity for example. Evil? Sin? If we attribute that to our animal nature, then why the taboo? Is it a sin because we culturally say it's wrong?

Let's face it; none of us is perfect; we all have what can be described as a Dark Side; some of us have extremely developed shadows, to the point of having that be our dominant characteristic. In others, it is more veiled and may take longer to surface.

In some cases, that dark side is just a seed and simply needs the right circumstances to flourish. Life often has a way of serving up curveballs that we are not able to cope with in ways that are constructive and the result is behavior that is DEstructive.

Before it even gets to that point, we start to notice those actions that are simply annoying: benign habits like toilet seat configuration, using the wrong fork at a restaurant or too infrequent deodorant use. Depending on your level of acceptance, that level of "undesirable" can usually be written off.

But what if it can't? What if that armpit neglect gets characterized as "Dude; you stink!" and someone's feelings get hurt? While there may be a kinder approach to that disclosure, what if it is done in front of others? You know, jokingly, but with a hint of truth?

I've seen this too often as a gradual devolution: from annoyance to disdain to disagreement to fighting to despair and even hate. What can we do to stop that downward spiral?

Later, when we get into the specifics of what comprises your individual relationship with someone else, we will look at destructive behaviors that can be labeled "non-negotiable": those actions that tip the scale from "this sucks" to "I am outta here."

"C'mon, What's the Worst That Could Happen?"

In trying my best to raise my daughter, one of the tenets I tried to impress upon her is that men and women are NOT enemies. But, as in most absolute statements about anything, that is not completely true. Some members of the opposite sex ARE the enemy, and they are to be avoided at all costs. Unless, like a true warmonger, you like that kind of thing, and you are convinced that when you engage in that war, you are gonna WIN.

If you are seeing the opposite sex as the enemy however, and yet, you are trying to have an extraordinary relationship, yours will be a battle in the jungle that no one is going to win; this will be your own emotional Vietnam.

Even if you are not enemies, there will be conflict in any relationship. How you negotiate those "events" will go a long way in determining the overall fabric of your relationship. And there is a huge difference between "events" and "issues." What I am suggesting is that you get as clear as possible about your role and your partner's role as you go into conflict. How important is this battle? Is it part of a war? If it is a war, do you think you are going to win? Is it important for you to win? Will your winning lead to extraordinary relationship? What if you lose? Will that lead to peace? Is peace even important to you? That may sound like a rhetorical question, but it's not; some people thrive on that conflict; it's fun for them, exciting, stimulating. Passionate, some will call it.

I'm not one of them.

I used to have the longest fuse in the world because of my conflict avoidance. While that has its advantages, there is a downside in that it allows resentments to build up. That avoidance and non-engagement can also be exasperating to others. It used to drive Lucy crazy. So she would "poke" me and push me to get a rise out of me, and when she did, I could see the glee in her demeanor that she had the ability to manipulate my state that way. So there I would be, all worked up, ready to engage (albeit late and in a negative way), and she would say, "OK, let's make up now." And in my (finally) adrenalized state, that was the very last thing on my mind.

All the images intertwined, vying for my attention at once: that first glimpse across the street, when I screwed up my nerve to introduce myself, how much better this was than the last one, she was so much fun, but how she would make me wait, and she was fit, everyone loved her but that was a problem too and it was her world but her world was all about the fun but it was still her world, and money, "that's because you don't have any..." and she couldn't cook but I could and the drama, so much drama and I hate that and then it would all be alright until the next time and now this: the dread, that feeling of failure...

Really? Like this? It's going to end like this?

I could see my breath, but couldn't feel the cold. I couldn't feel much of anything; not sure if the numbness was from the wine or the resignation.

She had done it again; pushed, not physically, but verbally, emotionally, like she liked to do, to get a rise out of me. Well, she did.

I had felt the adrenaline rise through my body as if it were shot through the soles of my feet, taking all of two or three seconds to rise all the way to the top of my head, at which point my body was going to want to move, react, do something physical. Fight or flight, baby. I knew what to do; turn around, get out, get away.

So I did. I turned away, bolted out of the living room, through the kitchen, grabbing the French knife off the counter, exiting out the kitchen door, into the night. The movement felt momentarily good, safe.

But it wasn't safe.

Fifty yards later, stumbling through the darkness, I sank to my knees in a cluster of shoulder high chamisa bushes.

They'll never find me here.

Just one swift, decisive stroke was all it would take.

Go ahead, you loser; it's over anyway. She's not gonna care. Nobody's gonna care.

My knuckles curled white over the handle of the knife, my thumb wrapped around the underside. That was all the motion I could muster. I was otherwise numb, inside and out.

This is going to make a fucking mess, *I thought.* How could it have gotten to this? What happened? It had all started out so perfectly. Alright, maybe not perfectly, but good, even great at times, and then gradually it all went to shit.

I don't remember how long I remained on my knees, not praying, though not exactly not not praying. Eventually, I could feel the cold, and the shivering started. Inside, it would take quite a while to feel much at all.

Fuck it; just DO it...

My grasp tightened on the knife handle and then, inexplicably, something shifted.

No.

Not like this. Not anything even remotely like this.

I pulled myself up, made my way through the darkness, back to the house, and tossed the knife back on the counter, where it clattered against the dirty dishes stacked with the food left over from dinner.

Shit, *I thought,* that knife wasn't even clean; I could've gotten an infection.

Funny how the mind works sometimes.

Lucy was still in the living room, facing away as I entered. As usual, she had no idea what she had precipitated. She turned and opened her mouth to speak.

"Don't," I said. "Not. One. Word."

I continued on into the bedroom, undressed and got into bed.

Fuck "not-going-to-bed-angry."

I'd deal with her and this and everything else tomorrow.

What happens "tomorrow?" How does it get to this point? From loving, euphoric, hopeful optimism to feeling like life itself isn't even worth living, over a relationship with another human being not meeting our expectation: that level of despair.

It's <u>that</u> important.

The good news is that, after a scenario like that, "tomorrow" is often when the change occurs, because you simply won't tolerate "business as usual." So there is opportunity in this type of conflict, but I am going to suggest we go about it differently, consciously, and hopefully before it gets to crisis mode.

For me, it was time to do some personal work; I had put it off for far too long. Therapy started out as couple's work, and then, not only did I get some individual counseling but started back to school to finish my Psychology degree and then get a certification in Hypnotherapy.

Were we "enemies?" It sure felt like it as some point. Others in my life would look at that relationship and her role in it and describe her as malicious and conniving, but in retrospect, I have come around to thinking that she was just trying to get her needs met. Unfortunately for me, there was very little consideration for mine in that equation. It didn't matter how much I gave, there was always a hand out for more. And while that didn't make us enemies, it certainly wasn't a recipe for extraordinary relationship. We were a bad, bad match, conducting ourselves at a very low level.

So, yeah, "What's the worst that can happen?"

It can get pretty ugly. I was "lucky" in that my depression and despair did not descend into physical violence. I had enough awareness to make that choice. Clearly, I was feeling impotent (no, not THAT way, although in some, that can surely manifest), but how did it get to that point?

Power Struggles

The TP Impasse

Yes, THAT TP; toilet paper. Let's have it be a metaphor for those truly unimportant things in a relationship that become issues because we have to be right. Over or under? Who cares, right?

Wrong.

Why DOES it matter to some? It's about being heard, it's about being in charge, it's about a sense of order, it's about having something to fight about, it's about holding your ground and not giving in. Maybe it's not the TP; maybe it's the way the dishwasher is loaded. Assuming that this chore gets shared, how much extra wasted effort goes into having the cups on one side and the glasses on another? And are you the kind of person who will deliberately misload the dishwasher just to get your partner's goat? (Not that I have ever done that, in a spirit of misguided mischief...)

Who IS the boss?

Who has the power in your relationship? What does that look like? Is it around money? Sex? Parenthood? Gender?

Who is more invested? There is a theory that purports that the person in the relationship with the least emotional investment has more power. Think about that for a moment. If you are more "into" your spouse than they are you, you have more to lose, therefor they have an advantage over you. Sounds kinda harsh, I know, but it bears consideration.

Angie, who had dabbled previously as a dominatrix (although that was not an overt dynamic in our relationship) told me towards the end of our time together, "Maybe you should stop seeking out these powerful women." I considered that for a moment, and realized that I did have that pattern in my choices.

But I also realized that I liked having a strong woman beside me. I have no desire to dominate anyone, or to have someone dominate me, but I have lost respect for women in the past that couldn't carry their own weight.

(What? Did I just kinda gloss over the Angie-as-a-dominatrix part? It wasn't my cup of tea, folks, really. Once, standing on a step that enabled her to be taller than me, she looked down at me and "ordered" me to get down on my knees. I just laughed at her. Nice try, Ang. Sorry; no 50 Shades here).

Have you ever had someone say, "He's just not that into you?" Or worse, "*I'm* just not that into you!" Very seldom are two people equally invested in a relationship. If there is a huge disparity, there is a tendency for there to be a massive power imbalance. How do we measure that? You may just want to ask, "On a scale of 1-10, how invested am I in this relationship?" And then do the same for your partner. And then, in the spirit of openness between you, have them answer the same questions.

First of all, in designing how to go forward, as a couple, you need to decide whether or not a power imbalance is a problem. Often, in relationship, individuals will end up taking the lead in one area or another, sometimes through mutual agreement, but often that's just how it shakes out.

These days, because our gender roles are less clearly defined, it's a delicate dance we do as partners around "who's the boss?" in a particular area. Sometimes one partner leads because they know how, or they are "supposed to." But what if they don't really know how? What if the person who is "following" knows more about the particular dance you are doing at any given time? This is an area where creating an agreement gets the partners clear on whom is leading or whom is following in any given area. There can still be joint decisions, but if you have one person "taking the lead," things can run a lot more smoothly.

Part of the problem comes in that in the existing paradigm (dance), the men generally lead. But, we are creating a new paradigm, remember? One in which the old ideas don't necessarily apply. ("Necessarily" being the operative word here; there may be areas where the man DOES take the lead, if that is what both partners agree on). If we want to beat this dance metaphor to death, consider that you both know different dances, and in order to become the best dance couple, the person who knows the dance best gets to lead. Makes sense, doesn't it? Well, it's not all that easy in reality; toes are going to get stepped on. It requires letting go, admitting that someone may know more than we do, allowing ourselves to look silly, inadequate, ignorant, less than...   But if we can't do this in front of our partner, who CAN we do it in front of? And that is part of what the contract is designed to do: get a sense of who's who in the relationship.

We have all seen couples that never get past this hurdle: they each need to be right all the time. And they bicker and snipe and their interaction is a constant struggle to get the upper hand. Is that fun for them? It must be, on some level, but is that what you want for *your* relationship? Consider too that in deferring to your partner in certain areas, some of the pressure of having to perform in this arena gets alleviated.

What happens if you are not trusting your partner to take the lead in a certain area when they are insisting they do? You have to ask yourself, "Is this coming out of a sense that I don't think they can do this (as well as I can)?" Or is it just that you are a control freak who doesn't want to let go of the reins anywhere in your life?

This is what a written agreement is for; write it in. This can be done with very specific parameters in place (i.e. the bills getting paid: how, when, from what account). And if the parameters are NOT met, don't turn it into an "I-told-you-so." Use it as an opportunity to switch the roles, or make suggestions on how to improve the system, for the good of the union.

Who's the "wife"? Alright, alright, before I get all you women's rights people up in arms, I have been the equivalent of the "wife" in a couple of relationships. And you know what? I didn't like it. But you know what else? I didn't (and don't) want to be the "husband" either. For me, the concept of extraordinary relationship is about partnership: being with someone who I am compatible with in many ways, but is complementary enough that she can take the lead in areas where I am challenged and vice versa.

Many power struggles revolve around money and income. Traditionally, the men brought home the bacon, wives were property and women had to play a subservient role. That's the way it was in my family of origin. What a joke. We were poor; my Dad didn't make enough money to support our family with four kids, but he "forbade" our Mom to work for money (not that raising four kids was not a full-time job anyway).

She worked anyway, doing odd jobs on the side. Oh yeah, he had the "power" in the relationship, but just as a figurehead. Mom was the brains AND the heart of the outfit, not that she was any great shakes as a parent, but really, neither of them had a clue as to what to do with four kids. Their great legacy has been how NOT to conduct a relationship or to parent. Honestly, if ever there were candidates for divorce, it was them; they were miserable, incompatible and horrible together.

Mom passed away at 52 years old; I believe that she felt she had had enough struggling and misery in her life. But she was a full time Mom, and was dedicated to parenting us with all the information that was available to her at the time, a lot of which got communicated to us in her Momisms. There were a lot of lessons in her Momisms, some of which were most valuable when ignored. One of her favorites was "Don't do as I do, do as I SAY." Well, Ma, how about if I don't do EITHER? All part of the evolution, I guess: learning from her negative example. But she did teach me to respect an intelligent woman, and I always have. Bottom line is that my Dad didn't know what a resource he had right under his own roof, but culturally, it was too early (and he might not have gotten it anyway...)

Let's look at power as it stems from communication and disclosure. Have you ever been in a situation where you disclosed a secret, and then that information was "used" against you? Didn't it make you never want to tell that person anything ever again in confidence? You granted them that power in the disclosure and then they abused that privilege.

Scary, isn't it? And yet, in the disclosure, there is an opening, a potential for sharing, connection, for growth, for camaraderie. Isn't that why we do it to begin with?

What about the opposite? When we have a partner who is uncommunicative? Women, is this sounding like your man? (OK, yes, I am painting a broad stroke here, but stereotypes exist for a reason...)

And you men, is this sounding/feeling even vaguely familiar? If you are one of those macho, grunting, Neanderthal types, you are probably not reading this book anyway, but for those of you who are open enough to consider it, are you communicating as much as you could be? Or are you one of those types who can "do it all on your own?"

How's THAT going?

But before I go getting all judgmental about how two people set up their agreement, if you both agree to a traditional male dominated arrangement, fine. The key is, what do you *agree* on? Within my coaching community, we had a heated debate around the subject of a woman "submitting" to her husband based on an interview on the "Today" show with Gabriella Reese. In discussing her book about her challenges as a mother and wife on TODAY, former volleyball star and fitness advocate Reece said she believes women being submissive in a relationship is a sign of power rather than weakness.

In "My Foot is Too Big for the Glass Slipper," she writes that,
> "to truly be feminine means being soft, receptive, and —
> look out, here it comes — submissive.

> I think the idea of living with a partner is 'How can I make their life better?' So if I'm the woman and he's the man, then yes, that's the dynamic. I'm willing and I choose to serve my family and my husband because it creates a dynamic where he is then in fact acting more like a man and masculine and treating me the way I want to be treated."

> "I think because women have the ability to set the tone that the ultimate strength and showing real power, I

believe, is creating that environment. I don't think it's a sign of weakness. I think it's a sign of strength."

Reece, who has been married to legendary big-wave surfer Laird Hamilton for over 17 years, also clarified her definition of being submissive.

> "He's not saying, 'Dinner on the table at six,'" she said. "We're not talking about that. I'm saying, 'Hey I'll lift up my side, and I'll do it happily,' and also the expectation would be, or the hope would be, that he comes with the same attitude. Is it a form of service? Absolutely. But I think it's the place I can express that part of myself and my personality."

I would suggest that that is not the definition of "submission" that I know. To me, submission means "to give over or yield to the power or authority of another." Another flaw in her argument is that she has an expectation that he would do the same thing. How is that not submission on his part, according to her definition?

I guess my objection to this concept of "submitting" is that I see power struggles as the core of so many problems in relationship. Maybe it's languaging, but I don't feel, in relationship, the need for anyone to submit to me or vice versa. Having always been attracted to strong, intelligent, vibrant women, the power "issue" has sometimes been a delicate waltz, other times a tempestuous tango. In looking for ways to express a balance, I have gradually gone from "submit" to "accede" to "allow" to "accept" to "embrace." Ultimately, I want true partnership, where we understand each other's strengths, communicate and celebrate them, side by side. No submission necessary.

The issue of power in a relationship is a huge stumbling block for many. For those that have never experienced any power in their lives, the drive to exact some small semblance of that can result in what can look like bizarre, contrary behavior. If you are experiencing some of that in your partner, go back to the chapter on "yes" and "no," and practice giving in once in a while.

Abuse

I was physically abused as a child.

OK, spanked.

Now some of you may be thinking, *Oh, well that's different.*

Is it? It's OK for a full grown adult to strike a child who is a fraction of their size? How is that OK?

My Mom used to tell a story about my Dad hitting us as children and she told him he was not allowed to do that.

No, that was HER job.

He never hit us again, and at some point, once she had meted out enough punishment, neither did she. She didn't have to, we had been cowed into submission.

Once, though, when we were a bit older, in a drunken rage, my Dad did attempt to hit my sister. About thirteen years old at the time, I stepped in and hit him, again and again, until he slumped into a corner. And while, seemingly, my rising up had put an end to the physical violence against us, their reign of terror would continue until we left that house; we lived in fear that the violence could erupt at any time. I was angry and felt like I had to protect my sister from physical harm, so to me, that justified <u>my</u> violence. But why should any thirteen year old be put in a situation where he has to protect his sister against their father?

Why is this rant in a book about relationships? Violence begets violence. It's certainly not OK to hit your kids, and not because at some point they may come back and kick your ass. It's not OK because it is an adult striking a defenseless child. Your child. Your flesh and blood. And if you are going to play the "spanking" card, I want you to consider that your argument is that if you strike a child in a different way, on a different part of their body, it's OK.

It's not OK. Never hit a child.

Never, never, never.

And by the same token, it's not OK to hit your partner. And now we come around to it, because if we are talking about creating extraordinary relationship, how can that possibly include either that you would raise a hand towards someone you love, or that they might even be afraid that you would do so?

It's time to change how we look at domestic violence.

Ray Rice was a professional football player. Somehow he felt like it was acceptable behavior to strike his fiancé when they were in an elevator and knock her out cold. Initially, professionally, he was suspended for two games. A short while later, security video from the elevator was released and he was fired by the team; apparently the vision of the actual violence was cause for further punishment.

Ray Rice was a good football player, and I am sure in the beginning he was being protected so that he could continue to contribute his athletic talents to the team and those involved financially could continue to profit from his efforts. Interestingly too, there were those who came out publically and suggested that his fiancée Janay was partially at fault for antagonizing him. Really? And that made it OK for a professional athlete to punch the woman he loves in the face and knock her unconscious?

We don't know the details of the personal life between Ray and Janay. They may have gone through this before and somehow felt like this kind of behavior was "business as usual." Whether or not it was, they decided to go on with their marriage plans. I'm fairly certain Ray was contrite and promised to never hit her again. I hope he never does and I hope they go on to have a wonderful fulfilling life together and serve as a model for how to overcome issues of domestic violence.

If someone asked me, "Would you get in the ring with Mike Tyson for a million dollars?"

Would I?

Hell, yeah: for a million dollars. I'd make sure he knocked me out the first time he hit me too. And I would very certainly NOT get up from the canvas. But it would be one time and done. Give me my million and I'll be gone. Janay has promised to stick around for the rest of her life, wondering, *Is he going to hit me again?*

I also believe that everyone deserves a second chance. They have an incredible opportunity to be role models. There is a silver lining to all this, beyond the impact it will have on the Rices personally. This incident created a public awareness around domestic violence that screamed, "This is not OK." Ray Rice's backhand contribution (albeit a forehand punch) to society hopefully will far outshadow anything he could have done on the football field. He has an opportunity to become a role model by simply never conducting himself in that same way again. By evolving.

And hopefully, in his example, we collectively evolve with him.

Statistics say that one in four US women have experienced some sort of physical abuse in their lifetime in this country. That is not OK. Women should not be walking around in fear for their physical safety.

Men, these are our fellow humans. If nothing else, as the larger of the species, we should be looking to protect our women and children, not hurt them.

How does this pertain to extraordinary relationship? I would suggest that ANY abuse in a relationship, whether it is physical, verbal, psychological or emotional is inappropriate.

What constitutes abusive behavior, though? How about name-calling? Have you ever called a partner "stupid" or "ugly?" Have you ever had that happen to you? What about an occasional "Fuck you!" tossed your way? What did that feel like? Have you ever been abusive in a relationship? Most of us have, sometimes in response to another abusing us. Or maybe being abused in another relationship and feeling like "I'm not going to be the victim anymore. It's my turn now."

Sometimes, especially when we are young, we don't have a framework for what constitutes abuse. If we grew up in a dysfunctional or abusive home, we don't have a framework for just how wonderful relationship can be. I was watching Dr. Phil's "Man Camp" on TV and he had a couple on that fought like cats and dogs: cursing, name calling, screaming. Both of them: the husband and the wife. In an interview with her, after she watched a video of one of the fights where her husband repeatedly called her a "bitch," Dr. Phil said to her, "Do you know how many times in all of the years I have been married that I have called my wife a bitch?"

"No, I don't," she said.

"Zero."

And the woman looked at Dr. Phil like he had two heads. She confessed later that she had never even considered that a relationship like that could EXIST! For her, the "better" (as in "for better or for worse") in her marriage didn't even consider a future that was not verbally abusive, because she didn't have a model for that.

There are angry people in the world, as well as those who are mean, aggressive, violent, selfish and uncaring. Are you one of those? Even part of the time? The question becomes, "In relationship, are you being abusive even some of the time, to the person in your world who is most important to you?"

We men have to deal with what could be described at times as an overabundance of testosterone. I am not offering that up as an excuse: more of an explanation. As civilized humans, that does not give us a free pass to abuse our partners. There are plenty of positive and productive places to channel aggression. Find one.

If I were a woman in our culture, I would be angry about having to walk around in fear, about making less money for the same amount of work, about being treated by a lot of men like I am a second class citizen. A lot of women are angry at these injustices; men are the enemy and it comes across in relationship.

So, two pieces of advice; if you are an abuser, stop. Find someone to partner with that you will respect and honor and treat that person as an equal, the way YOU would like to be treated. And if you are being abused, realize that, for whatever reason, there are abusive people out there, but YOU DON'T HAVE TO BE ON THE RECEIVING END OF THEIR AGGRESSION; there is no place for that in extraordinary relationship.

Period.

Incompatibilities

In all relationships, not just romantic or intimate ones, every way that we connect with others, every idea we agree on is evidence that we are not alone. While it is not universal, one of the potential perks of being in relationship is that we feel supported; someone has our back. We are "in this together."

Conversely, every disconnect is a potential wedge that can drive partners apart.

Let's consider sex (again). How's YOUR sex life? "Compared to what?" you might ask. What they are doing on the internet? One of my coaching clients was a 21 year old young man who had never kissed or touched a girl, but spent about 8-10 hours a day on the internet, indulging in way more than his fair share of porn. He called his mother a "whore" because she was having sex with her boyfriend. Do you think there might have been a distorted perspective on what sex or intimacy was for him? There is growing concern about the quality of intimacy among couples that have grown up with readily available sexual images that do not reflect reality.

So, yeah, the internet; it's a whole new world out there and all of this information and technology is building on itself, expanding exponentially, and meanwhile, we are supposed to find a way to make our relationships work. It is a reality of where we are now in our culture and it has to get factored in. How much time ARE you going to spend on the internet? Is your I-phone strapped to your hip for access at a moment's notice?

Turn it off! Turn your partner on instead!

So, things not going so well in the bedroom (or the couch or the kitchen table)? Just get on the net and have a go at yourself instead of communicating with your partner about how it could be better. What? You can't talk to your partner about sex?

Yes, you can. Is it hard? (Let me rephrase that so that we are not going down an unintentionally prurient path here). Is it difficult?

Yes, it can be very difficult; there are often tender egos and fragile self-images that can be injured by even the slightest suggestion that "you are doing it wrong." And sex is so SERIOUS. But it doesn't have to be. Bring a sense of lightness and playfulness to it and see what happens. And above all, try going into it with the intent of pleasing your partner.

Wait, what!!!!??? I know, that brings with it a whole set of its own complications; what if I'm not doing it right? For most people, that's even worse than your partner not doing it right. If this is an area of incompatibility in your relationship, consider starting over. With your partner, that is. Treat your lover like it is the first time again, but consider how you might do it differently.

Speaking of incompatibilities; I have to preface this next story by saying that I had lived in Santa Fe, the woo-woo capital of the world, for a long time and that this kind of thing, while somewhat rare even there, didn't really raise any eyebrows.

When Rita and I first started seeing each other, she would repeatedly say, "I don't like it here."

Usually, when I hear something like that, I have to figure someone is talking about a town or city they are referring to. Except when she said "here" she meant "herePlanetEarth."

Incompatible, indeed. Can I take this opportunity to let you be aware of the challenges of intergalactic relationship? In her defense, she was not claiming that she was dropped off at Roswell by some mother ship; it was that her consciousness was somehow transported here from some other place. In my defense, I didn't go running off in the opposite direction, calling her some kind of crackpot. I accepted this as her belief system. And for those of you out there that are rolling your eyes, ask yourself how much more fantasial this is than most religious belief systems.

Ultimately, everything "here" got compared to things "there," which incidentally was much like Pandora in the movie "Avatar." Consequently, much of what I brought to the table came up a little short.

Throughout the book, you will hear me talking about bringing your very best to the relationship, which often means there will be some measure of personal growth involved.

Which often means change.

Well, shit...

Just when you thought you had him exactly the way you wanted him, now he's going off and *changing*.

To keep a relationship dynamic and fresh, we want our partners to grow, to evolve, to become better. There are a lot of different ways this can happen. It can be along a career path, it can be personal, it can be spiritual.

This can often make for a rocky dynamic. Jeff Brown looks at it like this:

> "It doesn't matter how much two people love one another if they are developmentally incompatible, or if there is not a shared willingness to become conscious. This is why they call it a relationship instead of a loveship. Love alone is not enough. If you want it to last, you have to relate to each other in ways that keep the ship afloat."

Brown is placing a high premium on mutual personal growth here. And I agree; if one person is constantly trying to grow, and the other partner is not, they are going to get left behind. But this is just one area of potential compatibility. Some people like to maintain the status quo; their world is just fine the way it is, and you had better NOT be rocking their boat. Which are you? Is your partner the same way? Occasionally, a relationship can work where each person is accepting of the others stance on growth and change in general, but it's rare. But as we will explore later, this is an area of great importance: values and a general sense of how life should be lived. Sometimes we will see this around religion or spirituality.

I had this happen only once; Gloria dragged me into church. Well, not literally, but I wouldn't have gone by myself, and as it was, I went reluctantly. I think we both knew it was a test.

172

I failed. As churches go, it was pretty cool, with the rock band and the hip minister or pastor or whatever you call the main guy. This was a far cry from the Russian Orthodox regimen that we had to endure as children. But I just wasn't feeling the rapture, and by the time the service was over, we both knew it was the beginning of the end. This was important to her and she needed for it to be important to me.

I guess it was worth a shot, but in the end it was a dealbreaker for her.

The point is that there are a lot of ways to be different from your partner, but the more ways you are alike, the better your chances for a harmonious, extraordinary relationship.

Later, when we look at the list of potential areas to consider in your relationship agreement, you'll see how many ways there are to connect and disconnect with your partner.

Relationships with Others

There are over 322 million people in the United States, including 1.05 women for every man. According to ezinearticles.com, there are only 86 single men for every 100 single women. I will leave the math to you, but my point is that there are a LOT of women out there. And, despite the shortfall of males, that's still a LOT of men. Millions. So, it's no wonder that despite all of the obstacles, two people find each other through that mélange and decided to couple.

But now that the two of you are "one," how are you going to handle your relationships with all those other millions of other opposite sex humans out there? There's family, near and distant, co-workers, friends, acquaintances new and old, the person in the car next to you at the stoplight, the strangers you pass on the way to your office every day, neighbors that you've met and haven't and the hot blond flirting with you at the restaurant. Then there are your virtual friends, some of which you haven't even actually (physically) met. Some of you have large social circles, some small.

How much of your time do these others get on a weekly basis, and how much goes to your partner? And think about it not just in terms of hours and minutes, but the quality of that time and the focus. Some of us are extremely close with our family of origin, even as adults; there can be contact every day. Some of us have children and they deserve a huge portion of our attention. Some of us have a circle of friends that is the center of where we get our emotional support.

Who "feeds" you? Emotionally, that is. Who makes you feel important, significant? How much of your self-esteem is derived from members of the opposite sex?

Have you ever had an emotional affair? What an interesting concept this is, and relatively new. Not that the idea of it is new, because I believe this phenomenon has occurred for a long time, but the identification and recognition of it. And in these times, while an emotional affair can occur face to face, they are becoming much more common online; exes, old flings, chatters, facebookers, bloggers. Why, complete strangers are now competing for the attention that would (and arguably could or should) be going to your partner. The amount and quality of that attention to others goes a long way in determining the quality of the relationship with your partner.

One of the traps we fall into in relationship is that we expect our partner to satisfy all of our needs. Not only is that unrealistic, it is unhealthy and potentially damaging, not to mention time-consuming and unfair. Are you getting needs met by others? Is your behavior appropriate in the meeting of those needs? By your definition or your partner's?

It's not the same for every couple. Some partners get the bulk of what they need in terms of love and connection from their mate. Others have a rich and varied social life and the partner is less called upon to meet those needs. It's good to know not only where YOU fall on the spectrum, but your partner as well, and what the expectations are going to be going forward.

Personally, again and again, I have made the mistake of putting all of my emotional eggs in my partner's basket. Usually, it's a safe and familiar basket, so it's so much easier; they are right there all the time, you know what you are getting, it doesn't have to be spread around, I don't have to trust a bunch of other people (oh, we wouldn't want THAT now, would we...?)

In the long run, that's not fair to my partner and certainly not fair to the relationship, where it can place a huge burden. That's right, you, partner, are to fill the roles of best friend, lover, confidante, basketball-watching buddy, therapist, personIcanfartaround, person I wake up to (often overlaps with the last role), travel companion, fellow foodie, gossiper/gossipee, security blanket, pillar of strength, ardent supporter, gym buddy, concert goer, co-parent, nurturer, defender, co-habitor, and all-around-be-there-when-I-need-you person. Here's a toxic combination: someone who is looking for that, and another person who thinks they can BE that. You'd never leave the house or go anywhere. It is too incestuous and is bound to implode at some point (and invariably did, every single time I told myself I wasn't going to do it, then did anyway).

We are social beings. Granted, some less than others, and it is good to know where you are on that spectrum as well as your mate, and in the best of situations, to be accepting of both personality types. Easier said than done. For the introvert, at first, that gregarious date who does all the talking is a wonderful "fit." For both. But in a social situation, where there are others, that introvert is often left alone and feelings of resentment can arise for both parties. Others become a threat to your special, polar bond. And that threat comes from fear. Fear of loss, fear of not being enough: the two "biggies."

In a healthy relationship, spreading some of the love around to others can be beneficial, cathartic, therapeutic, even fun! But as we know (and some of you are probably already ahead of me here), HOW and WHERE you spread the love around is the key.

Having others satisfy some of your needs takes some of the pressure off of your partner; you end up seeming less "needy" to them. Family members, friends, buddies, girlfriends (we're only talking same sex here. We'll get to opposite very soon), co-workers, acquaintances can all satisfy some of the need we have for human contact. The question can become; is the amount of time you spend with others disproportionate to the amount of time you spend with your mate?

Again, what does your mate think?

Let's talk about how you interact with the opposite sex. What are the rules the two of you have for that? Well, the rules should be what you mutually agree on.

What? You haven't talked about that?

Is your behavior the same when you are away from your partner as it is when your partner is present? Or, is it "don't ask, don't tell?" Is there a double standard? How would you feel if you knew your spouse was behaving the same way you do? It may be OK, and if that is the agreement that you and your mate have, that shows a high degree of confidence in your union. Oh, it's a "silent" agreement? And she doesn't know about it? I see.

Are you a flirt? Do you get fed by the attention of the opposite sex? I see a lot of you shaking your heads out there. And I know that some of you are in absolute denial that you would ever behave in such a disrespectful manner to your spouses and partners, but you do it anyway, sometimes without even thinking about it.

I once told a partner that she had a love/hate relationship with men. Her reply was, "No I don't; I love men too much." I know; just what every boyfriend wants to hear, right? She LOVED the attention of men, but here's the thing: I knew she would never cheat on me. Well, I didn't KNOW it, but I felt like she had such a strong sense of loyalty and integrity, that she wouldn't cheat. And, I also didn't feel like she wanted to be with anyone else. But at the same time, she loved getting that attention. She loved having men want her. So I coined a phrase for that: "Cheap Trick." This is a level below emotional affair, where she was not really wanting to engage with someone else emotionally, but she wanted them to engage with her. Remember Cheap Trick's song, "I Want You to Want Me"? Well, there you go. She would flat out, to this day, deny that she was doing that. But sometimes, we know our partners better than they know themselves, don't we?

This is about wanting the approval of others, but not really willing to give of yourself, or only a limited amount. So, in some ways, this is a kind of tease. Is this flirtation? Good question; when does looking for attention cross over into flirtation? What has to get attached to male-female interaction for it to be flirtation? What is the line that gets crossed from simply interacting with another human being and enjoying their company to "inappropriate" behavior? And is flirting inappropriate?

Flirting is defined as, "to court triflingly or act amorously without serious intentions." "Serious intentions": hmmm... As in so much of what I discussed, most of this behavior occurs without any thinking involved. One person's "being friendly" is another person's "serious intention." And it IS a form of communication, and can be both verbal and non-verbal. Then where it gets tricky is not only in your intent, but the perceived intent of the recipient.

Are you a "toucher?" In our culture, we don't touch as much as they do on other, more collective societies; we are a country of individuals, so we must have our personal space. When that is violated, it can be interpreted as a sign of serious intent. When Laura and I first started going out, we had an instant, affectionate connection. We were so engaged that it took a while before we let others into our circle, but at some point I arranged for us to have dinner with another couple. If I were to cross over into hyperbole, I would say that Laura couldn't keep her hands off the guy. The truth is that she touched him around five times during the course of our evening (Was I counting? Apparently). I assumed that everyone at the table was as acutely aware of this as I was. Was that true? I don't know. I assumed that the other woman at the table was seething, having her man being "constantly" touched. The guy seemed to be digging it. Was Laura aware of what she was doing? We were so into each other at the time, I know she wasn't trying to pick this guy up. But what was her intent? And what got perceived at the other end?

This other couple were good friends of mine, and this was the first time that Laura had met them. I do believe that she was trying to make a good impression. Was it too good? And then it got me wondering if she was this "touchy" around other guys when we were not together. How did I feel about that? How did she perceive all of this, if at all? How did she think others perceived it? What was her intent? Was she "cheap tricking" them? And what if she was? Was I going to be OK with that?

I let those questions percolate (fester?) in my head without expressing them to her. "Why not just ask her," you might be asking. That is a good question. Was I worried that the question might be turned around on me? That my behavior might be called into question? Was I projecting?

Nahhh...

When I did finally broach the subject, Laura asked me if her "touchy" behavior made me feel uncomfortable. Honestly, at first, before we had a chance to discuss it, it did. But once I realized what was behind my discomfort (misplaced feelings of threat to our relationship), it quickly dissipated. I didn't want her to change; I wanted for her to bring to others some of that same joy that she brought to me.

Ay; there's the rub: "some." I didn't want her getting "juice" from other men. What if their "juice" was somehow better than my "juice?" That's all well and good in theory, but what if she is getting something she needs from someone else? What if it goes beyond that? What if she gets attracted to someone else? What if she finds herself spending time with someone else of the opposite sex in a way that she doesn't want me to know about?

"What if, what if, what if!!?" I decided that I would just have to bring the very best of my own juiciness and that was either going to be good enough or not.

Caroline and Wally had a long distance relationship for over four years. He traveled all over the world as a software developer, she owned a restaurant. Both of them have a lot of contact with others, especially her. We were discussing the trust element in their relationship and how key it is. He told me about a time when he was in Caroline's place and a guy was rubbing her shoulders and the guy noticed that Wally was watching and so he stopped. That's when Wally got perturbed: when the "masseuse" indicated his bad intent by stopping. Wally would have been fine if he had kept going, having it be out in the open. Interesting, huh?

How do we differentiate between what constitutes a "good friend" and someone that is commanding too much of our attention? And, is that definition different from our perspective and our partners? If it is congruent, no problem. If there is a gap in that definition, there is a potential snag. We may have crossed over into the realm of crushes and emotional affairs.

An almost certain indicator that your significant other is having an emotional affair is when you hear a name of their acquaintance being mentioned disproportionately often, especially out of context. There is a weird phenomenon around this (and I have been on both sides) where we know there is an inappropriate bond, but we have an almost morbid compulsion to want to disclose it to our partner. Rita had to tell me at some point that the IT guy from where she was working just loved to eat mangoes.

First of all, "What?"

Second of all, why am I hearing about this? Of course, in my insecurity, I imagined sordid scenarios of mango juice dripping down their respective chins, all teeth and tongue and slippery fingers and "Here, let me wipe that off for you..."

When confronted: absolute denial. She also had a habit , when we were in public situations, of finding the most nerdy, insecure wallflower and gush over him, touch him, get in his personal space, no doubt giving him masturbatory fantasies for months, if not years, to come (unintentional double entendre, but I'll run with it...)

This begged the question, "Is it me, or is it her? Or was it some twisted, dysfunctional combination of the two?"

At first, since it was simply easier, I blamed it all on her. But after her repeated denials, which I didn't believe anyway, I realized there wasn't anything else I could do to change her behavior, and I began to realize that my interpretation was part of the problem and that I *did* have some control over. I began to take a look at MY part in that dysfunctional relationship. Why was her seeking that attention from others so threatening to me?

Insecurities

In my work as a hypnotherapist and a relationship coach, I see time and time again how often our problems, issues, baggage and challenges can be distilled down to being caused by a sense of low self-esteem. When we are not feeling worthy of being with our partners, there can be resultant behaviors that are often embarrassing in retrospect. (I once followed a girlfriend on a Sunday morning, convinced that she was meeting someone clandestinely, only to have her pull into a church, which was, incidentally, where she had told me she was going...)

There are dozens, if not hundreds of books that have been written on low self-esteem. The best I have found is "Self Esteem" by Matthew McKay and Patrick Fanning. This book was instrumental in personally allowing me to shift not only the way I saw myself in the world, but the way I looked at others.

The first time I ever had sex I was a senior in high school. I had passed on several other opportunities before that, but despite knowing what had to be put where, I had no idea about how to go about doing that, so things would go only so far. Melissa would change that. She was new in town. We had met in the summer and had become quite an item by the time school started. We had been dropped off by some friends at Denton Lake, which was the big make-out spot, and I was anticipating doing just that. She had other plans: she got me down on the ground, got my pants undone, whipped out a condom, had it on me and then had herself on me before I barely knew what was happening. She had obviously done this before.

As it turned out, she had and continued to: not just with me, but with most of my "friends," although unbeknownst to me at the time. Being in high school, all that became quite a topic of conversation. So when a bunch of my buddies were speaking in hushed tones and then got real quiet once I approached, I got suspicious. It seems that she had discussed my inexperience with some of them. I think my already questionable self-esteem might have taken a bit of a hit over those numerous betrayals: my "girlfriend," my "friends." Typical high school nonsense, but those kinds of disloyalties can have far-reaching ramifications in the long run if it doesn't get nipped in the bud.

It didn't. Get nipped in the bud, that is. And trust became an issue for me. There ended up being many times over the years that I have considered that partners of mine were not being faithful. Sometimes those fears were warranted, sometimes they were extensions of my fears, imagination and insecurities.

How do we decipher the source of that? Very often those feelings of insecurity come at times when our energy level is low: physically, psychologically, psychically, spiritually. The first step is to recognize that we are indeed in the low place, and then to set up the habit of creating that shift to a more realistic perspective where the situation can be viewed more objectively.

If we are getting triggered, a good question can be, "What else could this mean?" Because often, we are being triggered by a set of circumstances that looks like something negative from our past. A photo of a guy on your girlfriend's phone for example. Now, if it's a naked picture, that might be legitimate cause for further discussion, but if it's just a photo of, say, her co-worker that you are feeling somewhat threatened by, say, playing the drums, is it worth bringing up, having it get into a fight, and having her think about what a pussy you are? While I am all for openness and honesty, some stuff you just have to work out on your own because, well, it's *your* stuff. Just because you get triggered doesn't mean you have to let that spiral down into unnecessary drama. That goes for both of you.

Now, my default when I get triggered is to consider that it's my issue. After all, I *am* the one getting triggered. If, after a reasonable amount of time spent processing, I determine that I am not solely at fault, then it becomes fair game for discussion.

If it turns out that YOU are the "culprit" in feelings of jealousy, time and time again, that is, YOUR triggers, YOUR past experiences, YOUR insecurities are the filter that everything runs through, get help.

I ended up living in Santa Fe, NM for over 25 years. They call it "The City Different" for numerous appropriate reasons including how accepting it is of those with alternative lifestyles. While that can be a blessing, it also opens the door to being a mecca for the downtrodden, the disenfranchised, the heartbroken and the wounded. Those souls would flock there to lick those wounds. It never ceased to amaze me how long so many people would wallow in their shit: indulging that feeling of "yes, I am a victim." And, yes, I understand how GOOD that can feel on some perverse level: the "knowing," the consistency, the "certainty" that this *is* how bad it is.

But, at some point, you gotta get over it!

As a reminder, this book is about evolution. As part of my early growth, my "getting over it," I vowed after that petty high school drama never to put someone else in the position that I had been put in; I was never going to betray anyone else. I was going to be the rock, the person who always did what he said he was going to do, the trustworthy one.

Well, I had good intentions, but as you will see, I had underestimated the negative long term effects on my self-esteem of not only my upbringing but those reinforcing early betrayals at the hands of my friends.

Jealousy

By the way; if you are having an affair, and you think you are "getting away with it," you're not. Partners know. They just fucking KNOW.

Aaahhh, that's not always true either; I've been cheated on and didn't know it at the time. So maybe you *can* cheat and get away with it. But is that part of your definition of extraordinary relationship?

Jealousy is a state that I have personally spent WAY too much time engaged in, as numerous, undeserving (as well as a couple of deserving) partners will attest to. Is it real? Is it imagined? Is it my partner's behavior or my perception that is making me feel this way? As I discovered while in the stranglehold of this, it has so many layers that cut through to the darkest parts of our psyches. For a real in-depth look at the phenomenon, read Nancy Friday's "Jealousy," all 539 pages of it. I did, because the monster gripped ahold of me and wouldn't let go. I obsessed, I stalked, I spied on, and as it turned out, the threat to my relationship at the time WAS justified, and not imagined, and it sent me into a pattern of mistrust for years afterward.

If this is an obstacle for you, you have got to come to terms with it, whether it is your issue or your partner's. Bottom line with this one is, if it exists for one of you, it exists for both of you, and it can be a relationship ender. Regardless of whether or not it is a relationship ender, it makes a relationship be MILES away from extraordinary.

What's on the other end of that spectrum?

Absolute trust.

So how do we get there?

When I think about my stance on jealousy in extraordinary relationship, it simply doesn't exist. NOTHING constitutes a threat to that relationship. I want to be with her, she wants to be with me. I WANT others to see her as I see her: sexy, smart, kind, vivacious. And I want her to feel them "get" that in her, and have it feed her. No restrictions on who she is, our relationship conducted on the terms we have laid out. Do I run the risk of losing her to someone else that sees her wonderfulness and having him want her, and then possibly her wanting him?

Sure. But it won't be because I haven't done my best to have her want to be with me.

Is getting ego-fed by the opposite sex necessarily bad? The whole "ego" thing has gotten a lot of bad press. But let's be honest; we are social animals, and the approval of others is important to us. Granted, more important for some than others, and if it gets extreme, it deserves all that bad press (attention narcissists...), but by and large, it FEELS good to be wanted, desired, approved of and thought well of by others. We ALL have a need for connection. So, what becomes inappropriate behavior in your relationship?

In this new paradigm, what's appropriate is what the two of you decide is appropriate.

That male-female attraction is a thread that runs through our daily lives in wonderful and sometimes distractingly annoying ways. How much time do you spend considering the opposite sex? Is it on a conscious level? Never? Or is it an awareness that runs through your existence on a low level at some times and not others? Do you like it, or is it invasive and distracting? When it occurs, does it include your partner? Do you want it to?

Ask yourself this; "What do you WANT your awareness of the opposite sex and resultant reactions to look like?" I have had periods in my life (usually in those "never-again" moments after a breakup) when I never wanted to see another woman again. Fortunately, those were short-lived.

If sexual attraction to others is an issue in your relationship and you don't want it to be, either behavior or perception of that behavior has to change. Which one are YOU in control of, personally?

Infidelity

The biggest deal breaker for most marriages is infidelity. It is a breach of trust that most couples are just not able to overcome, once it is out in the open. Some couples do stay together, and they either get the trust back or decide that they are going to go ahead without it, that there are enough other positives in place. Or that the alternative, being alone, simply represents too many negatives.

The Huffington Post reports that in men, 48% of men cheat because they want more sex than they are getting at home. 47% just want more sexual variety. For women, 44% cheat simply because they are attracted to someone else, but interestingly the next highest reason, at 32%, is that they want reassurance of their desirability.

For some, cheating is not a big deal, and around the world, in some cultures, it is accepted that marital partners are getting some on the side. In America, it is a big taboo, but if you look at statistics for infidelity, you are likely to pull your hair out for lack of any consistency. If I start to average out the different surveys though (how's that for some fuzzy math, huh?) it seem like about half of all married men AND women cheat. More and more we are starting to look like our promiscuous primate cousins, the chimps and the bonobos.

Statistics can be fun, but I generally find them moot when I am talking to anyone about THEIR experience. I think it would be safe to say that very few people LIKE to be cheated on (OK, there is a sexual subculture of cuckolding, where people DO like that, but it is a small percentage...)

So, unless you are creating a sexually open relationship, cheating: bad. Deal breaker? This is part of the discussion in creating your proposal. Most people go into a relationship never intending to cheat.

Then infidelity happens. "I didn't plan it; it just happened."

NO, it didn't "just happen;" we are conscious human beings and we make choices. The point is that circumstances of relationship CHANGE in ways we may not have anticipated, and we find ways to justify behaviors that we never thought we would. These changes usually come about slowly, but through communication with your partner, if the goal is extraordinary relationship, negative consequences can sometimes be headed off at the pass.

If you look at those reasons for cheating: not getting enough, wanting something different, being attracted to someone else, an assurance of desirability; if things are good at home, those distractions, even when they come up, are not going to have the same power than if things are shaky.

I spoke with a very sexually healthy thirty year old woman who was telling me about how she and her last boyfriend would have sex 5-6 times a day. Every day. Maybe she was blowing smoke, but I was inclined to believe her, within the context of our discussion. Her current boyfriend is 59 years old. And she explained to me that he is a different kind of lover.

No kidding.

And she was already looking around for some more action. When I asked why she didn't stay with the first guy (the sex machine), she said that it was only that way in the beginning.

Well, right. First of all, who has the time to be fucking 5-6 times a day, every day, forever? Nobody.

It changes. So let's figure out what's going to happen when it does.

Because it will.

First of all, if sex is that important to you, that's good to know. What's also good to get clear about is how you are going to get that need met. Is it going to be with one person, or numerous partners? Are you going to go in and out of relationships just for the sex, as long as it lasts, then jump out and find someone else? Are you looking for some sort of polyamorous arrangement?

Interestingly, you can have extraordinary relationship under any of those circumstances. Remember, this is the new way; we are throwing out a lot of the old rules and making up new, more flexible ones. But also remember, one of the guidelines is that for it to be extraordinary, we are going to conduct ourselves with integrity. So, if you are wanting to have "sexshul relations" (thanks, Bill...) with someone outside of your agreement, what should you do? Here are some options:

1. Don't. Just decide that your word is more important. Acknowledge to yourself that you have become attracted to someone else and congratulate yourself on your impulse control.

2. If the problem keeps arising (yes, I know it's a double entendre, but this applies to you potentially philandering women out there too), talk to somebody about it. And here's a suggestion that will give you a sense of just HOW important it is; if the thoughts and feelings won't go away, talk to your <u>partner</u> about it. That's right. Which scenario has more pain attached to it: confessing that you are hot for someone else to your partner or breaking that partner's heart?

3. Have the affair. Sure, go ahead. What's the big deal? We only live once, right? But know if you do this, you will be summarily dropped from the ranks of Extraordinary Partners Club.

I am not endorsing #3.

I never endorsed #3. As you may recall from the last chapter, I *vowed* to never do that.

Vowed. An oath-swearing promise to myself.

That is until I wasn't getting my needs met and everything I was doing was for others. My life was just a series of just-another-days. Was I just going to go on that way forever? I resisted for a while.

And then I didn't.

But it was OK, because Amanda was never going to find out; I had the perfect alibi, the perfect story...

Right.

She KNEW. And I mean KNEW. Knew where to find the photos (I know; stupid, right? Don't get me started...) She knew where I was going, had me followed, the whole bit. I've made more than *my share of mistakes in my life, but that is the one mistake I truly regret, and if I had it to do over, I would. Very differently. And not just because I got caught; I deeply regret all of the pain that it caused, but it taught me some valuable lessons because of all the pain that was attached to it. Somehow, despite my "vows" to myself, I was able to justify it at the time. As karma goes, that affair/relationship went on for 3 years and ended when she cheated on <u>me</u> (cue Justin Timberlake's "What Goes Around Comes Around"...)*

Interestingly, a year before she cheated on me, she had actually written on the leg of my torn up jeans, "the honeymoon is over." And I laughed and made a joke out of it, not considering for one moment that there could be any truth to it.

Huh? Communicate much? Not at that point, I didn't. When she finally moved out and I drove to her new place the next heartbroken, earlyearly morning after a sleepless night and heard her with her new lover from outside her bedroom window (no, I wasn't stalking; it just so happened that her bedroom window was on the way to the front door), I went into total denial about what I had heard. After I searched the entire house (he hid from me, the pusillanimous bastard), somehow I made myself believe he wasn't there, and I sat and talked on the front steps with Sally for two hours.

Not my finest moment. Or hers. Or his (hah; thinking about it now; that fucker had to hide wherever it was he was hiding for two hours! I showed him!)

Conversely, get clear if you are deciding to engage with someone who is cheating on their partner. I know; when you are in the throes of new infatuation, getting clear is one of the hardest states to achieve. But here is another downside to infidelity; if you are going into this new relationship because now you have found your "true love," you had better be clear that you are hooking up with *someone who will cheat on their partner.* "Oh, but he/she will never cheat on me. Our love is true."

Bullshit. In some brief, elusive window of lucidity, you should wonder about just how trustworthy they are. And the flip side is valis as well; if you are the infidelitor, they should wonder that about you.

Years later, I discovered another downside to <u>my</u> role in these betrayals. Previously, I NEVER thought I would cheat on someone. I made that pledge, remember? I had looked in disdain at anyone who would even look at others outside of their partnership. But I did it, and in every relationship after that, I suspected my partner of cheating. Every single one. And yes, I got cheated on (and I had that coming), but even deeper than that was the realization that, if *I* could cheat, *anybody could.*

That distrust followed me around for years after that. I not only saw it in places where there really *were* potential threats to my relationship--in behavior that was flirtatious, soliciting attention from others. But I also saw it in places where I had no business seeing it, from women who were absolutely devoted to me, and as a result, it drove a wedge into our relationship and took it in a direction far from extraordinary.

Get clear. If trust is important to you, be just that: trustworthy. And find someone who has shown in their actions that they can be trusted.

"But," I can hear some of you saying, "If that is true, then no one should trust you." (Meaning, me, your formerly philandering author).

Thank you for paying attention, reader. None of what is written here is written in stone. The silver lining in my infidelity was that it taught me a hard clean lesson: don't do that anymore! Some of our lessons we have to learn the hard way, but those are the ones that stick.

Substance Abuse

I am only going to touch on this briefly as it has played a rather large part in my early development; both of my parents were alcoholics. My father was a binge drinker on the weekends, my mom had bottles of vodka stashed around the house and drank all the time. I can remember coming home from school and dreading seeing one of her drinking buddy's cars in the driveway at three in the afternoon.

Simply put, alcohol changes your state. That is why most people imbibe. For some it is a social lubricant, for others it allows them to forget, for others still, it is a way to have fun. But alcohol is a depressant, and eventually, in excess, it will turn you into another person.

If you are finding that most of your arguments and challenges come as a result of being in an inebriated state, then it is time for you to monitor, make adjustments to and manage your drinking. For some of you, that will mean you have to quit, because for whatever reason (and it may just be your compulsive personality) once you start, you cannot stop.

But for others, it just means that you have to teach yourself when you have had enough. If drinking more than a couple of drinks makes you stupid, or depressed or mean or argumentative, stop it! Rita and I used to love drinking wine together. But it was almost invariably into that second bottle when we would start to fight. Once I had that realization, I imposed a limit (on myself, and she could choose to refrain or not). Some individuals can do that. Others cannot.

If you can't do it yourself, get help, and that can possibly be from your partner. I have seen alcohol absolutely ruin relationships, in that it can bring out an aggressive side of personality that should not be directed at your partner. Ask yourself, "Is the person I become when I drink the person I want to be?"

The same goes for other drugs as well, obviously. As of this writing, the laws around marijuana possession are changing. I only smoked pot twice in my life; once I fell asleep, the other time I got a splitting headache. I realized that maybe that drug was not having the desired effect. I understand that behavior while under the influence of marijuana is different from being drunk, but again, if your indulgence is creating a problem within your relationship, it may be time to make a choice. Which is more important, your altered state or your relationship? If you are finding that you are frequently needing to change how you feel, it may be time for an assessment of what is going on up to this point in your life that makes you want to alter perception, change who you are.

To hide.

WHO ARE YOU?

I am asking the question here so that you can ask it of yourself. We all have many parts to ourselves, many of them incongruent. What I am asking you to do here, relative to relationship, is to get clear about who you are. How do others see you? How do you see yourself? How do you think others see you? Are those three images consistent? Are you sure?

Socrates, a long time ago wrote, "The unexamined life is not worth living."

Most of us have experienced introspection on some level. What I am asking you to do here is to do that around the subject of relationship.

Who knows you best? Can you go to them and seriously ask that question (who am I?) and be able to hear a truthful answer? We tend to be secretive in our culture and as a result seldom get that kind of honest feedback. Usually, others are afraid they will hurt our feelings, or that we will think badly of them because they are so judgmental.

What do you believe in? What is "true" to you? Is the world "fair?" Is money the root of all evil? Are men smarter than women? Can astrology predict your future? Did we really put a man on the moon? Do you believe if you work hard, you will be rewarded?

I'm reminded of the soliloquy by Crash Davis in the classic movie "Bull Durham" when Annie asks him "Well, what <u>do</u> you believe in then?"

"Well, I believe in the soul, the cock, the pussy, the small of a woman's back, the hanging curve ball, high fiber, good scotch, that the novels of Susan Sontag are self-indulgent, overrated crap. I believe Lee Harvey Oswald acted alone. I believe there ought to be a constitutional amendment outlawing Astroturf and the designated hitter. I believe in the sweet spot, soft-core pornography, opening your presents Christmas morning rather than Christmas Eve and I believe in long, slow, deep, soft, wet kisses that last three days."

Most of us could not be quite so poetic, articulate and succinct when asked that question, but why not? What would be your Crash Davis rant if you were the character in that scene? Write out fifteen items; take your time, because this is important, this is core to who you are. And then, once you have it, ask yourself if you really believe all of that, or if it is simply recycled regurgitated axioms that you have adopted over the years.

If you are just beginning a relationship, you know very little about the other person, and the dynamic between the two of you is usually best foot forward. Sometimes that person doesn't show their true colors until months later. Wouldn't it be great if we could sit down with someone after a first date and get an honest assessment? OK, maybe not, if it didn't go so well, but really... Wouldn't you love to hear what she tells her girlfriend about you tomorrow? The truth is that we get so used to ourselves that we don't know what we are presenting to others.

Jack was a friend of mine who once described himself to me as an "alpha dog." Nothing could have been further from the truth. I thought he was kidding, but no; that was somehow how he saw himself. What he didn't see was the version I saw when I once introduced him to a woman; he cast his eyes downward, gave her a limp handshake and mumbled something incoherently. I called him on that sometime later as I was trying to help him through his dating woes. He offered up some lame excuse about "going through a tough time," but he was like that a lot. He got pissed off at me and defensive and before I knew it, he rewarded my honesty with that modern insult of all insults; he unfriended me on Facebook.

That's another reason why we aren't honest with each other; most people don't want to hear it. And there can be negative consequences to our honesty.

My point here is that it could be time to get honest with yourself. The problem is, that is hard to do. Are you better at this point in your life than you have ever been? If yes, great! If not; why not? Can you be better? The answer to that is always "yes." Always; I don't care who you are. So why not do that? The biggest reason is that often we don't know, we aren't aware of how lacking we are, but other times, without knowing it, we are simply afraid of what personal growth might mean to us.

Get Clear

Consider this; there is one common denominator in every single relationship you have ever been in.

Ever.

That is YOU.

That's right; YOU are the constant in all of those "failed" relationships. If you are bringing your same old self to every relationship expecting a different result because it is with someone new, that is folly. And don't refer me to the Einstein "doingthesamethingandexpectingadifferentresultisthedefinitionof-insanity" chestnut. To me, that is not the definition of insanity, it is the definition of STUPID.

Granted, if you are going into a new relationship, there is a large part of the equation that is different: someone new and different. And yes, every relationship IS different, but if you have a legacy of "failed" relationship, it is time to look at what YOUR part is in that trail of broken hearts (whether it is yours or theirs). And again, "failed relationship" we are redefining not so much to mean that it didn't LAST, that it wasn't fulfilling on some levels, that it wasn't productive, or you didn't both grow, but that despite your best efforts (and hopefully your partner's as well) it was not a match that you both wanted to have continue.

We know we can't change the past, but we can change the future, and right here, right now, we are going to engage in a pattern interrupt. Yes, we are going to do things differently.

And by differently, I mean by "of your own design."

I had a client in his 50s (let's call him Gary) who was telling me about leaving his girlfriend of two years. He said he did everything to keep her, but then HE left HER. (I know; I was confused at first too). He gained 50 pounds over the course of their relationship (despite her being a fitness freak) and he turned into a needy and whiny mama's boy when she wouldn't spend every single moment with him. Oh, also, he missed her toned and fit body (but did he ever stop to wonder if she missed his?)

(OK, so maybe the "needy/whiny" characterization was a little harsh there, but as a coach, it is part of my job to be honest and sometimes even blunt, because most people don't ever get that, even from family and friends. Besides, I'm sure at the time I was a bit gentler [but just a bit] in describing his behavior back to him).

He didn't leave her; he lost her. He thinks he ended the relationship by leaving, but he really ended it by not meeting her needs. As a result, she checked out, and let him end it. Did any if this occur consciously? Very little; these were not manipulative, calculating, cold people. They were two intelligent semi-conscious adults trying their best to make a relationship work. Was this a case of not-realizing-what-you-have-until-it's-gone? Well, yes and no. Once he stopped meeting her needs, she stopped meeting his and it all unraveled because there was a severe lack of communication in this relationship, not to mention awareness, both self-awareness and awareness of the wants and needs of the other.

And while I am not the arbiter of who-should-be-with-whom, in terms of what was important to each of these two people, they were not a good match for longevity. This is an important distinction in the new paradigm. Just because a couple decides to no longer continue as a couple, it does NOT mean that that relationship was unsuccessful.

This relationship is a good example. Did they have fun over the two years together?

Yes they did.

Did they both grow and learn new things about themselves as a result of being together?

Yes, they did.

Will they have new information about themselves as they go forward into another relationship?

Yes, they will. Hopefully.

Gary didn't have a true sense of who he was going into this relationship. He did know he wanted someone communicative. Unfortunately, Angie couldn't meet that need for him. Fitness in her partner was important to her, as well as someone in their masculine presence. He didn't meet those needs for her.

Was this relationship salvageable?

Absolutely.

But it was going to require a reset on both of their parts—and I am not sure they were both willing to do that, or that they even had the awareness about what it was that the other truly wanted. Hopefully, in retrospect, they both have a better sense of who they are and what is important to them.

Did they try everything they could to keep the relationship together when they were in it?

The answer to that question is almost always going to be a "maybe." How do you decide how much is enough? In the old paradigm, in its purest form, you never gave up. And there is a part of me that would argue that perseverance is a necessary component for success. But it becomes a question of how we define "success." If you define it in terms of longevity, then they should NEVER give up. And if you go by the letter of the law, in marriage specifically, there should be no divorce, especially if you "agreed" to stay together "for better or for worse, 'til death do us part."

What does that phrase actually say? It says, "I don't care what happens: how boring, stupid, hurtful, abusive, apathetic, different, lying, untrue, unappreciative, unattractive, overweight, you OR I become, we have to stay together. Let's have the vows say THAT and see how many people sign up!

But most people don't think that that is going to happen when they first start out. The experiences of millions of people before them do not matter. Because their love is "true." Now, I know I am painting a bleak picture, with a very broad stroke. Yes, there ARE loving, giving couples out there that lead satisfying, fulfilling lives together. My contention is that there are not enough. And in this new paradigm, we are going to be shifting our focus away from "how long" to "how extraordinary."

There could be, and should be many, many more incredible unions, and I contend the reason there is not is because we don't try hard enough to make it extraordinary, and the reason we don't try hard enough is because we don't know how.

Now, let's get away from the idea that if you have been in multiple relationships that you are a failure. In one sense, that is the purpose of this book. Granted, if you have been married and divorced, that means that you have promised someone you would spend the rest of your life with them, AND YOU (ummm... and I) HAVE GONE BACK ON THAT PROMISE. OK, that's bad; if you promise you are going to do something and you don't, that's not good; that makes you untrustworthy. So, feel bad about that for a moment, and then get over it. There's nothing you can change about that now, well, except for one thing: who YOU are in relationship going forward. You could never change your former partner (as much as you may have wanted to!), but I'd be willing to bet there were things you can do differently going forward.

So, the first question becomes, "What would extraordinary relationship look like to you?" Let's define terms first.

"Extraordinary." Extra. Ordinary. Not meaning "really" ordinary (because how boring would THAT be?), but the Latin "extra" meaning "beyond." So, beyond the usual.

And "relationship." That is, the act of two people relating. Relative to each other.

Relating to another in a way above and beyond what is commonplace.

So, what would it look like for you to relate to someone in a way that is beyond ordinary? And along with that question should be, "What are YOU willing to bring to the table (and possibly other articles of furniture) to make that happen?"

Get clear on what you want, get clear what your partner wants, operate from a place of integrity, with a focus on what YOU bring, all in a spirit of open and honest communication. (Well, shit; it didn't say it was going to be EASY!)

The alternative is what most of us are doing now and have doing since time immemorial; just let it "happen," make it up as we go and have it turn into a sad, pathetic anti-Indiana Jones adventure where, in making it up as we go, not only do we not get the girl, but she doesn't get us. Real life ain't Spielberg, folks.

In getting clear, it is useful to look at the obstacles that keep us from pursuing that which we KNOW we should be going after. Why do we do that?

Fear

I'm gonna go with a sports metaphor here. Andrew Luck is the quarterback for the Indianapolis Colts of the National Football League. He has an uncanny ability to "forget" when he performs badly and not let it affect his subsequent play later in the game. The sports announcers like to say he has a short memory and that his ability to forget mistakes on the field does not affect his later performance. Most of us are not like that. In fact, we "learn" as a defense mechanism to protect us in the future, otherwise, every trip out our front door would be an adventure (and for some, it is...)

Unfortunately, we often make associations about future events that tie us to past events that were unpleasant and it tells us to avoid them. Sometimes, that's a good thing, sometimes not. If we stick our hand in the fire and it burns, we learn not to stick our hand in the fire. Ah, that all our lessons could be that clear cut and simple! When we start mucking up the water with human interaction, you can throw all simplicity out the window. But that doesn't mean that we can't learn from our past relationships: quite the opposite.

First, through that experience, we can learn about what we want and don't want from being with another person, and more than anything, it teaches us about ourselves, and who we are evolving into and what we bring to the relationship table individually.

In going through the stories in this book, it's obvious that one of the demons I had to wrestle with was jealousy. While self-esteem is at the very core of that, there are other aspects in jealousy scenarios that can allow that emotion to surface: the behavior of others, interpretation of those behaviors, how we communicate around them and then our resulting actions going forward.

Central to all that is the issue of trust. Most of us have been in love at one time or another. And most of us have also experienced the pain of a broken heart.

So, yeah, most of us have had someone mash that sucker flat. What do you attach to that phenomenon? Is it that all men (or women) suck? Or was it that other person's fault that your relationship became just so much emotional roadkill? How often have you uttered these words in the aftermath of a once googly-eyed debacle: "Never again?"

Right? Because we stuck our hand into that fire we call LOVE, and it HURT. So, not doin' THAT again...

But, "THAT" what? Love? Relationship? Men? Women? Or maybe just that situation, which was what? Transition-guy-on-a-summer-fling? Screwing-the-wife-of-your-bosses-ex-brother-in-law?

What?

That's just it; we're often not sure what it is we are supposed to avoid. So some of us get gun-shy about all of it. But c'mon... you gotta go out there and live life and so, invariably, you will probably go out there and commit some version of the same disaster all over again.

The good news is that sometimes we DO learn, and we decide to get back on that horse again because, (and remember this phrase),

"This is not that."

(Yes, "This is not that." C'mon; where else but here are you gonna get this level of esoteric, deeply complex, soul-searching philosophy?)

But let's get serious for a minute. We all have fears, and we can let those fears dictate how we experience life. And it's OK to be afraid. But at some point, if you want to live a full life, you have to push beyond those fears. That's what courage is.

Besides, *your fears may not apply in this situation.* Just because it looks or feels like whatever happened in the past on some level, this may be different.

Or not, in which case you should use your hard earned wisdom and RUN in the opposite direction.

How do we decide, then, whether to engage or not? Ideally we want to have our wits about us in ALL major decisions, and choosing who to spend time with certainly falls into that category. I don't have the answer to that question. Love comes in all shapes and sizes, and sometimes it pays to go beyond our comfort zone if what we keep doing is not getting the results we want.

But it's fun and that's why we do it. Like Woody said, "We need the eggs..."

So, do you have the courage to trust? And if we start to drill down into that question, invariably for me, the question comes up, "Trust what?"

And the answer comes up: trust that another person is going to do what they say they are going to do. And this is not just in the area of our romantic relationships, but in other areas of our lives. How many people in your life do you trust implicitly? If the answer is zero (and I can imagine that it is for some of you; there have been times in my life when that would have been my response).

There are two sides to that response: first, that there are no people in your life who can or should be trusted, and second, that even if there are people who can be trusted, you aren't willing to risk that, because you envision a potential negative outcome.

Once you examine your inability to trust, you can make a determination to go forward into the land of the living (and loving) or you can turn into your own version of Uncle Alex. But have it be a conscious decision, not a reaction based on your subconscious fears.

This brings us around to our "stuff." Yeah, we all have it: stuff, baggage, issues, challenges, call it whatever you want; if it is holding you back, it is fear-based. So before you go forward, how about cleaning house? How about taking some responsibility instead of blaming others for your life not being all it could be? Don't get me wrong, it's very easy to blame our exes for why your relationship with them wasn't fulfilling and it IS almost always the other person's fault (right?), but how about that one little thing that you wish you might have done differently... ALL of the times you've done it?

Because you were afraid...

To recount another area where fear dictated my behavior, let's consider how often I had inserted jealousy into places where it wasn't appropriate. I did it repeatedly. Why? Well, to protect myself, number one, but then, (and perhaps more importantly) to show I was RIGHT! Confirmation bias. We will look for "evidence" to "prove" what we already think is true, whether it is or not.

Right about what, you ask? How about that people are not to be trusted?

And while yes, it sucked then to not be able to trust anyone, at least then I knew; this is how the world works.

I was RIGHT!

But is that how I wanted to live the rest of my life?

No, it wasn't. So when I would start to feel those pangs of jealousy, I would ask, "What else could this mean?" And around jealousy in particular, that photo of someone's co-worker on her I-phone could have a much more innocent explanation than the heinous scenario my jealousy filter had cooked up.

As you may have realized, a common thread running through this treatise is personal responsibility. We've all seen (or possibly have been in) relationships that are abusive and we wonder how that person stays and puts up with it. They have rationalizations around it (oh, he's really sorry, it'll never happen again...) but at some point, if they really decide to look at it, and STILL stay, then what they are saying is that they are willing to accept being abused: that whatever they see the alternative as, abuse is better. I know abusive situations are never that simple: quite the contrary. But in some of those situations, people are being abused because they think this is what relationship looks like.

I know a young guy who's getting knocked around by his girlfriend. Something is keeping him there; either the sex is REALLY good or maybe he thinks this is as good as it gets (Ah, "As Good as it Gets:" one of my favorite movies with Jack Nicholson, where Nicholson plays Melvin Udall, an OCD writer who he plays to the hilt as the consummate asshole. There is that classic, though not very credible scene as he is leaving his psychiatrist's office, storming out through the waiting room full of clients, where he stops, looks at them and asks, "What if this is as good as it gets?") But I think this young guy simply doesn't realize that being smacked around by your girlfriend is not how most people live. Or maybe it's fun, or "passionate." (Oh, I'm sorry; did those quotation marks seem sarcastic or judgmental? Yes; I know some people like it rough. Then there are those who like it rough because that's the only way they've ever had it. But that's another book. Or maybe the 50 Shades industry has covered that for you...)

Yet another aspect of the abuser that bears mentioning here is that most abusers have been abused themselves. Does that make it right for them to inflict that on someone else? Of course not, but it does explain that behavior, to some extent. Very often, if you are being abused in a relationship, you are bearing the brunt of anger that should be directed at someone else, and it's being directed at you sometimes just because you happen to be there, but usually also because the attacker believes that they can get away with it. This is a very clear boundary to draw right away, especially around physical or sexual violence. Zero tolerance is a tough rule, and it should be. Domestic violence is not only a serious matter, but think about it in terms of what it is: one partner physically harming the person that is most important to them in the world. It should NEVER even get close to that point.

By the way, that young guy who was being knocked around ended up in the hospital after an overdose of sleeping pills. For him, that was a way out: to just end it all. He had felt powerless to leave in any other way. He survived those experiences. Hopefully there is enough pain in that experience that he never has to return to that type of scenario again.

Which brings us around to self-esteem again. For whatever reason (maybe it's all that anyone has ever told you and you believe it as "true") you think that nobody else will want you. Most people that are abused do not deserve to be treated as such, but they put up with it because they feel like they don't have a choice. History has shown that as human beings, we have the will and the ability to tolerate ANYTHING (yes, anything; think about it...) But at the end of the day, if you are suffering in your relationship, you have got to consider that if nothing else, you are better off on your own.

What fears do you want to take forward, and which do you want to leave behind? I have done a self-hypnosis visualization where I am at an airport terminal at the baggage claim (are you seeing already where I am going with this?) And going around on the carousel is ALL of my proverbial baggage. From there, I am going forth in my life, and choosing which bags I want to take. And I will say, there are quite a few bags that I have left behind, circling in perpetuity. I also go back from time to time and drop other bags off.

Yes, I am traveling much lighter these days.

We can use this same concept around relationship in general. If we are truly going to create something new, we have to leave the old behind. That is the beauty of this new paradigm; we are looking at everything differently: total redesign if that is what is necessary. But we don't have to throw the baby out with the bathwater; if something IS working, by all means, let's keep that.

In the restaurant scene from "As Good As It Gets" Nicholson insults Helen Hunt yet again and she asks him to pay her a compliment or she is going to walk out. After much hemming and hawing, he recites one of the great movie lines of all time:

"You make me want to be a better man."

Think about the dynamic behind that scene, and how it gets repeated in our daily lives. If we are in relationship with someone whom we don't respect, don't like, don't really care if we are with, there is no incentive to get better. If the relationship ends, so what? No big loss. But if you are in a relationship with someone who is "above you" in the hierarchy; you have something to lose by having that person leave. This is one of the reasons for relationships of ALL kinds; it encourages us to grow, to evolve, to go beyond where we were before.

Jessie told me as we were leaving our first date, "I have more testosterone than you."

At first, that came across as an insult; very few men would be comfortable hearing that. But after reflecting for a few seconds, I realized she was right. She was non-stop, achieving this and winning that, making money, classic over-achiever, gettin' shit done. But she wasn't happy. And I realized from the context of our conversation that night that I was perhaps the perfect complement for her. And she for me.

Was our "reverse" polarity going to create some challenges for us? Potentially, yes. This was outside of traditional male/female roles. But maybe at that particular point in our lives, she was needing what I was offering (an opportunity to slow down and smell the roses), while she was offering me the opportunity to push the envelope and get more accomplished.

"You're right" I said, "You got a problem with that?" (Once again, in my now-defunct Jersey accent).

"No; I moved here to become an underachiever."

"Well, here, let me help you with that..."

For the record, she ended that relationship after two (what I thought were) great dates. Apparently, we were "not a good Match" (yes, it had been internet-initiated). That was all the explanation I got. Apparently, she wasn't quite ready for the level of testosterone she felt I wasn't producing.

Was she "afraid" of slowing down and not being the best? I don't know; we didn't get a chance to know each other. Interestingly, I saw on FB that she was dating Jim, the self-professed "alpha-dog." I would have placed cash money on how long that one was going to last.

Get Help

It is not within the scope of this book to provide the means to overcoming some of the more challenging situations that can arise between you and your partner. Before you resign yourself to being an Uncle Alex, though, consider this: If your love life is not what you would like it to be, and the two of you are having trouble reconciling that yourselves, there are qualified counselors and coaches out there who can help for either individual or couples counseling. That being said, there are lots of them out there who do as much harm as good, and there are those out there who are perfectly capable of helping, but are not a good fit for your particular issues or personality. If you do enlist the help of a coach or counselor, and it's not going well, try another one. Try up to five, because I feel that as many as three out of four counselors shouldn't even be in the field. If, after five, you're still feeling frustrated, consider that you don't really want to be helped and that you might need a shift in perspective around THAT. Maybe all that drama and fuckedupedness is actually working for you on some level.

One other word of advice in the area of personal growth: keep at it, keep moving forward. There is no bigger proponent on the planet than I around getting rid of your demons however you choose to do that. But one of the worst paths you can take is one that ends IN THE PROCESS. In my hypnotherapy training we talked about clients who would go through life displaying their "treasured golden wound." You know the type; they blame their parents, or their upbringing, or their spouse: somebody, anybody, anything rather than taking personal responsibility for their actions as adults.

This is an area where a little bit of knowledge can be harmful. As just one example, "I have abandonment issues" can keep you from extraordinary relationship because you are defining yourself a certain way. If you have been in therapy for a number of years and you are still talking about the same old shit, then you are probably using your therapist as a professional best friend rather than a therapist. Time to try something different.

Instead of "I have abandonment issues," how about something more along these lines: "I used to be afraid to commit because I have lost others who were close to me, but now I am willing to do whatever is necessary to have others close to me. I am making a difficult but courageous choice for my life to be better."

Get over it, come out on the other side and get on with the rest of your life. Bob Newhart did a very funny skit as a therapist with a unique short term, on-size-fits-all approach. Check it out: https://www.youtube.com/watch?v=qmrGUVbaaRs

RELATIONSHIP AGREEMENTS

Let's do THAT! (An Overview)

So, you've done some of your personal work, and found someone who has done some of theirs and it's looking like the two of you are boarding the train for Coupleville. Now, in the old paradigm, you got on that train and just let it take you wherever it was going to go and when you arrived, Coupleville pretty much looked like it had in the past. What we are going to change, through the mighty power of metaphor, is that now your destination will be one of your collective creation.

But first, a story to illustrate how I came around to this way of thinking.

Having moved back to the East coast after my initial sojourn that ended in New Mexico, I decided to take a construction job to learn about the building industry. My job on the Jersey shore required about a 45 minute commute, and as most Jersey jokes go, I had to travel either the Garden State Parkway or the Turnpike to get around. Tired of the traffic at the end of one work day, not wanting to use Exit 109, I decided to take local roads home and travel down the shoreline, which pretty quickly got me lost. I wasn't in any particular hurry, so I started to look for a place to eat and came across a place called Frankie's in Pt. Pleasant Beach. The parking lot was full, but quiet and it was just starting to get dark. As I pulled open the front door I was greeted with an almost deafening noise level. There was no music; it was all just voices in conversation, but elevated, animated. The place was jumping.

It was like a scene from "Cheers," with a circular bar, only three times as crowded and not a "Norm" in sight. Somehow, I managed to find a seat at the far side of the bar, ordered a burger and a beer (in a frosted mug) and waited for my meal to arrive.

I struck up a conversation with the guy sitting next to me:

"Hi; I'm Roman."

"Brian"

"Wow, this place is really hopping."

"Yeah, it's all locals. We come after work and hang out, watch the game. It's a good crowd."

It was a great place to people watch. Most of the patrons were twenty or thirty-somethings, professional, attractive and the energy level in the room was palpable.

From my vantage point, I saw two women enter the room. They were obviously regulars, greeting numerous others as they worked their way around to the side of the bar where Brian and I were sitting.

As it turned out, one of them was Brian's girlfriend, the other her best friend. Since I had to eat, I didn't give up my seat, but we were all situated very close and at some point, in between bites I inserted myself into their conversation.

Renee (the one Brian and Sandy would eventually try to hook me up with) was talking about ice cream and for some reason that seemed appropriate at the time, I made a remark about how while ice cream was just fine for eating, sometimes situations arose where it could be topically applied as well (obviously something about this place was bringing out the "randy" in me).

Sandy had her back to me, but she turned, looked at me, then looked at Brian and then back at me and said, "Who IS this guy?"

Brian made the introductions, then Sandy said, "Do you know him?"

"No, we just met a half hour ago here at the bar."

"Sandy locked eyes with me for a couple of seconds, laughed and just said, "Ice cream, huh?"

We all exchanged some daring dairy innuendoes and from that point on, I became part of their group and a regular at Frankie's. They tried setting me up with Renee but it never really worked out. She was very attractive, and both being available, we took a running stab at a relationship, but there was just something missing between us and it never got off the ground.

Frankie's became a regular stop on the drive home (once I actually found a more efficient way, that is, Exit 98) and the four of us were part of the regular scene there.

A few months after that initial introduction into their world, on Christmas Eve, I got a phone call from Sandy.

"Brian and I broke up."

We had all become good friends, and while I knew they were having their problems, I didn't think they were at a stage of breaking up. Sandy was very upset. Apparently, this was not the first time this had happened, and to have it happen during the holidays was especially distressing to her. She asked me to come over to her house, which I did, and that became the start of an at first clandestine (we didn't want Brian to know, even though they had broken up), then open and passionate relationship that was fraught with obstacles, not the least of which were local history and the fact that I had been contemplating a move back to New Mexico.

Sandy and I had "The Juice" at its absolutely most intoxicating. But the rest of it didn't look like The Faerietale at all, outside of the intense infatuation we had for each other.

Still, we considered a future together and talked about rewriting the Faerietale to make it fit our circumstance.

I suggested, "Let's do this; we will each write down a version of the Faerietale as it applies to our relationship, no holds barred, being completely honest, and then we will exchange them, and see how it matches up."

"Great; let's do that."

Once we compared them, it became painfully obvious that we were NOT a good match for long term. First there was staying in

New Jersey, which I was opposed to, and then there were issues with kid's Dads and family members and church. Somehow we had the presence of mind to end it before it all unraveled. Our parting was extremely painful, but somehow we both knew that this was as far as we were going to go together.

But in that exchange of potential futures was the seed of an idea: why not be this proactive in every relationship? Why not have this level of communication and openness and honesty? Why aren't all couples this pro-active in their approach?

At first they were rhetorical questions, but eventually when I started to look at them objectively, I realized that fear played an important part in not doing this. What if it turns out the way it did for Sandy and I? That we were NOT meant to be together? Who wants to own up to that? Especially in the midst of a wild, passionate affair? Not many. We were thrust into that position by my imminent move to New Mexico, so a major life decision had to be made. Do I stay or go?

In the end, we were left with a very bittersweet, "Casablanca" type ending to our story, complete with an airport and our version of Paris (alright, it was Pt. Pleasant, and while that doesn't have the same exotic ring to it, "We'll always have Pt. Pleasant," our time together never had the chance to get ugly and so has remained romanticized, including, but certainly not limited to, a special place in my heart for chocolate/peanut butter ice cream).

But what if our circumstances were different, in that more of the pieces lined up, and we did decide to stay together? There would have been numerous areas where compromises would have had to be made. With us, there were some non-negotiables right from the start, not the least of which was where to live.

Whenever two people decide to spend time together in relationship, compromises are arrived at, often without any verbal exchange at all. They become agreements, contracts, vows. Marriage vows are a contract of sorts, whether they are spoken to the ears of God, a justice of the peace or an assembled group of family and friends. The idea here will be to have the areas of agreement be <u>much</u> more specific than "for better or for worse." In this chapter, we will look at many aspects of modern life to be considered when two lives come together, ways to determine whether or not conciliation is possible, and how to go about negotiating it.

There are other types of relationship agreements, some written, some spoken and some unspoken. While the concept of the pre-nuptial agreement is familiar to most, it is reserved for those that have the resources to "protect" should the "promise" to spend the rest of their lives together somehow reverse; basically, "should this not work out, you can't have my stuff."

One of the highest profile relationship contracts has been between Facebook creator Mark Zuckerberg and his then girlfriend Priscilla Chan. According to the New York Times:

> "Priscilla Chan famously detailed her requirements of Mark Zuckerberg in a relationship contract before moving to California to be with him. Notably, she requested 100 minutes of shared time (neither to be spent in his apartment or in the Facebook headquarters) per week. Additionally, she required one date night per week."

Wow. 100 minutes a week. Wait; let's synchronize our watches... and, begin...

But, hey, judgment about that aside, the idea here is that whatever the agreement is between two parties, it be consciously entered into. (And btw, Mr. Zuckerberg and Ms. Chan have gone on to be married and parents. They have also decided to share their $$$ with the world, including pledging Three Billion Dollars to accelerate basic scientific research towards eradicating all disease in the world by the end of the 21st century. I'd say their agreement has expanded considerably beyond those hundred minutes).

I am going to suggest that at some point, it all be put into writing. Not so that at some point, when someone is not holding up their end of the bargain, you can berate them with a barrage of "You said"s... While a written contract can give you some ground to stand on (though not legal ground) the idea is not to have a piece of paper to wave in your partner's face when they inevitably "forget" to do something they said they were going to. The idea is to get a sense of what those wants and needs are and to begin a dialogue about what is most important for the both of you, and what you are willing to provide, not just in financial terms, like a pre-nup, but in emotional and practical terms. If nothing else, writing it down can remind both of YOU of what it was YOU collectively agreed upon.

Interestingly, same sex partners have been constructing relationship contracts for some time now, because there had been nothing else in place for them in terms of legal marriage. I talked to a lesbian couple recently that had gotten married in New Mexico about this new paradigm and one of them said, "Oh yeah, we've been doing that for years."

I wondered, now that they are married, if they would slip into some of the same complacency that plagues heterosexual couples. Hopefully theirs is not a be-careful-what-you-ask-for situation.

One area that has been the target of spoken agreement between couples over the years has to do with one partner working while the other finishes schooling for an advanced degree in law or medicine, for instance. This often becomes a bone of contention if the relationship dissolves. Financially, what is that partner's sacrifice worth in financial terms, now that the new doc or lawyer is raking in the dough? Unfortunately, that negotiation is hardly ever entered into proactively because it is just assumed there will be no end to the union.

In this age of texting, DTR is an acronym common among younger couples that means "Defining the Relationship." While common among couples new to relationship, this is often a first step towards solidifying a bond, or at the very least, getting partners on the same page around their level of commitment. Are we "going steady"? BF/GF? The terms change as we get older, but the concept is the same: are we "exclusive?" Are we "seeing other people?" So, verbal contracts in relationship are not new, but they have been very limited in scope and detail. And, what often happens is that issues are dealt with on a need-to basis, that is, issues that are important to the future or even ongoing success of a relationship don't come up until they need to be, and then, in crisis mode, often the best decisions do not get made going forward.

Again, the idea here is to be proactive about what you and your partner do and don't want going forward. That being said, creating a relationship is a bit of an adventure and so the agreement can be looked upon as a broad stroke to begin with, and the details getting filled in as you go. How broad and how detailed will depend on the personalities of the participants.

Let's take a look at varying degrees of commitment as we approach this dialogue. Commitment is defined as "the state or quality of being dedicated to a cause, activity, etc." For the sake of semantics and also to allow for different levels of duration, engagement, intensity and interest, we should probably be using different words at different times: if you are committed to something, you are going to do what you said you are going to do.

Some people live their lives dictated by a very high degree of commitment. For those of you who have children, and are conscious, devoted parents, you KNOW what that means: these children are my responsibility and I will be there for them, period.

What if there is something going forward you are not so sure about? What might you call it then? How about "promise?" That's the same thing though, isn't it? Propose! That's it! Webster defines "propose" as "to form or put forward a plan or intention."

Now, "propose" carries with it the traditional matrimonial association. But really, when you think about it, that's what a marriage proposal is: "Let's consider that, at some time in the future, we will make a commitment." Somehow I don't think that creating and signing a relationship agreement will elicit that same over the top, enthusiastic, showing-the-engagement-ring-to-your-girlfriend kind of outburst as, "He proposed to me!" That pie-in-the-sky optimism, born out of naiveté, not just on the part of the bride-to-be waving her engagement ring around, but also the prospective groom, very often says, "Yes, at some time in the (near) future, I will commit to spending the rest of my life to you, come hell or high water," usually with little idea how hot the hell or how high and treacherous the water.

In the beginning of this process, there is usually a discussion, an exchange of ideas. Then, if everyone is on the same page, there is an agreement, along with promises to do and not do.

And then (and this is one of the most important parts of this whole process) you gotta do what you say you are going to do.

Yes, that is dubious advice coming from someone who has married and divorced twice (but we are all supposed to be learning from my mistakes, right?) but that's how those new neural pathways get created.

The great philosopher James Brown (yes, THAT James Brown, "I feel good"...da-duh-da-duh-da-duh-duh) was once asked in an interview, "What is the quality you like most in a man?"

His reply was, "Integrity—that takes care of everything. Take care of your kids, watch your family, try to be a good man, walk as close as you can to what you believe in."

I love that last part: "...walk as close as you can to what you believe in." It allows for us to be human, to make mistakes. Conduct yourself with your very best intent, from your highest place possible, as often as you can.

Do your damned best...

And here's a kicker (and this ties in with personal integrity); how many people that you know, on a daily basis, conduct themselves in a way that is congruent with their intentions? How many people truly "walk their walk?" Most of us have good intentions, but let's face it, some people will agree to do things without ever having any intention of following through. Then there are those who have every intention of keeping their word and at the first obstacle, throw up their hands and quit. Or, maybe it's not even an obstacle, but some shiny new distraction that pulls their attention away. ("Hey, I could have ADD! Yeah, that's it; I have ADD... I got distracted. That's why I'm a failure...") (BTW, I have a problem with that diagnosis as an excuse. Not that some people don't have short attention spans; I had serious challenges dealing with someone who had the hardest time making ANY decisions, because all she could see was the one option in front of her. Couple that with the fear that she would make the WRONG decision and her decision-making mechanism was paralyzed. We would agonize over a vacation, for instance, make the plans to go and then a month later, we were looking at something totally different because, well, for no other reason than, there it was: another option. How exasperating was that? Plenty. And did I know this about her before we got together? No; it's not the kind of information that comes out on a first date, or a Match.com profile. As a matter of fact, she will swear up and down to this day that she doesn't do that. ADD? To a clinician, you bet. To me? No. Does she have a short attention span? Uh, yeah... Reason to not be together? No, not by itself, but it did go on the "cons" list at the end of our time together...)

So, what DOES get decided early on?

I would suggest starting with the positives: what would you like to have included? Then, as the process unfolds, you can each delve into the darker side, the aspects that maybe you have experienced before, and don't want to again, like the heinous behavior that your last partner displayed that became non-negotiable. It takes focus, and attention and perseverance, but again, intimate relationship, extraordinary relationship, is one of the most important endeavors we will ever undertake.

Early on with Barbara, I suggested that we be monogamous. This is a fairly common spoken agreement in couples (whether they adhere to it or not is another topic for discussion). She responded with an enthusiastic, "Yes, Let's do THAT!"

What I didn't know at the time was how difficult the rest of our decisions together would be. And some of that had to do with where we were in our lives.

Stages of Life

All of this information will mean different things to people at different stages of their lives. A lifetime commitment at 20 years of age is a whole different equation than one at 60. Unfortunately, at 20, when you know everything, including the everlasting nature of your love, it's hard to imagine that your relationship could possibly be anything remotely like the millions of others that have come before you. But then, well, you are probably not reading this book because you ARE all-knowing and of course, YOUR relationship is not like everyone else's and your love WILL last forever.

Are children in the picture? Be they current, future, your own or somebody else's, if there are little ones to consider, the whole picture gets that much more complicated, especially if you decide to take your role as parent (and/or step-parent) seriously.

If you are midlife (and the definition of that is changing as we all get to live longer), this is all a different equation. Very likely, this is the first time you have examined the choices you have made in your life. *Truly* examined them, that is. You have gone through the first part of your adult life on automatic pilot, living by the rules and examples of your family of origin and other early influences, and some of that isn't working for you. (If it was, you wouldn't be examining it).

And if you are like most Americans, both men and women, you are probably feeling "old." Well, the sooner you get over that (and you will) the better. You are in the prime of your life. Don't waste it!

Midlife crisis? Without going all Zen on y'all, (how's that for combining East and West?) I like to look at midlife not as a time of crisis but opportunity. A time to really design how you want to live your life; to look at the standards, rules and tenets, as well as your resulting behaviors, then decide what is working for you and what is not. Very likely, you have had some missteps and that has brought you around to this period of introspection.

Good for you. Maybe your parents set a bad example and you followed it, thinking this is how you were supposed to do it. Your life is as fucked up as theirs was and it has put you in crisis mode. The good news is that you don't have to do that anymore. Yes, it does feel really good when you stop banging your head against that proverbial wall. Hopefully, this book will provide some alternatives for you around relationship, if that has been a problem area for you.

Past middle age, or getting near that? Raised some kids maybe? Empty nester? Divorced after 20, 30 years? Again, good! It's not over; now you have a chance to make some sense of it all and really enjoy yourself and have others enjoy you as well. Isn't that what relationship is for?

Are you a "senior?" I will let you define an age range for that. In our golden years, true companionship can be more important than ever before (cue Mark Cohn's "True Companion"). What might you want that to look like?

Types of Relationship Agreements

Where are you in terms of relationship? Are you in one now, and want to revive it, or make it better? Are the two of you just starting out? Married? Or are you in between relationships? Alone? Interestingly, those last two options are the same except for your outlook. You could be coming off of a bad break-up and be in never-again mode (in which case you are probably not reading this book).

I've been in never-again mode numerous times in my life; for me, it didn't last. If you do slip into that temporary abyss, that's OK, but I would suggest only wallowing there for a short while. If you attach so much pain to relationship that you decide to stay there, hopefully you can devote your energies to *something* productive otherwise. Let's consider some different scenarios that you might be starting from.

New Relationship

So, you are just starting out with a new partner and want to be proactive about the outcome. Excellent! Maybe you have been in other relationships that turned out to be less than extraordinary. The good thing is that now you have some ideas about what has worked and what hasn't. If you are just starting out, you may want to choose "sparingly" from the list of options to consider focusing on, since you may not know your prospective partner all that well. I certainly don't endorse bringing a checklist with you on a first date, but realistically, that is what we do anyway. That first date is often like an interview, especially if one of the daters is actively seeking relationship. I know of one serial internet dater who had a date like that; she came armed with questions about everything-- from who he had voted for to favorite book. While that sounds a little contrived, that approach can be a good icebreaker, especially for those that find first dates a bit intimidating. Unfortunately for her and her prospective partners, she was a bit too bossy about it, limiting answers to one sentence. Do you think any of her dates had any flags go up about control issues?

New relationships are the perfect place to implement this new paradigm. It's tabula rasa, baby: the perfect time to see just how you line up with another person and discover who they are and want to be going forward.

Existing Relationship

Usually, there is going to be one party who is more invested in this process of extraordinary relationship than the other. Logically, the person whose needs are not being met is looking for a new way for the relationship to be. The other partner may be perfectly fine with the way things are, and therefore may engage in some foot dragging.

Are you in a relationship right now that is struggling? How much does it suck? I mean, do you wish he wouldn't want to have sex all the time? Or at all? Does the idea of getting between the sheets with him have you thinking more about having to do another load of laundry than any kind of ardor? Is your partner simply getting on your nerves or has it gotten to the point where you can't stand to be around her and you look forward to those times when she has to work late?

Generally, if our situation is a little uncomfortable, more often than not, we will tolerate it rather than stir the pot and try to affect a change. But when anything gets enough PAIN attached to it, it's actually a blessing, because that is when change occurs. So, yeah, if your flesh is crawling over the mere suggestion of connubial co-mingling, you're in luck! Yes, it falls into that category of sometimes-things-have-to-get-worse-before-they-get-better.

As part of this new paradigm, the first concept you may have to get your head and heart wrapped around is that your current relationship may have a limited shelf life. But that is not where I want you to start. There needs to be a very clear assessment about what is not working for you, and this has to be clearly communicated to your partner. If this is not well received, or not received at all, that is, not taken seriously, then you need to consider that most of your needs are probably not going to be met in this relationship and decide if you are willing to accept that.

More optimistically, you may present your case to your partner and they may not have had a clue that anything was amiss, and are willing to consider how they can make it better.

Married

When you got married, you entered into a contract with your spouse. You promised to, well, what did you promise? To "love, honor and obey?" That one, especially the last part, is a bit outmoded. "Love?" What exactly would that look like? "Honor?"

Same thing? Did it include "'til death do us part?" If that were carved in stone, divorce would not exist. Did you create your own vows? What did those include? Have you lived up to them? Original vows are a great place to start, but they are often too vague. Lots of people have taken those vows and not lived up to the letter of the law. How about "for better or for worse?" Could that be any more general? If you are reading this book, you probably didn't anticipate that "worse" would look like it has. Well, now you do, and maybe, going forward, that gets added to the list of what to avoid. Or, if you are an optimist, you can look for the opposite.

Incidentally, early on, most of us copy our parents' model of what relationship looks like. And if they were married, we probably assumed that eventually we would get married too. I am not against marriage, if you do what you say you are going to do when you take those vows. If you are promising the rest of your life to someone, then divorce should not be an option. I have talked to couples that have been married for thirty, forty, fifty years and more. Whenever I hear two people have been married for a long time, I ask what their secret is; we can all stand to learn something from those that have come before us, in their positive example or otherwise.

Sometimes the answer is "faith." And I can see that; if your belief system says that you have made this promise in the eyes of God and you faith is strong and pure and congruent with how you actually live your life, you probably WILL stay together, especially if your spouse shares those views. Will it be extraordinary? I have spoken to some couples for whom it is.

Others, not so much... I asked one couple about their "secret" for longevity and the husband said, "She does everything I tell her to." I looked at the wife, wondering if she was going to give me any clue as to whether he was joking or not. She returned my gaze with a practiced, thin, wan smile hiding gritted teeth, didn't say a word, and spoke volumes. Just because two people stay together doesn't mean it's a healthy relationship, or that either of them is happy or fulfilled. But they have their "agreement," probably spoken a long time ago, in vague terms, for better or for worse, 'til death do they part.

Granted, I am extrapolating a lot from a husband's seven word reply and her silence. For her, perhaps the security of what their marriage provides satisfies her most important needs. But I would be willing to bet that she would not describe their relationship as extraordinary, although he might.

I had one wife tell me, "There is an element of luck involved. But really, I married my best friend."

Another man, "Listen, give and forgive."

It would seem that in many of the success stories, a certain measure of cooperation is involved.

But What if My Partner Doesn't Want to Go Along?

The process of even considering a contract, in and of itself, can be a challenge when one person in the equation is happy as a clam the way things are: there is likely to be some resistance. Or, what if they are just paying lip service to what they promised to bring?

Yeah, I hate that...

After all, if it ain't broke, why fix it? There may be an absolute total cluelessness that there is a problem at all (is this starting to sound familiar?)

So, to address personal accountability here; what are you responsible for if your needs are not being met? You can't control the other person, you can't MAKE them do anything. But, you can express to them what your needs are. You may be in a situation where you have no (perceived) power in the relationship. Let's consider a worst case scenario; you pour your heart out, and your partner looks at you and says, "Really? Well too fuckin' bad; this is who I am and if you don't like it, you know where the door is."

Hmmm, you may have your work cut out. Is that a real threat? Or a bluff? If repeated attempts at communication meet with this resistance, you can offer to get help: counseling or a family member. But if you are getting this kind of resistance to change, then your responsibility to yourself and the relationship is to decide whether or not you are willing to accept these terms. You cannot assume that this person is going to change. But isn't that going to tell you something about your partner, who they are and how much they are invested? Maybe you already know that, and that is why you have initiated this process. It'll also tell you lots of things about yourself.

The bottom line, in this or any other relationship, is that your behavior is the only thing you have any control over. And even then, there are times when we do things and have to scratch our heads and wonder, "Why did I just DO that?" Consider that your partner does the same thing (that is, behaves sometimes in ways they are not aware of) and cut them some slack.

Some.

Old habits die hard, and sometimes creating new habits takes doing them repeatedly and with support. On the other hand, new boundaries may need to be created. Your partner may not have the same vision as you, or that vision may have changed.

After Rita and I separated the first time and we got back together, she remarked how now she felt like she was going to have to be on her "best behavior" (if we were going to stay together).

My first reaction was "No; you just keep being who you are. We want for this relationship to be authentic. I don't want you to change."

Really? Isn't that saying let's-do-the-same-thing-and-expect-a-different-result? (We already know how I feel about THAT!) But I said it anyway because, well, it was a pat answer. But in retrospect, isn't that what we SHOULD be doing? Being on our best behavior? Why wouldn't we, in the most important relationship of our lives?

In that moment, I guess what I was saying was, "I want to be willing to accept you as you are (Was that ambiguous enough, do you think?) In my defense, at the same time, I had owned up to my part of the relationship unraveling, and I was saying to her, "I am going to bring MY best."

Of course, that begged the question, what constitutes "best behavior?" If that meant that she was going to sublimate herself to me, do my every bidding, deny her strongest urges and basically become someone she was not just to please me; that was obviously not healthy. But if that break for us presented an opportunity to grow and look at new ways to communicate and relate: great!

If it meant I-am-temporarily-going-to-do-what-he-wants-to-placate-him-and-eventually-we-will-get-back-to-normal-that-is-doing-things-MY-way, there was obviously a problem there.

Some things we do for our partners because they want us to, and it's not a big deal to affect that change. But when does that tip to where it is too much?

There is obviously not a single answer to that question since every relationship is unique, but the answer should come from a place of conscious consideration.

You and your partner can write out your agreements separately. This is one approach to creating the joint agreement, but not the only one; the two of you can also sit down jointly with the checklist and see what applies or start by having a conversation about what each wants, based on past experience (both good and bad).

This brings up a key point in this whole discussion about what the two of you want the relationship to be. How much will each of you be expected to sacrifice, give up, sublimate, change, hide and deny in the name of extraordinary relationship if you really don't *want* to change?

This is where I think compatibility becomes so important. It just stands to reason that the more ways two people are compatible, the less chance there is for conflict, disagreement and disharmony. But it also stands to reason that if you are TOO alike, there isn't going to be much growth.

In the past, in those instances where we ended relationships with others, we basically made a determination that we were either giving up too much or not getting enough (or both) and that those circumstances were not going to transform.

Part of the problem has been that even though marriage vows cover a wide range of possibilities for adjustment, both positive and negative ("in sickness and in health," "for better or for worse," "richer or poorer") they are not specific enough. What if instead, they were more graphic? It makes me think about how when our populace was first presented with the specter of deviating from the delicate balance that is our ecology and the powers that be decided to label it "global warming." I remember hearing that and thinking, "Cool that doesn't sound so bad. I wouldn't mind it being a few degrees warmer." Instead, from the get-go, a more appropriate label would have been something closer to "CATASTROPHIC CLIMATE CHANGE." (Always in caps, btw...)

So we could have something in the wedding vows that was a bit more foreboding: "whether I cherish you or grow to despise the very ground you walk on," "whether I turn to you for solace in my time of need or come to recognize you for the soul-sucking emotional vampire that you may become," "whether our life is bliss or ends up sucking beyond any reasonable imagination."

Clearly, that is not going to happen, unless you have a couple with macabre senses of humor. But we are looking to create a new paradigm, right?

But since the two of you are creating this agreement, have it say whatever you want. And mean it. Want to get married? If you cannot think of a single scenario in which you would leave your partner, you are probably still infatuated or you have a belief system that supersedes any heinous behavior on your partner's side. If that is the case: great. How about marriage with no option for divorce? I now believe that divorce should not be an option if you are going to promise to spend the rest of your life with someone. I realize that people change and circumstances change. Maybe the challenge of how changeable our lives are at this time in history coupled with lifelong commitment in the face of that is the thorny part (for me, but obviously for so many others too).

If your other half is digging their heels in around the idea of change, it's probably because their needs are being met, and they may have gotten complacent about meeting yours. But what if that safety net of "'til death do us part" was not a part of the equation?

If Not "'Til Death Do Us Part," Then How Long?

There has been considerable debate among friends and colleagues in discussing this new paradigm around whether or not an agreement should have a term attached to it. My contention at the beginning was that since we have been working with an undetermined, open-ended length of time ("forever," "always," and the heart-warming and gee, do-I-ever-look-forward-to-that "'til death do us part") and that was NOT working for most people, then we should have a shorter, finite length of time, not unlike a lease, with an option to renew.

While that made perfect sense to me, I have come across a fair amount of resistance to that idea.

Some individuals scoff at the idea of a limited term. Here is my advice; if you are uncomfortable with the idea of a term in the agreement, don't include it. If your partner wants one, and you don't, then the two of you need to have a conversation about that because there may be a difference in the level of commitment between the two of you.

Or, it can be argued that, regardless of how well things were going, the end of that term could be viewed as a potential ending point for the relationship. That is a large fear. A fear of distrust, a fear of abandonment.

But let's revisit the original premise here. Despite one of my exes once having asked me, "How is your book on short-term relationships going?" I am not proposing or supporting the idea of short term relationship, unless that is what the two of you agree on. The original idea had been for there to be pro-active, short-term, renewable periods of co-created relationship, that, if continually made extraordinary, will want to be renewed by both parties, over and over again. While I do believe the concept has merit, I think it will be some time, if ever, before that becomes the default. So the focus has shifted away from the length of the agreement to the quality.

There is one scenario where I see a finite time period being of distinct value, though, and that is in the case of a relationship that is on the rocks and ready to be disbanded. In that case, unless both parties are ready to walk away (in which case, just do it), usually there is one party more attached to the idea of staying together. Then, I recommend that at least a 90 day contract be entered into, with a review not only at the end of that time, but along the way, to try and recreate the bond that was once there and eventually go beyond.

In marriage, we celebrate anniversaries. Well, sort of. I believe those "celebrations" don't go far enough in continuing to create a relationship that is extraordinary. I believe that a scheduled review, an in-depth, up-close and personal examination of "How's it going?" can keep issues from falling through the cracks, and allows for changes to be integrated into the fabric of the relationship as they arise.

Co-creating the Actual Agreement

A contract!? That doesn't sound very romantic! Well it's not, so, forget it... Let's just go into this relationship willy-nilly (yes, it IS an actual word) and we'll just make it up as we go. It'll be an adventure!

And that's what we do, and yes; it IS an adventure. And while we WANT our relationships to be exciting, spontaneous and passionate, there is another part of us that wants them to be secure and comfortable, predictable, harmonious, loving, giving, trusting: a harbor in the storm.

I once sat down with an attorney, consulting on a contract of a different sort. What he explained to me was that contracts are really for when things go in the shitter. In the beginning, whether it is a business partnership or personal, things generally look rosy and optimistic (otherwise you wouldn't be entering into it, right?) But what he explained was that HIS job was to think about all of the things that could go wrong, *ahead of time,* and head them off at the pass. While we will integrate some of that thinking into this project, we are also going to consider more of what can go RIGHT and be moving towards that.

You got your carrot.

You got your stick. (Spoken in my no-longer-existing Jersey accent...)

While we don't want to ignore the stick, let's have the stick be those relationships from your past that were less than outstanding, and have the carrot be the new extraordinary bond we are looking to create.

To facilitate the process, I will provide a template, but by no means will it be comprehensive. Together, you can pick and choose what you want to include, what you don't want, and what simply doesn't apply. And it doesn't all have to be done in one sitting. I have found that the process can be drawn out over weeks, or even months, as different aspects of "what's important" get discussed, considered and brought forward into your collective consciousness. It becomes a proactive selection process around what you both want, what you (specifically) don't want, and whether or not you are willing to meet those needs for your partner. And that to me is the most important aspect of the contract; what YOU are willing to bring to the relationship.

Yes, we all need to get our needs met, and hopefully as a result of this process, you will. But if you go into the process with just your laundry list of "wants," it is a recipe for failure, and not just failure of the relationship to last, but for it to be extraordinary at all.

On those topics that warrant it, I have found it useful to ask the question: "How would you rate the level of that NOW, in the relationship, on a scale of 1-10? And, if it is less than 10, what has to happen for it to reach a 10?" Because, if we are striving for extraordinary, is anything less than 10 what we should be shooting for?

But if we are realistic we know that there are going to be those areas that won't be 100, no matter how hard we try, because there will some compromise in not only the process but also the outcome. What will become apparent are the ways in which the two of you are different, and the ways the two of you are the same. This includes not only differences in personality, but differences in interests and WAYS of doing things.

I find, in true partnership that it is important that there be a sense of fairness. This does not mean it is the SAME for both parties, but that it be equitable and that there not be a double standard. An example of this could be time apart. If he wants to spend his time apart visiting his family, and she wants to have a girl's night out, that's OK, as long as it's agreed by both. Very often though, double standards come in around behavior with others of the opposite sex. For instance, if he is having drinks after work, socially, with women, she's got to be allowed the same option, if she so chooses.

Gloria loved to salsa dance. When we first got together, we considered my being a part of that until we, (she, actually), realized not only that at some point I would be having physical contact with dancers other than her (women, that is), but it might curtail her contact with other men:

Gloria: 'Well, if it were just us, that would be fine, but I don't want other women pressing up against you."

Me: "But you have other men pressing up against you, don't you?"

Gloria: "Yeah, but that's different."

Me: "How is that different?"

Gloria: "blahblahblahblah"

It didn't matter what she said, because it was bullshit. There was no difference. She wanted there to be, but there wasn't.

So, in our "wisdom," she ended up giving it up and I never started. I'm not sure how that decision came about. Did I impose that on her? No, but I had expressed my dissatisfaction with the double standard. As a result, she ended up not pursuing an activity that she enjoyed.

What would have been the "healthiest" solution to all of this? There are a couple of them, I think. We could have been an "exclusive" dance couple, which would have made the most sense (but she didn't seem to like that option). We could have put aside her jealousy about other women dancing with me and shared salsa as a community activity. Or, I could have put aside my pedantic over-analysis aside and encouraged her to continue on her own, regardless of whether or not there was some aspect of getting some sort of inappropriate "juice" out of these guys asking her to dance. If she needed that, on some level, why not let her have it? At the very core of the matter, she genuinely did love to dance.

But we didn't choose any of those solutions. We let our life become smaller and both of us harbored resentment about it. We both lost. Instead of our relationship growing as a result of an opportunity (or challenge), we let our insecurities and baggage loom over the situation and as a result, the relationship got smaller and considerably less extraordinary.

She stopped dancing and before too long, as Metaphor would have it, so did we.

Compromise ends up being an integral part of any relationship, and there are different ways to go about it. Utilizing the aforementioned sense of fairness can be a delicate dance that can quickly turn into a power play. If you sense that happening, stop and consider ways to have it be a true compromise.

The next chapter includes a list of areas to consider including in your agreement. Some will apply, some are so obvious you may not have even thought about them, some will (hopefully) open up long discussions and then there are others that I haven't thought to include (but you can).

The Laundry List

Before diving into the list, I would recommend scanning over it in its entirety, paying close attention to those areas of greatest interest to you, whether for positive or negative reasons and to choose ten of them to plug into a prioritizing grid. The one I have found most useful was created by Richard Bolles in his brilliant book, "What Color is Your Parachute." His grid can be found in his book or you can access others by Googling "prioritizing grid." The reason behind this exercise is simply to find out what areas are most important to you going forth in relationship. This information will not only be enlightening to you, but especially to your partner.

Priorities
Relationship/Career/Family/Friends/Hobbies/Outside
     interests?

Relationship

Term?

Review Periods

Negotiation/renewal

Dissolution

Non-negotiables

Physical violence

Addiction

Infidelity

Illegal activity

Other

Rules of "Engagement"

Appearance (clothing, hair; decisions about)

Standards – expectations around how much travel and other luxuries

Communication

How to handle conflict/differences/break in agreement

Options for therapy/coaching/mediation

Requests for communication

If not now, person refusing schedules time?

"Going to bed angry"

Discussion of past

Temper, anger

Listening (vs fixing)

Willingness to give up being right to fully get the other's view

Marriage

Careers

General ambition and goals

Decision Making (Individual)

Decisions that impact both partners

Joining the military

Relocation

Selling assets

Changing religions

Relationship Rituals

      Ceremony

      Rings

      Name change

Life-changing events/circumstances

    Catastrophes

    Unexpected shit you never saw coming

Interests/activities/hobbies

    Community Service/volunteering

    New interests; individual/joint

    Television, video games, watching sports

    Outdoor activities

Behavior

    Support

    Drugs/alcohol, prescription

    Violence, abuse

    Personal safety

    Violence towards others

    Emotional abuse

      Defining

    Privacy

    Computer

    Journals

    Secrets

    Answering questions

    Withholding information

Outside relationships (Joint and Individual)

    Family

    Same sex

    Opposite sex

Emotional affairs

Jealousy

Behavior towards the opposite sex when partner is present and apart

Personal Growth

Relationship Growth

Option to consider regular coaching (or HOW is the relationship going to keep growing??)

Planning vs. seat-of-the-pants

Relationships with exes (including co-parents)

Sex /Intimacy

    Exclusivity or Open?

    Frequency

    Kinks/Aberrations

    Porn

    PDAs

Pet peeves

Gambling

Sense of humor

Teasing

Sarcasm

Name-calling

Values

Religion/spirituality/belief systems

Attitude – positive/upbeat or resigned/cynical

Biases

Living Arrangement

Cohabitation

Areas of responsibility

Cooking

Cleaning

Paying bills

Shopping

Home maintenance

Yard maintenance

Vehicle maintenance

Laundry

Entertainment

Technical

Separate homes

Shared time/location

Relocation

Change/goals?

Daily Life

Eating habits

Pets

Waking/sleeping schedules and conditions

Physical environment – temperatures, lighting

Daily routines

Standards for cleanliness - common area

Separate spaces / shared spaces

Time & Schedules

Alone time

Apart time

Conduct

Behaving as if the other person were there

Compromising the relationship/Inappropriate behavior

With opposite sex

Disclosure (don't ask/don't tell?) e-mails, texts?

Vacations

Holidays

Children

Yes/No

Birth Control

How many

When

How we handle birth defects

Adoption

Unwanted pregnancy

Last name

Parenting

Step parenting

Child Support

Defining age-appropriate boundaries

Secrets/ disclosures

Discipline strategies

Goals for children's lives

Daily care

Custody

Health/hygiene/medical

Bathing/deodorant (!)

Short-term illness

Medication

Mental Health

STDs / STD testing

Long-term illness/disability

Politics

Party Politics

Saving the planet

Voting

Financial, legal

> Major purchases (define amount)
>
> House title
>
> Car titles
>
> Ownership of property acquired during the relationship
>
> Loans/credit/debt
>
> Shared expenses
>
> Pre-nup?
>
> > Debts acquired prior to/after relationship
> >
> > Assets acquired prior to/after relationship
>
> Wills / estate executor
>
> DNR
>
> Power of Attorney
>
> Inheritance
>
> Insurance
>
> > Health
> >
> > Life
> >
> > Home
> >
> > Car
> >
> > Umbrella
> >
> > Beneficiaries
>
> Gifting
>
> Charity

IRS – Claiming deductions

Head of household

Taxes

Common Law States

Education, payment for, return on

Extended Family

Care for aging parents

Death

    Funeral/Cremation

ADDENDA (You add to the list...)

Quite an agenda, isn't it? And it's certainly not comprehensive. Here's another question: what, for you, is the most important item on the list? The opposite of a deal breaker: that which, for you, if that need is met, carries more weight than anything else. For some, this can overshadow everything else, for instance: a comfortable living situation, great sex, affection or creating and nurturing a family.

AND, what is most important to your partner? Because, this is your mission (should you decide to accept it) (this book will not self-destruct in 30 seconds, however...) You now know what is necessary to fulfill your partner's needs. It has been spelled out, literally.

I would suggest too, that there be a sense of lightness, even humor, in creating the contract.

For instance, here is a sample detail in the area of health and well-being:

We are each personally responsible for our own physical wellbeing while being open to suggestions from our partner about alternative care. We will maintain an attitude of wellness as the default. We'll communicate any ailments or discomforts. No ear coning for (________). No needles or hospitals or doctors for (__________) (unless bones are sticking out of her flesh).

(__________) does not want to be doted on when sick. (________), however, would be open to a reasonable amount of doting.

Medications are personal responsibility, but open to suggestion.

In case of emergency, call 911. No, really. In the event of hospitalization, (________________) will make sure (__________) is treated in the least invasive manner. No lobotomies. No life prolonging machines for (________). Brain dead? Pull the plug on either one of us!

Maybe that version is a little too flip for the two of you. But the creation of your agreement should not be an imposition. If this is a chore for one of you, it could mean that you are a seat-of-the-pants type who prefers for life to be more spontaneous. That is not only OK, but is information that is extremely valuable to your partner. On the other hand, if your partner is suggesting things be spelled out a bit more, that means details are important to them. Then the question becomes, "How do we compromise in all of this?

If your partner is vehemently resisting this process, it suggests that their life is just fine where it is: why upset the applecart? It suggests that person may be anticipating they are going to have to give up or do things they don't want to: their needs are being met and since when did you have needs!!? If that is the case, I suggest you get extremely clear on what your priorities are and how much of current behavior you are willing to accept.

This is more common in couples that have been together for a long time and life has settled into a predictable routine. In one case I know of, a woman was concerned that her husband was drinking beer all day on their yacht, every day, as well as overeating. When she sought to address these issues, he didn't want to hear about it.

How much can we read between the lines there? At the risk of generalizing, I'd be willing to bet there are issues of power, money, affluence, body image, sex, health and safety.

Usually, one person is exposed to this idea before the other and is maybe more invested in it, but let's say both parties are on board. There may be some new ground in all of this for one or both of you. So, pay attention to hemmingandhawing and footdragging; it signals an area of discomfort, but that may just be because it is new ground. Hopefully there IS new ground in this for both of you. That should be one of the reasons that the two of you are together: to GROW. Another area to remember though is that this is not Moses coming down from the Mount with the stone tablets. Remember, this is not about the contract itself; it is about the synergy of your relationship and what you are trying to create, together. There may end up being something new that doesn't feel right (ouch; you're on my hair!) but now you have a framework in place to communicate about that.

Re-negotiating/ Re-Upping

If you have considered/agreed on a term, made it through, and both of you want to continue, celebrate! Whether it's blind luck, compatibility, in the stars, cards, circumstance or hard work, you have gotten to a point where you want to remain as a couple. If your current agreement is working and firing on all cylinders, by all means, let it ride. Obviously, for the time being anyway, you have come across a system that works for both of you. If it ain't broke, don't fix it!

You may even want to consider upping the time period, but make sure there are check in times, just to make sure that you are allowing for changes or complacency.

Maybe things are going pretty well, for the most part, but there are some areas that need tweaking. If that is the case, it's time to get out those communication hats and sit down and renegotiate.

Maybe your agreement didn't include a term period. Regardless, it's not going as well as you would like. Or, things are just peachy for you, but your partner is feeling a bit, oh, let's say "less so"...

It's working, but maybe some things have changed...

Wait... CHANGE???!!!   What? You didn't sign up for that?

Well, sorry; change, probably more than anything, is what is going to make that whole matingforlife more challenging. Think about it; if everything stayed the same in your relationship as it was in that beginning, blissful, honeymoon stage, it would be easy for it all to last forever. But consider all the variables: first of all, outside influences. Yeah, all that external, reality stuff: the economy, politics, accidents, poor health, disaster, the weather! All the shit you have NO CONTROL OVER.

Then, compound that with internal change (Oh, no! Not internal change! Not growth!!!) and not just _your_ potential growth, but your partner's. Or, maybe yours and not theirs, or theirs and not yours (not sure which would be worse...)

How many times have you said this or had it said to you, in some form or another: "No, I don't want you to change..."?

Right. Total pat answer. When the reality is, if you have been with anyone else for any time past that honeymoon period, there's _something_ you would change about your partner if you could. Even if it's just that peskytoothpastesqeezingpreference (or those sloppy wet kisses). So, what if you were to straight out ask your partner what they would like for you to change? I know, right? Scary, because what if they told you what they actually felt? Like, really TOLD you? As in, actual, open, honest communication?

Here's the thing; people change ALL the time, but they hardly ever change because WE want them to. But, y'know; sometimes they do, given the proper motivation. YOUR responsibility, or expectation, for that matter, is not to change anyone. Your responsibility is to communicate to your partner what your wants and needs are, listen to what theirs are, decide if you are willing to fulfill those for your partner and then decide how much of your partner's shortcomings you are willing to accept.

Have you expressed what your deal breakers are?

You might discover something about yourself that you didn't even know that you might be perfectly willing to change. I was informed that I have a tendency to not close cabinet doors. OK, not a big deal, I know; but I was completely unaware that I was doing that. So, if I am unaware about THAT, what else am I doing blindly just out of habit that I would be willing to change? Of course, it begs the question, "What if she asks me to change something I don't WANT to change?"

You don't have to alter your behavior just because your partner is requesting it. You can always say "no." Or, maybe there is a compromise of some sort to work out. What you don't want to do is to get into a trading scenario.

I once promised, on a first date no less, to consider reversing my vasectomy in exchange for being able to watch NBA basketball any time I wanted. It made for a great, over-the-top-I-can't-believe-we-are-talking-about-this-on-a-first-date-conversation, but, seriously involved months later, I ended up being reminded of it. While I did very consciously consider it, I realized I would be doing it for the wrong reasons (unlimited NBA notwithstanding). And while I was being flip about that agreement on our first date, it was a very serious proposition when it came around the second time, an incredibly difficult decision to make, and ultimately, a deal breaker for her when I said "no."

As another, more serious example, (than the terrible innocuous noncabinetdoorclosing trait), it was pointed out to me how incredibly live-for-today I am. Now, I wasn't totally unaware of this trait in myself, because I AM a child of the 60's. When the Grassroots sang, "La la lalalala live for today..." I took it to heart. (For you Buddhists out there, you are saying, "Well, isn't that the way you're supposed to do it?" That treatise will NOT be covered within the scope of this book). And, as part of my adult version of myself, which IS by my own design; I LIKE that part of myself. I like smelling the roses, I like being in the moment, I like not planning every little thing. I like going to the grocery store without a list (cue that cartoon screeching tires sound). I don't want to have to think about what I am going to eat 5 days from now. My MO at the grocery is buy a bunch of stuff I like, in that moment, (doesn't the salmon look great today?) and eventually, it'll all get eaten.

What's the downside to that? Very often, the one thing I went to the store to GET, I forget.

One partner I had, on the other hand, HATED going to the supermarket. She would plan the entire menu for the week, and have an ongoing list. The upside? Nothing was EVER forgotten. The downside? I might not be in the mood for rice and beans next Thursday.

Was her position valid? Sure. First of all, a list is a great tool for not forgetting things (I just have to remember to make one, first of all, then remember to bring it with me, and then remember to consult it when I am at the store, which is a lot of work, yes, but worth it so that I don't forget the sour cream for the Beef Stroganoff, for instance...) but then, just because there is a list, it doesn't mean that I can't take advantage of the salmon looking really fresh.

Salmon aside, for someone who is a planner, my cavalier attitude towards the future can be exasperating. What about retirement? (What? Retirement? That's for old people... Oh...)

The obvious solution is compromise. And there are different ways to compromise. There is the compromise where you meet in the middle (we can bring a list, but it doesn't have to be carved in stone) OR compromise where it is done one person's way and the other person has to accept it (YOU are going to the store, with your list and I will eat rice and beans whether I want to or not OR I will go to the store and dinner will be a surprise and something might be forgotten).

One of the best books I have read surrounding this kind of compromise (and understanding, and resultant acceptance) is "One of Us is Crazy, and I Am Pretty Sure It's YOU." Not only do the authors, Tim and Joy Downs, provide revealing insights into personality types and WHY we argue, but they give some sound advice on how to stop that cycle and get yourselves REALLY communicating.

Here's another very common example: you start going out and the two of you are like two rutting wild boars in heat. Twice a day, every day. Well, guess what? That's not going to continue, and at some point, one of you says some version of, "Not tonight, honey; I have a headache."

Beginning of the end, right? If that kind of sexual gluttony is a priority for you, it just may be. But would you be willing to accept once a day every day? How about every other day, with an afternoon quickie on Sunday? How about twice a week and you agree to put your hand down his pants when he's doing the dinner dishes? (Sounds like a win-win to me...) This particular example, around sex, is a major bone of contention between partners with conflicting sex drives, and it's not always the men that are wanting more. If this is a high priority for you, and I mean HIGH priority, this needs to be communicated and an agreement worked out about how that need is going to be met when it changes (and it will).

I am not suggesting that your relationship starts to look like a scene from a New Delhi bazaar where you are bartering to get your every need met. Very simply; go in to give, be committed to what you are bringing to the table, and know what you are willing to accept in your partner's behavior.

Another way to look at this is that instead of your partnership being the "traditional" 50-50. Strive to have it be 100-100. I know that adds up to 200%, but we are shooting for extraordinary here, aren't we?

What happens, though, in a situation where the two of you are beyond compromise and you are locked in a stalemate?

In any relationship that is struggling, there comes a point when there is an evaluation of sorts that comes down to a basic "isthisworthstickingaroundfor? kind of decision. Whether you do a pros/cons type of comparison or assign a percentage to it (this is one of my personal favorites for decisions of any type; i.e. on a scale of 0-100 percent, how much do I want to attend this Shakespeare Festival? 95/5? (5% to catch up on some nap time?) So, more specifically as it relates to staying or going in the relationship, what percentage, what part of me, wants to stay? I find this to be a good starting point for those of us who like to quantify. But then it helps to *qualify* also. For instance, let's say that 70 percent of the time, things are going OK, or even very well. But the other 30 percent is spent in conflict that is just awful: soul-swallowing, down and dirty fighting coupled with sleepless nights. Quantitatively, 70/30 sounds pretty good, but what if that conflict is bone-crushingly awful? And what if you are conflict avoidant (YOU, reader, not me; we already know where I stand on that...) Is that enough to call it quits?

To me, this came down to (alright, it WAS about me, but maybe you can identify with this...) a quality of life issue. To me, to be arguing and at odds 30 percent of the time was WAY too far removed from extraordinary relationship. So here is part of the beauty of having a contract. What are you fighting about? Is this something that was covered in the agreement? Is someone not holding up their end of the bargain, or is this something new that has come up that neither of you could have anticipated? If it was considered as part of the original agreement, the dialog has already been started. One of you has committed to a certain set of rules or behavior and they are not adhering? Why not? There may be a perfectly good reason that could change the way you end up framing how you feel about it.

If it is important enough to dialog or redialog about, you may want to consider ahead of time, "How important is this?" Is this potentially a deal breaker? If this behavior continues, is it grounds for termination?

Let's talk about dissolving the agreement. There may be terms in the contract about non-negotiables; those acts or behavior that are grounds for immediate voiding of the contract (for some, infidelity, or physical abuse, but it really comes down to what you both decide). As human beings, we are capable of tolerating anything. Truthfully, anything, no matter how heinous, given the proper incentive. So, really, we make choices about what we are willing to accept in another's behavior. How do we communicate that?

Communication 101 tells us that we should stay away from "you" statements, name-calling and overgeneralizing ("You selfish idiot; you never meet any of my needs" is probably not your most effective way to start this conversation).

The time structure of a contract gives us a tool, though, for negotiating those behaviors that have become or are approaching, non-acceptable status. Let's take a couple that include social drinking as part of their accepted behavior, but one of the partners has begun to exhibit problem behavior associated with over-imbibing. And let's say it is getting serious; drunken driving, verbal abuse, maybe even physical abuse, health issues. For some individuals, some of that behavior would be non-negotiable. For others, it could represent a situation where their partner really needs their help and support to help through a difficult time. Let's say a couple is on a one year contract, and this drinking problem has reached proportions that warrant a serious discussion that could become deal breaking. If it is coming close to the end of the contract, the conversation could go something like this, "I am concerned about your drinking getting serious and your behavior around it is affecting our relationship. This is VERY serious to me, in a way that, if it is to continue, I will not re-up our contract to continue as a couple."

I realize that this is not a simple subject. Substance abuse is an extremely difficult problem that has many layers: physiological, psychological and social. My early exposure to the perils of this issue (Mom, Dad, would you like to stand up and take a bow?) has made me realize the value of early and open communication around this BEFORE it becomes a problem. I also understand the level of denial that usually exists around addiction of any sort. It is very likely that outside help will be required in dealing with any addiction problem. It is important to realize when anyone gets addicted to anything, that behavior is filling a very strong need for them. There are also those out there that have a compulsive side to their behaviors, and are more prone to addiction. All-or-nothing approaches can be rechanneled into very productive avenues. One of my real life heroes went from a debilitating cocaine addiction to creating a successful business that he would not give up on through the hardest times. Perseverance can carry over to relationship too. If someone can channel addictive tendencies to relationship, they will never quit.

One person's polar thinking is another person's perseverance.

This is also a good time to look at the threat of not re-upping as a negotiation tool. For me, throughout this whole process of creating an agreement, ideally there is a foundation of openness, honesty and integrity. In the spirit of all of those, I would contend that manipulation through idle threat is not a path to follow here; that is a low level approach to conducting a relationship.

But, what if not wanting to go forward is a serious consideration?

No Mas   (Gotta throw in a little Español for all my years in Santa Fe...)

If you end up spending the rest of your life with one person, by definition, that will be the last relationship you will ever have. If you are like most people, you didn't marry the first person you got involved with or engage in a life of wedded bliss, so it stands to reason that you have had relationships end before. While it may seem like the end of the world at the time, you now know that it isn't.

The premise behind relationship agreement is the same for marriage; you have a contract, you have agreed to DO something, now do it. Hopefully, there is enough interest by at least one of the parties to continue up until the end of the term (if a term is part of your agreement). But what if there isn't? Well, if BOTH parties want out, that indicates that there probably wasn't enough communication in the beginning to anticipate what could go wrong. Or, maybe it was SO passionate that the blinders were on, all the flags were up, your conscious, rational mind was saying, "Uh, dude, really...?" But you went ahead anyway (not that I have ever done this, mind you...) That being said, life does have a way of presenting minor molehills that can turn into what seem like insurmountable mountains that you no longer want to climb.

So, when DO we end it? When do circumstances cross over into the realm of not acceptable? Let's look at the concept of acceptance. This perspective comes to me as a result of a recorded seminar on relationship by Steve and Nancy of the Landmark Forum. One of the ideas put forth is that we are 100% responsible for accepting our partners.

Or not accepting them.

They are who they are, and our part in the relationship is to either accept them or not. They suggest that as humans, we can choose to accept anything. Anything. And when you start to think about it, it's true. You can think about the most monstrous behavior of another human, and you can come up with a scenario where you would accept that in them if it somehow serves your other needs.

That brings us around to personal responsibility. Here is what I propose: that you don't go into this (either of you) promising "I will do this if you do that." But rather that you go into it saying "I am committed to doing this. This is MY end of the bargain. 100%."

But what if you bring your 100%, your partner does not and that is not acceptable to you?

What can happen that is immediate "grounds for termination?" What may seem obvious to some may not be to others. Physical violence? Some couples see that as conflict resolution. Cheating? Not in an "open" relationship, and maybe allowable as an unspoken arrangement. Addiction? Maybe, but might you want to help your partner through something like that? If both partners are indulging, then it is just part of daily life. Illegal activities? Might be OK if you don't get caught. Taking a job in another city or country? Maybe, maybe not.

Suppose you run into something as a couple that you hadn't anticipated. This can happen even with couples that have been together for a while but it is a lot more common with two individuals that are still getting to know each other. Even with the very best of intentions, I have seen the whole ball of yarn unravel. Let's say, in the full spirit of this new paradigm, two people go into an agreement situation disclosing, in good faith, how they see themselves, but in that subjective view, some of the "dark side" gets omitted. And slowly but surely, that shadow starts to reveal itself.

Hopefully that has been communicated along the way, before the end of the agreement. And if it was, and your needs are still not being met, and it is grounds for non-renewal, so be it. But if you do what you said you were going to do, that's all you can do, and you can walk away knowing that you held up your end of the bargain, and the fact that the other did not is unacceptable.

When Barb and I first created our relationship contract, we inadvertently stopped short of discussing our modes of conflict resolution. What I realized before too long was that I wanted harmony while she thought it was perfectly OK to not only fight, but rage about what seemed to be total non-issues to me. I was hoping to show her a different perspective from the abusive relationships she had experienced in the past.

The first incident precipitated one morning when she raged at me for being in the same general area of the house as the bathroom she was using. This was in my house, btw, as I was getting our second cup of coffee to share in bed on a Sunday morning. That was the first red flag for me.

At that point, it seemed as though her anger towards men in general started to be directed at me and I actually said to myself, 'Take her punches; they are not intended for you.' (Understand, I was referring to verbal blows, both psychological and emotional. But, yeah, I really said that).

And I did. For a while, when I was in my highest place.

The second time occurred after we had just spent a week together in a cabin in the woods. We were preparing to go back home and I got a call from a male friend who wanted to get together.

She was vehemently not in favor of this: "I'm not ready to give you up yet!"

It turned into a huge fight. I made the mistake in that instance of acquiescing to her original stance and not going to meet my friend (meanwhile resenting it).

And when we got back home, words got said in anger that couldn't be taken back and we broke up.

She was not willing to accept any responsibility for her rages; I was "causing them," and they were simply her "getting upset." What was her way of communicating amounted to verbal abuse to me and it was a deal breaker. I was not willing to have that quality of life, I was not willing to walk around on eggshells, wondering when the next rage was coming on. Ultimately it was more important to her to be her passionate self than to have me around. So, I had to create that boundary, express it and then follow it up by leaving.

It was all very dramatic, since I had been spending a lot of time at her place and it had progressed beyond just having a toothbrush there; I had my own space in the walk-in closet, books scattered about and underwear mixed in with the laundry. In the moment of that decision, soundlessly, we scurried about (oh yes, she was "helping"; she wanted me out as much as I wanted to be gone) gathering up any evidence of my quasi-cohabitation. It looked like we were trying to cover up a crime scene; it's a wonder we didn't wipe down fingerprints. Isn't it interesting too how something is always forgotten, some article, some shred of evidence that turns up later to remind us that, yes, that DID actually happen, we WERE together? Interesting too is how, depending on your perspective at that point, how those boxer briefs that got flung behind the dresser or those cotton balls under the bathroom vanity can be either a sad reminder or a welcome relief about what once had been.

I think it is safe to say neither one of us was in our highest place.

The next day, I don't remember if she called me or vice versa, but in the cool gray light of dawn, it seemed to both of us that we had made a mistake. It was probably me that called; Barbara was never one to admit she was wrong (nor was "I'm sorry" a sentence that ever slipped past her lips), but she did agree that maybe we had been a bit rash in ending it so abruptly.

We decided to extend our contract for another three months and then re-evaluate at that time to see if we wanted to continue. While our relationship was only about 5 months long at that time, we both felt like there was enough working between us to continue.

Things were back to "normal," not being really sure what that was between us, but we were on our best behavior. I remember Barb saying something to that effect, which I guess to her meant that she was trying to corral that bucking stallion that would rise up in her. For my part, I was committed to not doing anything that might let the bronco out of the chute.

We tried, but it didn't go far enough, we weren't being ourselves, and when on vacation she decided to come after me because I neglected to wait for her crossing a deserted six lane boulevard in a foreign country, citing that as proof that I didn't love her, I knew we were back in trouble.

Once we got back home and sat down to talk about it, I had two questions for her: "Are you willing to accept any responsibility for your rages?" and "Are you willing to go to couple's counseling with me?"

Her answer to both was "No."

Me: "Then we're done."

Her: "Well, pack your stuff and get out."

Silence.

Deafening fucking silence.

So I got up off the couch and proceeded to pack up my shit.

Again.

I had told her that I was not going to do on-again, off-again. So this was it.

I would have persevered if I had gotten a "Yes" to either of those questions, but clearly, that was not forthcoming. So I left. Again. And for good.

Was that the "best" decision for us? Well, we'll never know, will we? Maybe if that packingthestuffandgettingoutofDodge part had been delayed, she might have considered that maybe counseling WOULD have worked. And I might have factored in those aspects of the relationship that *were* working.

But no; we went ahead and made a decision in the heat of the moment. In the section above, I went on a bit of a rant about honoring a contract. In this case, we still had time to go on our extension. But she said get out and I did. And I guess we could have called the next day and patched it up, when cooler heads were prevailing. But I didn't and neither did she.

I thought I could get her to change. I thought that by presenting her with the promise of a relationship that was considerate and giving that I could heal all the wrongs that my gender had heaped on her. I realize now that was not my responsibility. But the caveat was that she was going to have to change: and in the meantime (and it was Mean Time) I was going to have to be the whipping boy for all that past hurt, coupled with her contention that *our* problems were all *mine*, it became non-negotiable.

I paid a huge price for leaving that relationship. Not only were there parts of the relationship that were gratifying, but I had all of my eggs in her basket and was in a place where I was dedicated to making it work. When I decided to leave, my life was turned upside down but it wasn't like I didn't anticipate it. In retrospect, that was simply the amount of time we were going to spend together. Did that relationship "not work?" It certainly didn't last, despite how "conscious" we were about trying to make it extraordinary. I think we both grew as a result of being together and we had some wonderful times. That was just as far as we were going to go.

When I packed up my stuff (again) and left, I was in shock, even though I was the one leaving. And at the time, I was so full of adrenaline and whatever else that I was celebrating: "That's right;

fuck this fucking shit. I don't have to put up with this. I'm better off by myself. I didn't sign up for THIS!!!"

Yeah, well... the next day reality kicked in and I realized what I had done; I had gone back on my promise to BE THERE.

Then I quickly got defensive; wasn't she going back on HER promise? (Wait... was she? Did she promise not to rage, or did I just really hope she wouldn't?) It doesn't matter; I had gone back on MY promise: to be there when it got hard. And I knew, on some level, that things had gotten out of hand, and that we should take it up another day, but did I listen to that voice? That voice of reason? That voice of compassion?

Nope. I went straight to fight or flight. Actually, I got a two-fer: I fought AND fled!

Maybe we should have taken a time out, or I should have "taken a step back" instead of walking away.

Let's look at stepping back. It has been my experience that very little ever gets solved in a highly emotional state. The problem ends up being that when we are agitated, it's very hard to make rational judgments about what we should do or not do. And so we react. And often react in a way that addresses old needs in old ways. But we are trying to create a new way, aren't we?

Aren't we?

So, how could this have been different? (I once actually had that question presented to me by my then five year old daughter who had been taught conflict resolution in her pre-K class. I know, right?)

Somebody has to have the presence of mind to stop the downward spiral. And we are not used to doing that, but we HAVE to get used to it! We *gotta* learn how to argue, we *gotta* learn how to have differences of opinion, we *gotta* learn how to say no, we *gotta* learn to listen and then, sometimes be willing to say, "You're right;

I never saw it that way before," and other times learn to say, "I hear what you are saying, but I still disagree."

And have all of that be OK.

(No wonder there are so few extraordinary relationships out there; this shit is HARD!)

Bottom line here is: if you have an agreement, go beyond your very best to honor it. If something comes up that needs renegotiation, renegotiate it. If something comes up that is so dreadful that you couldn't even imagine it going into a contract because it's so, well, heinous, that's a different story Extreme abuse, for instance. And alright, let's look at that concept: "extreme abuse." I was originally going to write "abuse." In the situation with Barbara, I quit because I felt like I was being verbally abused. Was I? It sure felt like I was; I mean, after the way my parents fought all the time, and I promised to never have a relationship like that. Was she being abusive? Not in her mind. She was being passionate. She was angry. She wanted to make sure that she could vent. That she could be heard. And that is how she was used to doing that. Abuse? It depends on which side you're on. I've known other people that have had those "passionate" relationships where they would fight and yell and then have great make-up sex. And it was all "business-as-usual." They would probably look at my scenario and wonder what the big deal was. But that's the whole point; in your couples' agreement, you mutually create the boundaries that you will operate under.

Were Barb and I a good match? Fuck no. In retrospect, I'm glad I finally left. Could I have done more? Probably, but I decided I had had enough.

What is "enough?" The question to ask at that point is, "Have I done everything I can to make this extraordinary?" Because at the end of the day, our own actions and behavior are all we can control (apologies to all you "manifestors" and control freaks out there; I'm sure you will take me to task on that last statement. You create it ALL, don't you, even the perfect mate? And how's all of that going, by the way? I would argue that for all of those that get their "created" outcomes, there is probably an equal amount that don't. How do you feel about a 50/50 chance?)

Are you meeting your partner's needs? You know, the ones that she has TOLD you she would like satisfied. Maybe you have. Remember "givers" and "takers"?

This is the type of relationship that eventually comes down to the "Incredulous Breakup." Tell me if this sounds familiar (from either standpoint): "What???!!! What do you mean you want to break up? It's going so well!" For those of you on the "taking" side of that scenario, may I suggest Empathy Camp, or even starting with Listening 101.

For those of you on the giving end; you have to decide if living your entire life for others is working for you. If it is, great, but then, you probably wouldn't be reading this book if it were working so well. On a limited basis, it CAN work. But if EVERYTHING you are doing in your life is for others, it's not healthy, it's not balanced, and ultimately, it's not going to work.

Are you taking care of yourself at all?

That's right; figure out what it is that YOU want or need, and figure out how to get it.

Wait; WHAT??!! Tried that? Asked for some attention, didn't get it? Went out and had an affair instead? Ok, maybe that's a bit extreme, not to mention counterproductive, but it got you out, didn't it? Ah, conscious living at its best... Alright, so maybe you regret that one; chalk it up to another of those fucking growth opportunities, but c'mon; is this how you are going to live the rest of your life?

I was once in a relationship I wanted to end that I described to my partner as "not good enough." I thought I was being kind in describing the relationship that way as opposed to HER not being good enough.

Nice try. Good intentions and all that. What she heard was "YOU'RE not good enough." All of my effort towards proper language and effective communication were for naught; she was hurt. The bottom line is that despite our intentions, sometimes our communications are going to fall short. But that can't stop us; we have to do the very best we can. How many times have we stayed "too long" in a relationship because we were "afraid" of hurting our partner's feelings? The question often becomes, "How long is too long?"

With Rita, I was at a point in my life when I felt like perseverance was the key to success, and I felt that there had been times where I had quit too early, so I stayed, and tried, on-again and off-again, to make it work. Five times. Did I stay too long? Well, maybe, but I am glad that we tried for as long as we did. The best part of this was that when we were finally done (and I mean DONEdone,) we KNEW we were done; there were no maybes about it. We both sprinted away from that one.

But still, let's pause here to look at that statement: "make it work." What does that mean? "Make it last?" "Make it better?" "Make it good enough?"

I had had enough awareness at that point in my personal development to consider "extraordinary relationship" with her. THAT'S what I was shooting for, and time after time, I felt like I kept coming up short. And then I realized the problem: I wasn't coming up short, WE were. She didn't have the same vision of what that was that I did. It was who we were together that we were struggling with. We had our good moments, it wasn't abusive but we both wanted more. Part of the problem was that her version of "more" was different from my version of "more."

But too often, we don't get to that place of the relationship (or our partners) crossing the line into non-negotiable, and we end up in a relationship that is just barely "good enough." And too often, that is better than being alone, so we stay. And it never gets any better.

Confused yet? There are those who argue that confusion is good, because you are considering different options. Yeah, well I am here to tell you that, around relationship, and whether or not it should go forward, confusion SUCKS!

"What if I leave and that's the wrong decision?"

My perspective around "right" and "wrong" decisions is, in the moment, neither assessment exists. That judgment can only be made when you get to the future and see the outcome.

And then it's too late.

So, basically, around decision making, we're screwed. All I can say is, gather up as much information as you can, ask yourself if you've done your due diligence (then actually DO it), decide, and then OWN IT. As the future becomes the present, take responsibility for the outcome, for as much of that as you can. That is to say, again, we have to make decisions constantly without fully knowing what the result will be. How many times have we made a decision, some other factor gets involved that we had no idea about, and we end up thinking, "Well, if I had known THAT, I never would have made that decision"? The New Jersey lottery used to have a slogan that said, "You can't win if you don't play." And that is true. Every lottery winner EVER has bought a ticket. So, in relationship, you gotta buy a ticket, you gotta engage, you gotta play.

Let me go back to the "gather all the information you can part" because that is a place where a lot of us get stuck. It is easy to get caught in the trap of not wanting to make the "wrong" decision. One of the tools that helped me when I was having to make one of those potentially "wrong" relationship decisions was a book by Mira Kirshenbaum called "Too Good to Leave, Too Bad to Stay. The sub-title is, "A Step-by-Step Guide to Help You Decide Whether to Stay in or Get Out of Your Relationship." And it IS step-by-step. She asks probing, yet empowering questions that provide genuine clarity into what your priorities are and how it all stacks up, including the all-important "What is this going to realistically look like if I DO leave?"

Like in so many other life situations, the only factor we have control over is how we conduct ourselves: our thought processes and our behavior. Kirshenbaum's book is one of the best tools I have seen in getting the clarity necessary to make what is usually a life-altering decision. But I will argue it's not about the end result, but the journey, how you walk the path and who you are becoming.

If you end up going your separate ways, that means that even if the relationship was extraordinary for a while, then it became so much less so that now you either have to start over or live alone.

Well, right...

I never promised you a rose garden.

And this applies to walking away too. In that same spirit of openness, honesty, integrity and personal responsibility, can we add dignity to the list? It amazes me that so often, two people that once professed (and promised) to love each other can get to such of point of rancor, venom and even hate. I think it often gets to that point because of poor communication skills and arguments that get out of hand where things get said and done that are hurtful and irreparably harmful.

Remember, you can still care for someone very much and not want to partner with them. Hey, maybe your relationship should be less involved. Maybe the two of you are better off NOT living together: having your own separate places. Maybe the sex is good and nothing else. Why not just be lovers?

But look; if you did your best and so did he and it didn't work, at least you both gave it your best shot. And if you gave it your best and he didn't, you have to come to terms with the fact that you had no control over his behavior. I'd be willing to bet that there were some extraordinary moments though, because YOU created them, and that's as much as you can ask.

For some, ending it is quitting. And I have to agree, up to a point. I know a married man who was having an affair that he knew was destructive on numerous levels. But he kept going because, as he put it, "I don't know when to quit." He was being rhetorical, but looking at it objectively, from the outside, it was true; he literally didn't know when to quit. It was easy for me to look at his situation and see that he had passed a point long ago when he should have thrown in the towel. Unfortunately, it's much easier to make that decision for someone else than ourselves. For him, he still had his wife to go back to. But what if he didn't? What if he ended that affair and unbeknownst to him, in the arrogance of Icangetawaywithanything, his wife knew about the affair and now wouldn't take him back? And he was going to have to be, y'know...

alone?

Being Alone

Wait; this is a book about relationships. Why talk about being alone? Well, the reason we are creating this new paradigm is that, as incredible as you are, you may come across a partner who just doesn't recognize your gifts and you may find yourself "in between" relationships. And it doesn't matter who broke it off; you are still alone.

My recommendation?

Celebrate! You have no one to answer to now. You can do whatever you want. You can hang that toilet paper on the towel rack if you want; it doesn't matter. Maybe you want to wallow, if you got dumped (but for some of us, being the dumper can be even worse). Sure, go ahead and wallow, for a while. But make it a short while; don't wallow in the wallowing. I have a friend divorced after a 20 year marriage. That's a long time. After 20 years, you gotta figure it's going all nine innings. SHE ended up leaving, because he became a problem drunk and wouldn't fix it. But when she was out, she said that it was going to take her 5 years to get over the break, because that's how long "they" say it takes.

I think you can see where I am going with this. If you think it's going to take 5 years, it's gonna take 5 years. Hey, if you WANT it to take 5 years, that's one thing, and that's valid. But just be clear about what you want and don't complain about being alone if that is not what you want. That horse is out there to get back on if you're ready to mount (sorry...)

Here's another quote from Jeff Brown:

"Because of all the pressure to be partnered, so many people walk around feeling badly if they are on their own, and many others stay where they don't belong for fear that they will be seen as a failure outside of relationship. Surely all of this misses the point. What is most important is that each of us lives a life that is true to path, whatever that means to us. For some, their sacred purpose is inextricably linked to love relationship. It is there that they excavate and humanifest their deepest meaning. Yet others are called in a different direction and find their purpose in their creative life, in their work, in their individual spiritual practice. Everyone's soul-scriptures are unique to their own journey. The important thing in life is not whether we find the "one," but whether we find the path. Peace with path. It's that simple.

Peace with path."

Instead of bemoaning your solitude, consider that it may be a path for you, even if you have gone your whole life coupled with someone else. You don't have to go complete "Uncle Alex" on us, but maybe being joined at the hip is not the best way for you to go. Figuring that out will require some self-examination, and the good news is; now you have the time to do it.

Let's face it; some people aren't cut out for coupledom; you may be one of them. You may like not having to answer to anybody, and there is nothing wrong with that, not under this new paradigm. Or, you can decide that your newfound solitude is just a transition period before you go out and create the relationship you have always wanted.

WHEN IT'S ALL SAID AND DONE

Having worked in the high end jewelry business, I had the opportunity to observe lots of couples interacting in their "natural habitat." On the surface, adorning one's self can be looked at as a vain endeavor, but once we dig beneath the surface there are a lot of levels to that embellishment: attractiveness to others (both same and opposite gender), personal confidence, self-esteem, feelings of indulgence and even power. While we sold both men's and women's jewelry, most of our clients were women. We had big easy chairs for those husbands that didn't want to engage in this activity that was obviously important to their partners. Very often, they were there just to give "permission" for their wives to be able to consummate their purchase. That was often an interesting manipulation in and of itself. There were those too, that were locked in power plays, with the husband having to approve a purchase seemingly based on aesthetics alone, when really it was based on him being the boss, regardless of how much the wife liked a certain item. I had one couple argue in the store about a purchase; even though she loved the necklace, he wouldn't "allow" her to buy it. They left, empty-handed and at odds, only for her to return later and buy exactly what she wanted.

On the other hand, for those couples that bought jewelry "together," it became another way to connect.

Him: "Wow; that looks beautiful on you. It makes your eyes look even greener."

Or her: "I only want to get this if you love it; I want to look beautiful for you."

It got to where I could tell which relationships were healthy, based on their interactions in our store. It was a little game I would play: "Rate the Relationship."

While working in a jewelry store can seem mundane, for me, as a student of human behavior especially in how couples interact, it gave me an opportunity to dissect a joint activity and apply that to how that partnership is working. Often, couples would come in looking for anniversary gifts, which would invariably elicit the question, "How long have you been together?" Not that longevity for me any longer is the barometer of relationship success, but I always found it interesting to hear responses to the follow up question, "What is the secret of your relationship success?"

We can all stand to learn something from those that have come before us, in their positive example or otherwise. One husband responded, "I'm away a lot," and while that prompted some chuckles, it made me wonder about whether that was more about absence making the heart grow fonder or whether he was getting his needs met elsewhere. Another couple had been married for 58 years. The wife was a pistol. With a twinkle in her eye, she described her husband as her "sugar daddy." He good-naturedly went along with it and bought her a bracelet for her aged, withered pencil-thin arm. They left the store leaving a wake of warm and fuzzys behind.

I met Stoney sitting at the corner of a circular bar eating dinner. Now in his 90's, he approached the bar laboriously, took his seat and proceeded to open his MacAir and type away. At some point, he engaged us in conversation and, completely unsolicited, proceeded to tell us about his marriage to Dorothy.

They met in Pasadena, CA in 1941 at the Civic Auditorium where Benny Goodman was playing a dance concert. Despite having taken dance lessons Stoney had never asked a girl to dance before. He chose whom he considered the most beautiful young woman up on the stage to be his first. As it turned out, Dorothy was quite the dancer, a professional, and knew all the latest dances, including the jitterbug. At the end of that night, Stoney asked her out again and she said, "Well, you have halitosis and you can't dance, but sure, I'll see you again."

In all their later years of dancing, she would always lead. After a year, they eloped and worked together at Goodrich Rubber in the war effort.

Dorothy had passed away three months prior to our meeting Stoney that night after 69 years of marriage. Sometimes even bad breath and two left feet cannot stop the progress of true love.

One of my favorite couples had been married for 23 years, but it was a second marriage for both of them. Beth explained that when they got together in their mid-forties, they decided to go in with no assumptions: "tabula rasa" as she described it. And they decided to look at what they had done in their prior relationships and take forward what had worked and leave behind what didn't. What a concept (someone oughta write a book...) She used the words "proactive" and "positive."

"But more than anything," she said, "we really like each other, and there is a certain gladness we have around that."

"Gladness." I found that to be an interesting choice of language. To me, that speaks to an appreciation, not just of each other, but of the relationship itself. And if there is a common thread in all of the success stories it is that: appreciation. Appreciation not just for the other, but for what the two of you have together, the union. So, it stands to reason that if you are going to appreciate someone, you have to respect them, even admire them. Which means finding a partner that, in your perception, is at least as high as you or maybe even above you on the hierarchy scale. Which then means that you had better keep growing and evolving to continue to qualify for that person. It's not a magic formula; there are circumstances that can come up that can throw the whole thing in the shitter and there is an element of luck and serendipity in all of it. But hey; that's what makes it so much fun!

Happy Endings

There is no magic formula for success in this new paradigm. In any decision, we take what information we have and we go forward, as adults, and accept the consequences. Unfortunately, all that ends up being a bit of a crapshoot when we don't know what the outcome will be. The problem is, we are often faced with ultimatums that either require us to make a choice or have it made for us. Hopefully we learn from our mistakes and the mistakes of others. That is why I have included the stories here that I have: to come up with ways to create deeper, more profound relationships.

I have always pursued long term relationship; I have never gone into a relationship thinking, "Ah, I'll just stick around for as long as it's fun." But now my perspective has changed. I don't <u>assume</u> it will last, but I still WANT it to; it's my nature. So I'm going to do everything in my power to make it extraordinary.

Jeannine Callea Stamatakis, a psychotherapist and psychology instructor, wrote in 2011 in Scientific American MIND,

"A range of nonbiological factors can help pinpoint which pairings are built to last—those who communicate openly, respect each other, share common interests and maintain a close friendship, even when the intense attraction wanes."

Those are certainly good places to start, as well as the relationship being a priority for both partners. So, pick an extraordinary partner. I know; not always easy, but have it be a priority and not just based on physical attraction but those qualities that matter in the long run, whatever those are for you. Even more importantly, BE a good partner: the very best you can be. Communicate: be courageous in that, go beyond your comfort zone.

Give.

FORgive, in those times when your partner falls short. And this forgiveness should be not so much in the big transgressions, but the little ones: the forgotten anniversary, the omitted "I-love-you," the stolen glance at an attractive woman, a joke that hit a sore spot. Not that the big ones shouldn't be forgiven as well, but that should lead to another discussion about whether or not that behavior will be accepted and/or repeated.

Referring to Dr. Morris May again,

> "Forgiveness, according to my father, Dr. Archibald Hart, is defined as 'giving up my right to hurt you back.'"

When I first read that, I had to think about it. Is that right? But yeah, you hurt me and at least a part of me wants to hurt you back. And yes, through an "eye-for-an-eye" perspective, I have a right to do that. But, in true forgiveness, I am consciously choosing to not do that. For the good of the relationship. It's an interesting perspective that I had not considered before.

Have faith in all of this: trusting that you WILL achieve favorable outcomes, forgive yourself when you don't get all of the ones you want, and forgive others too, because, after all, we are all just out there trying our best to get our needs met.

That's all we can do: our very best. It begs the question, when it all looks like it's going south, "Have I done everything I can?" That ends up being somewhat of an unquestion to yourself, because it could be argued that you can always do more, you can STAY, you can tolerate, you can "know" that it's going to get better, you can let yourself be abused, you can turn a blind eye to the fact that your life sucks, all because you have bought into the idea of everlasting love. So maybe that is not a fair question. Maybe a better question is, "Have I done everything I am *willing* to do to make this an extraordinary relationship?" And maybe you have and it IS extraordinary. For your partner, that is, but not you. Then you have to make a choice about whether or not that is the way you are going to live the rest of your life. Maybe you like being a martyr. Maybe you like always doing for others and that makes you feel so good about yourself that all else is secondary. That is valid. Is it enough though?

Ultimately, your decision may end up being that the relationship has run its course, and as painful and heart-wrenching as that may be, it is not the end of the world; it does NOT make you a failure. Maybe you are better off by yourself: unfettered, footloose, not having to answer to anyone else. I would suggest that both of those perspectives should end up being part of this new paradigm.

What I am proposing is that you make conscious choices about how you move forward. And then allow for the idea that it is all subject to change and that your transformation can come from outside sources, your partner, or even from you. At the pace that our modern world is spinning, that shift is much more likely to happen than in generations past. We need to make allowances for that, and somehow maintain our humanity and our compassion.

So, be more conscious, be more giving and loving and kind. Put yourself on the list of those you take care of.

And although at times it is more of a challenge than others, live as *happily* as you can.

And maybe, just maybe, *"ever after"* will take care of itself.

RECOMMENDED READING

Branden, Nathaniel The Six Pillars of Self Esteem Bantam 2011

The Psychology of Romantic Love Penguin 1980

Chapman, Gary The Five Love Languages Northfield 2010

Collins, Susie and Otto www.passionate heart.com

Deida, David The Way of the Superior Man Sounds True 2004

Downs, Tim and Joy One of Us Must be Crazy... and I'm Pretty Sure It's YOU Moody 2003

Friday, Nancy Jealousy William Morrow 1985

Gottman, John Ph. D. and Nan Silver The Seven Principles for Making Marriage Work: A Practical Guide from the Country's Foremost Relationship Expert Harmony 2015

Hendix, Harville Getting the Love You Want Henry Holt and Co. 1988

Kirshenbaum, Myra Too Good to Leave, Too Bad to Stay Dutton 1996

Manson, Mark The Subtle Art of Not Giving a F*ck Harper Collins 2016

May, Sharon Morris Ph. D. How to ARGUE So Your Spouse Will Listen Thomas Nelson 2007

Mckay, Matthew, Ph.D & Patrick Fanning Self Esteem MJF 2000

Patterson, Kerry with Joseph Grenny, Ron McMillan and Al
    Switzler Crucial Conversations: Tools for Talking When
    the Stakes Are High McGraw Hill 2002

Peck, M. Scott The Road Less Traveled   Simon and Schuster 1978

Puhn, Laurie   Fight Less, Love More   Rodale 2010

Robbins, Anthony   Awaken the Giant Within   Fireside 1991

Ryan, Christopher and Cacilda Jetha   Sex at Dawn   HarperCollins
2012

Sills, Judith, Ph. D.   The Power of No   Psychology Today,
November/December 2013

Welwood, John   Perfect Love, Imperfect Relationships
Trumpeter 2006

Zweig, Connie and Jeremiah Abrams   Meeting the Shadow: The
Hidden Power of the Dark Side of Human Nature   G.P. Putnam's
Sons 1991

www.romanramsey.com

Made in the USA
Monee, IL
07 July 2026